I0342154

WHY <u>ARE</u> WE HERE?

A NEW approach to studying the Scriptures clearly reveals

The Plan, Purpose & Meaning of Life

A non-denominational way to study using spiritual and practical 'keys' better to understand the Scriptures

INGREDIENTS:

PURE TRUTHS,LOVE,JOY,THE INSPIRATION OF GOD. TOOLS PROFITABLE FOR LEARNING CHRIST'S TEACHINGS ON

HOW TO LIVE AND THE MEANING AND PURPOSE OF HUMAN LIFE

Compiled by Brian H.Butler

Copyright © 2015 Brian H. Butler. 2nd Edition © 2023

All rights reserved. No part of this book may be used or reproduced by any means, graphic, electronic, or mechanical, including photocopying, recording, taping or by any information storage retrieval system without the written permission of the publisher except in the case of brief quotations in critical articles and reviews.

The English King James Version of the Bible is generally considered by most scholars to be overall the best translation despite its ancient English, and its many small errors of translation which can easily be resolved by the careful student. Quotations from the KJV form a large proportion, well over half of the contents of this book. The King James Version of the Bible is in the Public Domain.

Cover picture "Sunrise, Westport, Ireland", by Siobhan Guthrie.

Copies of this book may be obtained from Amazon Books

Brian H. Butler Author page.

Due to the dynamic nature of the Internet, any web addresses or links contained in this book may have changed since publication and may no longer be valid.

The views expressed in this work are solely those of the author. .

Perfect bound paperback book ISBN: 978-0-645-7342-0

Ebook ISBN: 978-0-6457342-9-4

The author of this book may be contacted at

bhb@ernestworkman.com

Typeset by Brian H. Butler

Formatted by: Angel Key Publications angelkey.com.au

Published by IngramSpark

Printed by: LightningSource

DEDICATION & ACKNOWLEDGEMENT

The Author would like to dedicate this book to the memory of Dr. Ernest L. Martin, Ph.D. The contents of this book, and the unique approach to a non-denominational study of the Holy Bible, were composed from 2013 onwards based on taped lectures given between 1977 and 1997 by Dr. Ernest L. Martin.

Dr. Martin was formerly the Head of Theology of a Christian denomination and training college. Dr. Martin resigned in January 1974 because of his unresolved doctrinal issues with the administration.

The Compiler of this book knew Dr. Martin well, and spent time with him personally as a colleague over a period of several years.

During his career as a theologian, Dr. Martin became renowned and highly respected as an historian and archaeologist by many scholars, in particular by Professors of Archaeology at the Hebrew University. He spent over a year of his life working with students on archaeological digs in Israel.

His authoritative book on the 'Star that led the Wise Men' to where Christ was, has been widely accepted by astronomers worldwide, as it contains details of the spectacular happenings in the movements of the heavenly bodies recorded at that time.

Another volume written by Dr. Martin detailed the exact time of Christ's birth from astronomical indications in the Bible. Thanks to modern means of tracking the movements of heavenly bodies in previous centuries it was possible for his calculations to be confirmed by astronomers worldwide.

Sadly Dr. Martin died in January 2002, a great loss to the world and to those who seek Biblical truth.

The Compiler of this book would also like to acknowledge with deep respect, gratitude, and awe, the knowledge and understanding he gained from the inspiration of Christ and the flow of His Holy Spirit during his many hours of prayerful study of the Word of God to produce this volume.

Brian H Butler

CONTENTS

Dedication & Acknowledgement   iii

Preface   vii

Introduction -- Essential Study Tools   x-xlvii

Chapter 1
    Fundamentals of Scriptural Knowledge   1

Chapter 2
    Principles of Chronology   19

Chapter 3
    The Importance of Geography in The Bible   37

Chapter 4
    Design and Development of The Holy Bible   52

Chapter 5
    Prophecy – & Christ's Marriages   69

Chapter 6
    Biblical History & Archaeology   89

Chapter 7
    Systematic & Dogmatic Theology   142

Chapter 8
    Essentials of Old Testament History   205

Chapter 9
    World Powers Decline - 6th C.B.C. - A 'New Age' Dawns   222

Chapter 10
    Origin & Goal of Western Civilisation   243

Chapter 11
    What Must 21st Century Christians Avoid Like
    The Plague?   268

Chapter 12
    The Meaning and Purpose of Human Life   281

A Short Autobiographical History   353
By Brian H. Butler

The English King James Version of the Bible is generally considered by most scholars to be overall the best translation despite its ancient English and its many small errors of translation, which can easily be resolved by the careful student.

Quotations from the KJV form a large proportion, well over half of the contents of this book.

The King James Version of the Bible is in the Public Domain.

The format of the manuscript is Letter, typeset in 12pt Arial with automatic headers, footers and pagination.

PREFACE

For over a year, I have had the opportunity to listen to more than one hundred and sixty of Dr. Ernest L. Martin's taped lectures on many different topics and doctrines. This involved more than two hundred and fifty hours, plus many more writing up the notes I took, and I have learned more 'Truth' in that time than I did in the previous sixty years of what I had thought was my personal "Bible Study".

I had thought that his Home Study Course would probably be for beginners, so I left them to the last to listen to the tapes. Without realising it, I had in many ways left the best to the last! This Home Study Course has provided much of the material for this book. The study methods he suggested are wonderful for beginners to set them on the right track, but it is also of incredible value to anyone who has studied God's Word for many years as I have. I have experienced an explosion in the amount I can learn from the Word.

Through the years, I have heard quoted the same verses on reading the Bible many, many times: 2 Timothy 3:16 All scripture is given by inspiration of God, and is profitable for doctrine, for reproof, for correction, for instruction in righteousness: and 2 Timothy 2:15 Study to shew thyself approved unto God, a workman that needeth not to be ashamed, rightly dividing the word of truth.

I had learned both these wonderful verses by heart from the beginning of my association with the sect I joined. Knowing them by heart is one thing, it is quite another to be able to study in such a way so as not to be ashamed of the work you do, especially when you find out how our studies should have been approached as I have now.

The problem was, despite my many years of study, I had never been told how to study the Bible. Although I was a member of a fundamental sect for years, and attended years of many Bible courses, I was never instructed in any practical or constructive detail concerning how to undertake my studies of the Bible.

The reason for that was that none of the ministers were themselves familiar with how properly to study the Bible, so there was no question of their being able to pass this vital information on to members or students! How do I know this? Because if the ministers had had the advantage of taking the Home Study Course to which you now have free and simple access, they would certainly have wanted to instruct their congregations and students on how to approach Bible study in a 'workmanlike' manner.

The principle of 'here a little and there a little' is a true Biblical fact, but was misused by the ministers to encourage members and students to look up the verses that they used to support the many incorrect doctrines of the Church, and thereby to obey the instruction given in 1 Thessalonians 5:21 Prove all things; hold fast that which is good.

The result was a whole group of many thousands of people who only knew what they were told to believe! This method of teaching, or so-called 'proving' by the Church, kept them all in a tragic state of ignorance of the glory, the wonder, the beauty, and the scope of the Holy Bible. Subtle or what?

This way of enslaving minds also kept those thousands firmly in the grip of a false Gospel, which actually denied them the full knowledge of who Christ really Was, the nature of the real life of Christ Jesus, the awesome reality of His sacrifice, and God's amazing purpose for all human beings.

I am not blaming anyone for my period of ignorance. I thank God for my previous associations which brought me to appreciate the Word of God as much as I did then.

I am also 'over the moon' as they say that God has opened my eyes wider to be able to appreciate more of the actual Glory of His Word in my later years.

Please begin by carefully studying the Introduction as it contains a summary of the 'tools' Dr. Martin used, and encourages others to have available in their study 'toolbox' in order to become a skilled 'workman'.

Sadly Dr. Martin died in 2002, but he left us with the manner of study he developed. This body of information is truly a unique masterpiece of instruction in the workmanlike procedures, methods, and the best ways to extract the most out of any time spent in Bible Study.

Accordingly, I urge anyone who has access to the material in this book to make a careful, diligent study of all the principles that are outlined, and use them as practical guidelines and a mental backdrop to all their studies of the Word of God.

Brian H. Butler

INTRODUCTION --
ESSENTIAL STUDY TOOLS

There is an old proverb which says: If you give a man a fish, you feed him for a day. If you teach a man how to fish, you feed him for life.

The spiritual fishermen needs special tools. The student needs to be well organized to 'fish' things out of the Bible. He or she needs to have an easy method to learn from the Bible, learn what the Prophets, the Priests, and The Living Christ have to say to us that is relevant to us today.

This is not what is happening among scholars, theologians or ministers in our era. Most of them seem to think that the Bible has been so worked over in the past centuries that there is not much to learn.

More and more, it is the opinions and ideas of men about the Bible, rather than a study of the Bible itself, or of the original manuscripts from which the English or any other language versions are derived.

Not that all men's ideas or opinions are wrong, but scholars quote scholars and scriptural references from the universities, seminaries etc., which are not always helpful in arriving at an accurate translation or the truth.

It is useful to remember that the King James Version was produced at the command of King James in 1611 A.D., and the manner in which this was done led to errors in translation.

1. The King gave the translators explicit instructions not to translate anything into English that would conflict with the beliefs of the Church of England.

2. There were 54 scholars involved, and there was always the possibility that their knowledge of the Hebrew, Aramaic, or Greek languages varied.

3. The translators inserted thousands of words that were not in the original texts which are printed in italics in the King James Version. It is important to be aware that these words are not in the inspired manuscripts.

4. It is also likely that their understanding of Church of England Doctrine may not have been perfect, and of course that Church was an offshoot of the Catholic Church with its different beliefs. So bias may have entered in.

5. Modern translations can be an excellent help to our understanding. It is well to remember that each one might reflect to a degree some of the beliefs or doctrines of the particular denomination the translator belonged to who was responsible for the new translation. They might have allowed personal beliefs to influence their translation of the original texts.

Whenever there is any question of meaning, it is wise to consult the text in the original language in which it was written. Every word in the original texts was directly inspired by God, YHWH, and His Son who became Christ, the Messiah. This is not true of translations by men into English or any other language.

However, The KJV is still probably the most reliable translation we have, so long as we use carefully all the tools at our disposal to check what a word or a verse or passage might mean as we go along.

This book will focus on what the inspired word of God, the Holy Bible says, not on men's opinions from over 20,000 differing denominations.

Introduction -- Essential Study Tools

A new manuscript version of the Bible in the original order is needed

The sacred names of God need to be properly translated because the divine titles are significant for Christians. Traditionalism is hindering understanding. In the billions of Bibles in the world, the books are all in the wrong order, and they contain many incorrect translations of words and deviations from the texts in the original languages.

A manuscript version of the books of the Bible in the correct order, with meticulous translation is crucial to a proper understanding of the Word of God. Such a volume has recently been produced, and anyone interested in obtaining one might contact: Congregation of YHWH, Jerusalem, P.O. Box 832, Carteret, New Jersey, 07008, U.S.A.

To enquire about obtaining a copy of the "Hebraic Roots Bible" which is in the correct order, and has been very carefully translated from the original texts, go to: http://www.coyhwh.com/en/bible.php where it is offered, with a request for a donation.

You may also want to contact www.askelm.com to enquire whether such a volume is available and is still in print from this site.

Here is a chart of the structure of the Holy Bible in the original order of the books as they should be presented in printed copies of the Bible.

This chart designed by Gary E. Arvidson is copyright.

Copyright held at www.askelm.com

© 1984 Ernest L. Martin.

CHRISTIANITY DIRECT FROM CHRIST – THE WORD OF GOD

THE HOLY BIBLE – GOD'S PERFECT STRUCTURE AND DESIGN

The Bible we have today has 66 books. The Old Testament contains 39 books. The New Testament contains 27 books. 39+27 = 66. This man-made structure and order obscures the perfection and completeness of the Holy Bible. God's Word to mankind. In the 4th/5th century A.D., Saint Jerome, commissioned by Pope Damasus in 382, made up the Vulgate version in Latin. Jerome avoided the original order. He put the Bible together in the Egyptian order as he thought fit. This confused the perfection and obscured the message of the Bible. This created chaos, so often the result of man's interference with the plan of God.

The Old Testament Canon was inspired by God, and arranged by Ezra in the 5th Century B.C. originally consisted of 22 books, one for each letter of the Hebrew alphabet. The New Testament 27 books were Canonized by John in the last decade of the first century A.D. after Jesus Christ had inspired him to write the book of Revelation. Revelation is the 49th book, completing the numerical perfection of 7x7. The first five books of the Bible, Genesis, Exodus, Leviticus, Numbers, and Deuteronomy are known as the Law. The number 5 is the number of Law. The 5 books, the New Testament Law, the Gospels and Acts form the exact centre of the Bible when all the books are in the Divine Order as seen on this chart.

Volume One — The Old Testament

3	Grand	Divisions
The Law	The Church (1st Rank)	The State (2nd Rank)
GOD (5 Books)	2. PROPHETS (6 Books)	3. PSALMS (11 Books)
1. LAW	**2. FORMER**	**5. WISDOM**
1. Genesis	1. Joshua – Judges	1. Psalms
2. Exodus	2. Book of the Kingdoms	2. Proverbs
3. Leviticus		3. Job
4. Numbers	**3. LATTER**	**6. FESTIVAL**
5. Deuteronomy	5. Isaiah	4. Song = Passover
	6. Jeremiah } MAJOR	5. Ruth = Pentecost
[The Old Testament Pentateuch is the beginning division of the Holy Scriptures. The following two divisions of the O.T. are subsidiary to the Law. The Prophets' division is superior in rank to the Psalms' (or Royal) division because the prophets were direct emissaries of God and were responsible for instructing and admonishing rulers and kings - the position shows authority of rank and teaching.]	7. Ezekiel	6. Lament. = Ab 9th
	4. MINOR	7. Eccl. = Tabernacles
	6. The Twelve	8. Esther = Purim
	1. Hosea	
	2. Joel	**7. RESTORATION**
	3. Amos	
	4. Obadiah } Assyrian Period	9. Daniel
	5. Jonah	10. Ezra-Nehemiah
	6. Micah	11. Chronicles
	7. Nahum	
	8. Habakkuk } Chaldean Period	[This third division is the Royal (state or government) section and was inferior in rank to the prophets (division two).]
	9. Zephaniah	
	10. Haggai } Restoration Period	
	11. Zechariah	
	12. Malachi	
Basic Law: 5 Books +	Priests & Prophets: 6 Books = 11 Books	Kings & Rulers: + 11 Books = 22 Books

⇐ 22 Books ⇒ — 24 Books

New Testament PENTATEUCH

1	2	3	4	5
MATT	MARK	LUKE	JOHN	ACTS
Jewish	Jewish-Gentile	Gentile	Universal	Universal – to Israel
4. GOSPELS & ACTS (5 Books)				
1. ON EARTH			**2. IN HEAVEN**	
Gospels (Christ on earth)			Acts (Christ in heaven)	
22 Books		5		22 Books
		5		
	New Testament Books			
	PENTATEUCH			
	"THE FOUNDATION" (I Cor. 3:11)			

Volume Two — The New Testament

3	Grand	Divisions
The Jew (1st Rank)	The Gentile (2nd Rank)	World Holocaust
STATE (7 Books)	CHURCH (14 Books)	GOD (1 Book)
5. GENERAL	**6. PAUL**	**7. REVELATION**
3. UNIVERSAL	**4. 7 CHURCHES**	**7. PROPHETIC**
1. James	1. Rom. } The ABC's of Christian Doctrine	Revelation:
2. I Peter	2. I Cor.	The Book of Sevens
3. II Peter	3. II Cor.	
4. I John	4. Gal.	1. Seven Churches
5. II John	5. Eph. } II The XYZ's of Doctrine	2. Seven Golden Candlesticks
6. III John	6. Phil.	3. Seven Stars
7. Jude	7. Col.	4. Seven Spirits of God
	8. I Thes. } III End Times	5. Seven Lamps of Fire
[These seven epistles were primarily intended for the Jewish people. Their theme is non-sectarian and intro-ductory to Paul's doctrinal epistles. They are placed as first position to fulfil the principle "to the Jew first" (Romans 2:10). They were written to Jewish Christians in general and not to specific churches. They were written by the "pillar" apostles with top rank over Paul.]	9. II Thes.	6. Seven Seals
	5. MILLENNIAL	7. Seven Angels
	6. MINISTERIAL	8. Seven Horns
	10. Hebrews } Temple Symbolism	9. Seven Trumpets
		10. Seven Thunders
	11. I Tim. } The Epistles for Professional Leaders	11. Seven Heads and Also Seven Heads
	12. II Tim.	12. Seven Plagues
	13. Titus	13. Seven Vials/Bowls
	14. Philm.	14. Seven Mountains
		15. Seven Last Plagues
		16. Seven Kings
		[The Book of Revelation has all the extracts of being the final book of both Testaments.]
II. High School	III. College	IV. Post Graduate Studies

⇐ 22 Books ⇒ — 24 Books

I. The First Christian Principles – Grade School
(The central historical division of both Testaments)

GOSPELS & ACTS (5) Books ← 49 Books → (7 X 7) ← LUKE

© 1994 Ernest L. Martin

Designed by Gary B. Arvidson

Introduction -- Essential Study Tools

xiii

To assist your studies, the reader may copy this chart onto 8½ x 11 or A4 for personal study purposes only. Suggestion, keep the .jpg print of the chart handy when you are studying, as it is a constant reminder of the perfection of the original structure of the Bible, and a great help to further our understanding of the organisation and design of the original scriptures.

Matthew 5:13 Ye are the salt of the earth: but if the salt have lost his savour, wherewith shall it be salted? it is thenceforth good for nothing, but to be cast out, and to be trodden under foot of men.

Each of us has talents, and it is our job to develop them. This is our job as Christians, to be about our Father's work, and to realise that we have a special task to do that as 'called out' ones. We are commanded to study in a skilled workmanlike manner. Proper methodical study is an essential part of life for every Christian. This book is only a beginning, but it is a start! We also have a responsibility to teach our children about God and our glorious future while they are young.

Deuteronomy 4:9 only take heed to yourself, and keep your soul diligently, lest you forget the things which all eyes have seen, and less they depart from your heart all the days of your life: but teach them to your sons and your son's sons;

So here is a command in the Old Testament Law that parents should teach their children at home before they were of school age. This should still be the case. Everyone needs to be in a learning mode all their lives.

At any time in history there have been only a few claiming to be Christians who have not 'bowed the knee to Baal', so to speak. Modern 'churchianity' is riddled with pagan symbols, doctrines, and heathen practices, but the followers of the thousands of denominations do not realise it.

Introduction -- Essential Study Tools

The Apostle Peter warned about the infiltration of pagan ideas into Christianity which was happening to an alarming extent only a short time after the gift of the Holy Spirit on the day of Pentecost just fifty days after Christ's resurrection and ascension. Christ sent the Holy Spirit on the day of Pentecost.

Acts 2:1 And when the day of Pentecost was fully come, they were all with one accord in one place. 2 And suddenly there came a sound from heaven as of a rushing mighty wind, and it filled all the house where they were sitting. 3 And there appeared unto them cloven tongues like as of fire, and it sat upon each of them. 4 And they were all filled with the Holy Ghost, and began to speak with other tongues, as the Spirit gave them utterance.

Acts 11:25 Then departed Barnabas to Tarsus, for to seek Saul: 26 And when he had found him, he brought him unto Antioch. And it came to pass, that a whole year they assembled themselves with the church, and taught much people. And the disciples were called Christians first in Antioch.

But it was not long before all kinds of false ideas and pagan doctrines had crept in to pollute the true Gospel.

2 Peter 1:16 For we (the true apostles and disciples of Christ) have not followed cunningly devised fables, when we made known unto you the power and coming of our Lord Jesus Christ, but were eyewitnesses of his majesty.

The matter of there being so many eyewitnesses is very important as many secular people tend to scoff, and suggest that none of the events of Christ's life really happened.

Jude 1:4 For there are certain men crept in unawares, who were before of old ordained to this condemnation, ungodly men, turning the grace of our God into lasciviousness, and denying the only Lord God, and our Lord Jesus Christ.

Introduction -- Essential Study Tools

At this time in the 1st Century A.D., the Roman Empire had many gods, but interest in them was on the wane. Initially Christians were thrown to the lions, or pitted against gladiators, to entertain the people by the Emperor Nero in 64 A.D. Then over the next two centuries, a form of Christianity, mingled with many of the popular pagan and idolatrous practices of Roman gods was gradually adopted by the populace of the spreading Empire. Then in the 3rd Century, around 312 A.D., the Emperor Constantine was converted to a form of 'Christianity' and it became more generally accepted.

Many Christians think that it is fine to celebrate Easter (Ishtar the Babylonian and Assyrian goddess of sex, eggs, rabbits etc., that gave rise to the English word Estrogen a sex hormone; otherwise called Ashtoreth - Hebrew, Astarte – Greek). Easter is nothing other than a slightly modified sex festival with so-called Christian trimmings.

Most think there is no harm in Christmas which is almost universally accepted as a 'Christian' celebration of Christ's birthday, but in reality is a period of excesses of sexual activity, food and drink, and often with violent behaviour. Christmas is clearly connected to ancient idolatrous Sun worship.

But there is surely no harm in those practices, is there? God says He hates them!

Isaiah 1:14 Your new moons and **your** appointed feasts my soul hateth: they are a trouble unto me; I am weary to bear them.

Jeremiah 10:1 Hear ye the word which the Lord speaketh unto you, O house of Israel: 2 Thus saith the Lord, Learn not the way of the heathen, and be not dismayed at the signs of heaven; for the heathen are dismayed at them. 3 For the customs of the people are vain: for one cutteth a tree out of the forest, the work of the hands of the workman,

Introduction -- Essential Study Tools

with the axe. 4 They deck it with silver and with gold; they fasten it with nails and with hammers, that it move not.

Sounds like God does not like 'Christians' learning and adopting the ways of the heathen. Many doctrines now generally considered 'Christian' are directly opposed to the laws of God. Doctrines such as the 'The Trinity', 'The Immortality of the Soul', 'When you die, you go to heaven', 'Christianising' Christmas, Easter, Halloween; 'Tithing', 'Confession to and gaining absolution from any man'; Statues, Pictures, Relics, Rites and Rituals in Churches, even some aspects of church architecture, and more, are all condemned by the Scriptures.

God does not like 'Christians' incorporating pagan idolatrous practices with watered down beliefs concerning what Christ taught, in fact He hates it.

Amos 5:21 I hate, I despise your feast days, and I will not smell in your solemn assemblies.

Sounds like God does not like 'Christians' worshipping Him with their own version of 'feast' days.

More will be explained about the false ministers, deception, counterfeits, and the false gospels of 'Churchianity' in this volume.

Can two billion 'Christians' worldwide really be deceived?

Yes they can be, and yes they are! This may appear to be an arrogant statement, critical in the extreme, and offensive to some, but it has to be said. If you knew someone was about to lose everything of value they owned through deception, if you could, you would naturally want to warn them would you not?

Do they know they are deceived? No they do not. Here is a sobering truth: **'a person that is deceived does not know they are deceived'!**

Introduction -- Essential Study Tools

Christ warned many times to be wary of deception. The problem is that people just do not believe Christ Jesus!

Feel like shooting the messenger?

Christ 'shot from the hip' when speaking to the top religious leaders in Jerusalem in the Temple. He pulled no punches. After all, the YHWH of the Old Testament who inspired every word the Prophets uttered was Christ Jesus, so when you read in any of the Prophets, ... and the Lord said... this is Christ talking to them then, and to us now. The reaction of the religious Jews then was to want to attack, stone and kill God's Prophets who were warning them of the impending destruction of Jerusalem and the Temple.

Moses was at times in fear of his life because of the antagonistic Children of Israel towards him and towards God.

Possibly the clearest example of God's messengers being treated badly is the Prophet Jeremiah. He was only seventeen when God appointed him to tell Judah and Israel that because of their deserting God, and for their abominable sins, God was going to allow Jerusalem to be ruined, the Temple destroyed, and they would go into captivity for seventy years.

Jeremiah prophesied for forty years, and during that time he was abused, put in the stocks, locked up in prison several times, frequently in fear for his life, thrown naked with no water into a pit with mud at the bottom. According to some historians, his life was ended by being stoned by a mob of Jews.

Here is Christ Jesus talking to the very top religious leaders in the Temple. He was telling them what they already knew from the Scriptures, and they could not deny it.

Introduction -- Essential Study Tools

Matthew 23:27 Woe unto you, scribes and Pharisees, hypocrites! for ye are like unto whited sepulchres, which indeed appear beautiful outward, but are within full of dead men's bones, and of all uncleanness. 28 Even so ye also outwardly appear righteous unto men, but within ye are full of hypocrisy and iniquity. 29 Woe unto you, scribes and Pharisees, hypocrites! because ye build the tombs of the prophets, and garnish the sepulchres of the righteous, 30 And say, If we had been in the days of our fathers, we would not have been partakers with them in the blood of the prophets. 31 Wherefore ye be witnesses unto yourselves, that ye are the children of them which killed the prophets.

32 Fill ye up then the measure of your fathers. 33 Ye serpents, ye generation of vipers, how can ye escape the damnation of hell? 34 Wherefore, behold, I send unto you prophets, and wise men, and scribes: and some of them ye shall kill and crucify; and some of them shall ye scourge in your synagogues, and persecute them from city to city: 35 That upon you may come all the righteous blood shed upon the earth, from the blood of righteous Abel unto the blood of Zacharias son of Barachias, whom ye slew between the temple and the altar. 36 Verily I say unto you, All these things shall come upon this generation.

Please do not get angry and think to shoot the 'messenger'; just believe what Christ Jesus our Elder Brother repeatedly warns His brothers and sisters to be very careful not to be deceived. But who is Christ warning us about today? The religious leaders who teach for doctrines the commandments of men, those who incorporate pagan idolatrous practices into the Christianity that they teach.

Matthew 24:4 And Jesus answered and said unto them, Take heed that no man deceive you. 5 For **many** shall come in my name, saying, **I am Christ; and shall deceive**

many.... verse 11 And many false prophets (not a few – many) shall rise, **and shall deceive many.** Verse 24 For there shall arise false Christs, and false prophets, and shall shew great signs and wonders; insomuch that, if it were possible, they shall deceive the very elect.

We can be thankful that currently there is nobody showing great signs and wonders, but when the world's 'Christians' see these 'miracles', and the person doing them is claiming to be Christ, many will be deceived. However, it will not be possible for Christ's elect to be deceived so long as they are close to Christ, because He will flood their minds with His Truth.

If anyone is getting their beliefs about Christianity, God and Christ from any 'church', or from any of the many thousands of organisations of men, they are in grave danger of being deceived because Satan has deceived the whole world.

Revelation 12:9 And the great dragon was cast out, that old serpent, called the Devil, and Satan, which deceiveth the whole world: he was cast out into the earth, and his angels were cast out with him.

The only way anyone can be sure they are not deceived is to get their information directly 'from the horse's mouth' so to speak. The Holy Bible, the Word of God is the only safe source of Truth. As we study we have to pray continuously for Christ's help to absorb His truth from the Bible, and to be protected from evil ideas. Remember the part of the 'Lord's Prayer'?

Matthew 6:13 And lead us not into temptation, but deliver us from evil (or the evil one): For thine is the kingdom, and the power, and the glory, for ever. Amen.

Christ has the Power to deliver us from the wiles of deceptive ideas. And will do so if we ask him. But if we just sit back and accept what we are told by often sincere and apparently well-meaning teachers, we can easily be deceived, but this does not need to happen.

Jeremiah 17:5 Thus saith the Lord (this is Christ speaking!); Cursed be the man that trusteth in man (or organisations of men), and maketh (human) flesh his arm (strength), and whose heart (mind) departeth from the Lord.

Billions of people think they are following Jesus Christ, but they are embracing idolatrous pagan idols, false doctrines, and forbidden images wholesale. As you study the Bible under the guidance of Christ Jesus with the help of the Holy Spirit instead of relying on men, you will see this scenario and pattern repeated a distressing number of times in the Bible.

God pleads every few verses for His children to love Him and be obedient to Him. What do they do? They do anything but. All through history, they turn their back on God, commit idolatrous spiritual adultery, and ignore His laws. Look around the world today, people obeying God's law of love delivered to us by Christ Jesus are sadly quite hard to find.

Matthew 7:13 Enter ye in at the strait gate: for wide is the gate, and broad is the way, that leadeth to destruction, and many there be which go in thereat: 14 Because strait is the gate, and narrow is the way, which leadeth unto life, **and few there be that find it.** 15 Beware of **false prophets, which come to you in sheep's clothing,** but inwardly they are ravening wolves.

Religious leaders do not appear to be dangerous wild animals, they look as gentle and as harmless as sheep, but do not be deceived.

God and Christ have always worked personally with a chosen few throughout history. With Moses and Aaron in

1500 B.C., in 1100 B.C., with Samuel who had a school for prophets, with the 'Major' and 'Minor' Prophets of the Old Testament up until the time of Ezra in the 5th Century B.C.

In the New Testament times, God was working with a selected few individuals, John the Baptist, Mary and Joseph, the disciples that Christ called, and of course Paul.

Paul lived in the university town of Tarsus and sat at the feet of Gamaliel who was a great Jewish scholar. In previous centuries only those over age 30 went to school. But Paul was called out to receive instruction directly from Christ Jesus and become an Apostle, and write under the inspiration of Christ Jesus fourteen books of the Bible.

Acts 22:3 I am verily a man which am a Jew, born in Tarsus, a city in Cilicia, yet brought up in this city at the feet of Gamaliel, and taught according to the perfect manner of the law of the fathers, and was zealous towards God as you all are I this day.

Paul had a great deal of 'undoing' and 'unlearning' to do, as dyed in the wool Pharisees were convinced they were right and doing God's work, when in actual fact they had long since departed from the Mosaic Law.

Over a period of two hundred years, they had gradually phased out strict obedience to Mosaic Law, and had invented a huge number of their own laws, extremely burdensome picky and petty laws and restrictions, they had embraced pagan ideas and practices, yet Pharisees still claimed they were representing Mosaic Law. Instead they were using the Talmud as their authority. They had totally deceived themselves.

Matthew 15:1 Then came to Jesus scribes and Pharisees, which were of Jerusalem, saying, 2 Why do thy disciples transgress the tradition of the elders? for they wash not their hands when they eat bread. 3 But he answered and said unto them, Why do ye also transgress the commandment of God by your tradition? 4 For God commanded, saying, Honour thy father and mother: and, He that curseth father or mother, let him die the death. 5 But ye say, Whosoever shall say to his father or his mother, It is a gift, by whatsoever thou mightest be profited by me; 6 And honour not his father or his mother, he shall be free. Thus have ye made the commandment of God of none effect by your tradition. 7 Ye hypocrites, well did Esaias prophesy of you, saying, 8 This people draweth nigh unto me with their mouth, and honoureth me with their lips; but their heart is far from me. 9 But in vain they do worship me, teaching for doctrines the commandments of men.

The Scribes, Pharisees, and other religious leaders were absolutely 'nailed' by Christ's words. As a result, they could not wait to get their hands on Jesus and have him beaten half to death and crucified by the Roman occupying forces. Not content with that, the infuriated Jewish religious leaders also stoned the naked Christ while hanging on the tree of crucifixion until his face was unrecognisable, and his body torn to shreds by the stones.

Isaiah 52:14 As many were astonied at thee; his visage was so marred more than any man, and his form more than the sons of men:

All this caused Christ to die sooner than the watching soldiers thought He would.

John 19:31 The Jews therefore, because it was the preparation, that the bodies should not remain upon the cross on the Sabbath day, (for that Sabbath day was an high day,) besought Pilate that their legs might be broken, and that they might be taken away.

Hard to imagine, but these fanatical religious Pharisees were concerned about the technicality of the law. Christ was crucified on the day before a Holy Day Sabbath, and as the afternoon drew on, they wanted Him taken down so they would not break the Sabbath as they thought. Religious they were, but certainly not Godly.

John 19:32 Then came the soldiers, and brake the legs of the first, and of the other which was crucified with him. 33 But when they came to Jesus, and saw that he was dead already, they brake not his legs: 34 But one of the soldiers with a spear pierced his side, and forthwith came there out blood and water. 35 And he that saw it bare record, and his record is true: and he knoweth that he saith true, that ye might believe. 36 For these things were done, that the scripture should be fulfilled, A bone of him shall not be broken.

37 And again another scripture saith, They shall look on him whom they pierced. Psalm 34:20 He keepeth all his bones: not one of them is broken.

Zechariah 12:10 And I will pour upon the house of David, and upon the inhabitants of Jerusalem, the spirit of grace and of supplications: and they shall look upon me whom they have pierced, and they shall mourn for him, as one mourneth for his only son, and shall be in bitterness for him, as one that is in bitterness for his firstborn.

This prophecy in Zechariah is most interesting as it refers to two periods in the future. The occasion of Christ's death, they, the Jews will I look on Him they had pierced; but also there is a time coming in the future when the whole of Israel, and the Jews in particular, will come to realise that Christ was indeed the Messiah, and they will be absolutely mortified at what was done, and will repent bitterly of their unbelief. At this time in the future, many 'Christians' will come to realise that their lives have not matched up to the true definition of what it means to be a Christian.

It is wonderful to know that true repentance is prophesied to come to many individuals who are currently deceived, and indeed also to the entire Jewish or 'Israel' people prior to the second advent of Christ.

So in effect, Christ suffered two death sentences, one by Roman crucifixion and the other by Jewish stoning. During the Medieval Inquisitions the Catholic Church tortured and killed anyone who did not toe the line issued by the Popes. Religious persecution has taken many forms over the centuries, and of course still exists today in many parts of the world between peoples of differing beliefs, even when they claim to worship the same God.

The pure essence of Christianity, and our glorious future

Romans 3:23 For all have sinned, and come short of the glory of God;

1 John 3:4 Whosoever committeth sin transgresseth also the law: for sin is the transgression of the law.

Christ lived a perfect sinless life, and died carrying the entire burden of all human sin to pay the penalty for the sins of every person that has ever lived, is living, or ever will live. Christ was dead for three days and three nights in the grave. He was dead. Lifeless, not conscious in any way. That is what death is.

Ecclesiastes 9:5 For the living know that they shall die: but the dead know not any thing, neither have they any more a reward; for the memory of them is forgotten.

Ecclesiastes 9:10 Whatsoever thy hand findeth to do, do it with thy might; for there is no work, nor device, nor knowledge, nor wisdom, in the grave, whither thou goest.

This is why the doctrine of the 'Immortality of the Soul' is so very evil. For if Christ did not actually die, then our sins were not forgiven, and the penalty of our sin would be death. Cessation of life.

But Christ did die, and we are forgiven. Christ was also resurrected from the dead, went to heaven where he sits on the right hand of the Father.

Matthew 28:5 And the angel answered and said unto the women, Fear not ye: for I know that ye seek Jesus, which was crucified. 6 He is not here: for he is risen, as he said.

Come, see the place where the Lord lay.

Hebrews 1:3 Who (Christ Jesus) being the brightness of his glory, and the express image of His person, and upholding all things by the Word of his Power, when He had by himself purged our sins, sat down on the right hand of the Majesty on high:

Paul writes in the hope that God will give all who seek Him, will give them the Spirit of Wisdom, so that as true Christians they can become part of Christ and in Him.

Ephesians 1:17 That the God of our Lord Jesus Christ, the Father of glory, may give unto you the spirit of wisdom and revelation in the knowledge of him: 18 The eyes of your understanding being enlightened; that ye may know what is the hope of his calling, and what the riches of the glory of his inheritance in the saints, 19 And what is the exceeding greatness of his power to us-ward who believe, according to the working of his mighty power, 20 Which he wrought in Christ, when he raised him from the dead, and set him at his own right hand in the heavenly places,

Christ Jesus is alive and sitting at the right hand of the Father in Heaven, and in a sense we who are true Christians are with him there. Exciting? More than!

Ephesians 2:6 And hath raised us up together, and made us sit together in heavenly places in Christ Jesus:

Clearly, we are not now physically in heaven sitting next to Christ, but we Christians who are **in** Christ, are **in type** with Him in heaven in this life. As human beings, we can and do enjoy a close relationship with our Lord, Master and Brother. When our time comes to die, and/or be resurrected to life eternal, we shall then actually be with Him in Heaven at the right hand of the Father as full members of the God family. Amazing!

True Christians, human beings who have the Holy Spirit, are the called out ones, Christ's 'ecclesia' or group, and what joy that should give us.

1 Peter 2:9 But ye are a chosen generation, a royal priesthood, an holy nation, a peculiar people; that ye should shew forth the praises of him who hath called you out of darkness into his marvellous light;

As we study the Holy Scriptures diligently, prayerfully, we will grow in Grace and Knowledge because of our minds direct Spiritual contact with the mind of Christ Jesus.

John 16:13 Howbeit when he, the Spirit of truth, is come, he will guide you into all truth:

If we listen to any human beings and their ideas, beliefs, and teachings, we lay ourselves open to being deceived by cunningly devised fables and untruths.

1 John 2:27 But the anointing (of the Holy Spirit) which ye have received of him abideth in you, and ye need not that any man teach you: but as the same anointing teacheth you of all things, and is truth, and is no lie, and even as it hath taught you, ye shall abide in him.

But Christ uses the Spirit of God in our hearts and minds to teach us only the truth. And only the amount of truth He deems appropriate at the time.

Romans 8:16 The Spirit itself beareth witness with our (human) spirit, that we are the children of God:

Job 32:8 But there is a spirit in man: and the inspiration of the Almighty giveth them understanding.

Introduction -- Essential Study Tools

All humans will die, but in due time they will also be resurrected to life. We do not go to heaven when we die. No human that ever lived has ascended into heaven.

John 3:13 And no man hath ascended up to heaven, but he that came down from heaven, even the Son of man which is in heaven.

Acts 2:34 For David is not ascended into the heavens: but he saith himself, The Lord said unto my Lord, Sit thou on my right hand,

John 3:14 And as Moses lifted up the serpent in the wilderness, even so must the Son of man be lifted up (crucified): 15 that whosoever believeth in him should not perish, but have eternal life. 16 For God so loved the world, that he gave his only begotten Son, that whosoever believeth in him should not perish, but have everlasting life. 17 For God sent not his Son into the world to condemn the world; but that the world through him might be saved.

Our job, our work as Christians is to believe in Christ, the Son of God, the Word, the Author of the Holy Bible, and to respect His wishes and His directions concerning how to live this life, that we are saved, and that we will receive eternal life in due time.

John 6:29 Jesus answered and said unto them, This is the work of God, that ye believe on him whom he hath sent.

Believing in Christ is work! But it is He who gives us the belief in the first place.

Romans 6:23 The wages of sin is death; but the gift of God is eternal life through Jesus Christ our Lord.

Because the penalty of our sin has been paid by Christ Jesus, He was, and is, and will be able to present every human being to God the Father sinless and without spot.

Ephesians 5:27 That he might present it to himself a glorious church, not having spot, or wrinkle, or any such thing; but that it should be holy and without blemish.

Philippians 3:20 For our conversation (citizenship) is in heaven; from whence also we look for the Saviour, the Lord Jesus Christ:

Even now it is still not easy to be a Christian, and in the 21st Century, Christians around the world are still the victims of personal attacks. In many areas, people belonging to different religious persuasions who have historically lived side by side peacefully with their neighbours, suddenly find themselves at war with them. Their differing beliefs about the God of Love are the fuel for hate. How can this be? We must never forget that at this time, God is allowing this to be Satan's world, and Satan hates to see people living peacefully, and stirs up hatred. And Satan uses the false teachings of many types of 'Churchianity' to create discord and hatred..

However, God is working with few individuals in our era, those who Christ is adding to His Ecclesia or group. Christ is building his group Himself.

Matthew 16:18 And I say also unto thee, That thou art Peter (a pebble), and upon this Rock (Christ) I will build my church (This word is not in the original texts, it is derived from a pagan god called Circe, so this should read Greek 'ecclesia' - group); and the gates of hell shall not prevail against it.

Christ is certainly not leaving it to any of the thousands of human religious denominations to build his ecclesia!

Christ inspired the writing of the entire Bible

It is of vital importance that all earnest students of God's Word appreciate that the Living Christ Jesus is God's Son, our Creator, and that He inspired every word in the Holy

Bible, so He was actually the Author. Believing that this fact is true, and having faith in the truth of that statement is a major key that opens our minds to understanding. Sadly so very few people actually believe that this is true.

John 1:1 In the beginning was the Word, and the Word was with God, and the Word was God. 2 The same was in the beginning with God. 3 All things were made by him; and without him was not any thing made that was made. verse 14 And the Word was made flesh, and dwelt among us, (and we beheld his glory, the glory as of the only begotten of the Father,) full of grace and truth. 15 John bare witness of him, and cried, saying, This was he of whom I spake, He that cometh after me is preferred before me: for he was before me. 16 And of his fullness have all we received, and grace for grace. 17 For the law was given by Moses, but Grace and truth came by Jesus Christ.

As has been mentioned, all translations of the Holy Bible have flaws, but Christ Jesus has ensured that every individual in His group, His 'ecclesia' will be able to overcome these issues with His help. When we use the tools covered in this Introduction and the rest of those in this book with care and attention, Christ will cause God's Spirit to guide us into 'all truth' that He wants us to have at any given time.

Also we need to appreciate that Christ really is God, so that when the prophesied restoration and the times of refreshing referred to in Acts 19 and Daniel 12 begin to occur, we will see that our personal and collective knowledge will increase.

The role of the Holy Spirit in our studies

John 16 tells us about the central role of the Holy Spirit in our lives. Jesus said in verse 12: I have yet many things to say to you, but you cannot bear them now. verse 13

Howbeit when he (it), the Spirit of Truth, is come, he (it) will guide you into all truth; for he (it) shall not speak of himself (itself); but whatsoever he (it) shall hear, that he (it) will speak; and he (it, God's Power) will show you things to come.

Note: The Holy Spirit is *not* a person, this is a totally fallacious and incorrect teaching of Satan in the Garden of Eden, and the many organisations of men to this day. The Holy Spirit is the essence and expression of God's Power at work.

As we grow in grace and knowledge, the essence of God's Power, the Holy Spirit will guide us into all truth that God intends us to have at any particular time.

The Holy Spirit will 'speak' to us as we study, not by audible sounds, but directly into our minds in terms of concepts, thoughts, ideas, new understandings, and feelings. It is impossible for the human carnal mind to appreciate God's Word without it. This is the 'language' of God's spirit working in our minds.

Job 32:8 But there is a spirit in man: and the inspiration of the Almighty giveth them understanding.

The 'spirit in man' is what sets us apart from the animals. It imparts the gift of consciousness, as well as many rudiments of God's characteristics, love, forgiveness, thought, mind power, design, creativity, imagination, patience, kindness, joy, sorrow, and so many, many, more.

Romans 8:16 The Spirit itself beareth witness with our spirit, that we are the children of God:

Animals have a spirit which defines their specific characteristics. God's Spirit can communicate with the human spirit and inspire us with the ability to understand that we have a 'family' relationship with the Great God.

When we study, we need to ask for Spiritual Gifts

Our spirit can only commune with God through the gift of the Holy Spirit plus the other spiritual gifts we need. So we ask that His Spirit will fill our minds, and guide us into truth; and that God will give us the gifts of faith, confidence, and belief. Ask also for the gift of true repentance and a contrite heart; and that we will grow in Grace, knowledge, understanding and wisdom.

Romans 8:4 That the righteousness of the (new Spiritual) law might be fulfilled in us, who walk not after the flesh, but after the Spirit. 5 For they that are after the flesh do mind the things of the flesh; but they that are after the Spirit the things of the Spirit. 6 For to be carnally minded is death; but to be spiritually minded is life and peace. 7 Because the carnal mind is enmity against God: for it is not subject to the law of God, neither indeed can be.

We do not need religious, pious, or ecclesiastical men of any kind, however sincere they may be, to 'help' us, as that only leads to our absorbing the confusion of different ideas of men. There is only One Mediator between us and God, and that is His perfect, all powerful Son Christ Jesus.

1 Timothy 2:5 For there is one God, and one mediator between God and men, the man Christ Jesus;

Understanding 'Progressive Revelation' is an important key

Over time spent with Christ and indeed after his resurrection, the disciples continued to grow in Grace and knowledge due to the reality of 'Progressive Revelation' which we can see in action throughout the Bible from Genesis to Revelation.

God has not revealed His entire Plan to His children all at once, but gradually over the centuries from Adam on, then through the Prophets and the Writings, and finally through the Word, Christ Jesus.

After Christ came to earth, He began a completely new phase of His revelation, firstly to His disciples, he gave the essence of the New Law of Love. Then latterly Paul was given the revelation that we, all human beings, were called and saved before the foundation of the world.

Ephesians 1:4 According as he hath chosen us in him before the foundation of the world, that we should be holy and without blame before him in love:

Then in 63 A.D. Christ revealed to Paul the Mystery hidden to humankind from before the foundation of the world that our future as Christians was to become fully born children of the Most High God.

Colossians 1:26 Even the mystery which hath been hid from ages and from generations, but now is made manifest to his saints:

Then finally, the capstone of the Scriptures was given to John by the risen Christ in the book of Revelation. These are all phases of 'Progressive Revelation'.

Here is an example of 'Progressive Revelation' in the Old Testament. In the Book of the Law, children were to be visited by the punishment handed down for the iniquity of their fathers to the 3rd and 4th generation. This is repeated at least four times in the Mosaic Law.

Exodus 20:5 Thou shalt not bow down thyself to them, nor serve them: for I the Lord thy God am a jealous God, visiting the iniquity of the fathers upon the children unto the third and fourth generation of them that hate me.

Exodus 34:7 Keeping mercy for thousands, forgiving iniquity and transgression and sin, and that will by no means clear the guilty; visiting the iniquity of the fathers upon the children, and upon the children's children, unto the third and to the fourth generation.

Numbers 14:18 The Lord is long suffering, and of great mercy, forgiving iniquity and transgression, and by no means clearing the guilty, visiting the iniquity of the fathers upon the children unto the third and fourth generation.

Deuteronomy 5:9 Thou shalt not bow down thyself unto them, nor serve them: for I the Lord thy God am a jealous God, visiting the iniquity of the fathers upon the children unto the third and fourth generation of them that hate me,

However, in Ezekiel, this consequence of law breaking being passed onto subsequent generations is clearly changed. In effect this aspect of that law was abrogated or repealed by the Christ inspired words of Ezekiel.

People who lack understanding of the scriptures might see this as a 'contradiction', but God never contradicts Himself, and the Scriptures cannot be broken. They can be modified, expanded, or brought up to date by the Author though!

Ezekiel 18:20 The soul that sinneth, it shall die. The son shall not bear the iniquity of the father, neither shall the father bear the iniquity of the son: the righteousness of the righteous shall be upon him, and the wickedness of the wicked shall be upon him.

Every human has to die because of sin. Progressive Revelation is intermittently continuous throughout the Bible as God has gradually over centuries revealed more detail of His Plan and Purpose to His children over time.

Here is another example of 'Progressive Revelation' which has been resisted by many 'Christians'. Many churches which have kept one foot back in the Mosaic Law often emphasise a verse in the Sermon on the Mount to support their so-called law-keeping practices and then enforce them on their adherents when Jesus said:

Matthew 5:18 For verily I say unto you, Till heaven and earth pass, one jot or one tittle shall in no wise pass from the law, till all be fulfilled.

But just a few moments later, Christ says:

Matthew 5:21 Ye have heard that it was said of them of old time, Thou shalt not kill; and whosoever shall kill shall be in danger of the judgment: 22 But (that is no longer the case, I am giving you a new law!) I say unto you, That whosoever is angry with his brother without a cause shall be in danger of the judgment: and whosoever shall say to his brother, Raca, shall be in danger of the council: but whosoever shall say, Thou fool, shall be in danger of hell fire.

So what does Christ mean when he says in verse 19...?

Matthew 5:19 Whosoever therefore shall break one of these least commandments, and shall teach men so, he shall be called the least in the kingdom of heaven: but whosoever shall do and teach them, the same shall be called great in the kingdom of heaven.

Which one of these least commandments is Christ referring to? Is He referring to the Mosaic Law? Absolutely not! Christ is explaining his expansion of the New Testament Law of Love to His disciples. He is emphasising the need to keep the New Commandments that He is in the process of giving them! He is showing them that the New Law is now spiritual, and even more binding (and more impossible to keep without His help!) than ever the Old Testament physical laws were.

The Bible Student's 'Tools of the Trade'

Workers need the right tools. Skilled workers develop a relationship with their tools, treasure them, as through them they are able to produce good work of which they can be justifiably proud.

In order to be a good worker in the field of Bible Study, there are quite a few 'tools' that we can use in order to get the most out of the time we spend studying the Scriptures. Using the many 'tools' listed here, and elsewhere in this book, will help us gain greater knowledge, understanding and wisdom, and enjoy the satisfaction of learning well.

Instead of Bible Study perhaps being something we may feel we ought to do, with the help of the Holy Spirit, it will become an exciting journey of ever increasing discoveries. The Word contains so much information, the more we delve into the Bible, the more we will discover of the deeper and vital meanings that are hidden from those whose eyes are even partially closed.

Dr. Martin was a 'master' craftsman of his trade, and we have here part of the legacy he has left for those who want to become as proficient as he was. An exciting time is ahead of those who apply themselves to the principles in this book.

Rightly dividing the Word of Truth

2 Timothy 2:15 Study to shew thyself approved unto God, a workman that needeth not to be ashamed, rightly dividing the word of truth.

Our emphasis needs always to be on 'rightly dividing the Word of truth', but how do we do that? There are methods of study explained here that we can adopt to ensure that we do this as efficiently as possible.

When most people read the Bible they usually just read the text. There is a more scholarly approach we can use. We can use methods which will enable us to get a deeper understanding of the scriptures. This will enable us to get more "fish" so to speak.

1 Peter 3:15 but sanctify the Lord God in your hearts; and be ready always to give an answer to every man that asks you a reason of the hope that is in you with meekness and fear.

We need to teach ourselves by studying the Bible and asking Christ Jesus to give us open eyes and understanding hearts. We also need to be ready to help others understand the true meaning of the scriptures, always recognizing our need to be guided by the Holy Spirit.

If we are to be ready to give an answer to those who ask, we need to be truly workmanlike in our study of the scriptures.

We can be scholarly and methodical in our approach to study, but technical and complex matters can be and should be simplified. We need to develop our own system for ourselves, and not just mimic anyone else.

We need to learn principally from the one Book, the Holy Bible, with the help of the Holy Spirit, finding the unity and of the constant thread that runs through the whole book.

Always bearing in mind that The Bible is the one and only standard we can rely on, so long as we can understand what Christ who wrote it is telling us that is relevant for us today as we study.

Scriptural education was put on the back burner in 1859 when empirical and pseudo scientific thinking, Greek philosophies, and the study of nature and evolution took precedence. This is even more true today, as Scriptural Knowledge classes are being removed from the school curriculums, and the theory of evolution is taught instead.

Knowledge shall be increased

Daniel 12:4 but you had O Daniel shut up the words, and seal the book, even to the time of the end; many shall run to and fro, and knowledge shall be increased.

The Bible is 'sealed' to the average person. Why is that? Only God knows, and we can be sure that what He does is always for our ultimate good.

Hosea 4:6 My people are destroyed for lack of knowledge.

Lack of what knowledge? We live in an era of a technological and 'scientific' knowledge explosion never before experienced by human beings, yet we are systematically destroying ourselves and the earth as well. What this world needs is knowledge of God, Christ, and His Word, and His wishes concerning how we should live, dress and keep this Earth.

There is much in the Bible that has been sealed for centuries, but in our time, knowledge is being increased. In verse 10 of Daniel 12 it says none of the wicked shall understand, but the wise shall understand.

Who are the wise? Those who heed God's instructions. Understanding the principles of study leads us to greater knowledge and understanding, and God gives us the Wisdom by means of the Holy Spirit.

Proverbs 1:7 The fear (deep profound respect) of the Lord is the beginning of knowledge: but fools despise wisdom and instruction.

Studying what the Bible has to say on the subject of Wisdom is very interesting indeed. Even if a person simply reads all the scriptures that contain the word 'wisdom' in the Books of Proverbs and Ecclesiastes, they will gain great insight into the subject.

Use the Internet for locating scriptures, & historical knowledge.

Using the Internet can save an enormous amount of time. Bible Gateway is an extremely useful program. www.biblegateway.com. It has dozens of versions of the Bible to choose from, and many other powerful tools to help you with your study, and it is free to use.

You only have to type in a word or a text, or just the book and the chapter, and it will find all the occurrences in the version of your choice. The compiler of this book uses the King James Version (KJV) on this site for this work almost exclusively.

There is also another site which says the program it offers is free, but be careful not to finish up paying for it without realising it. Maybe they charge for the 'Android' version. So beware. However this tool enables you to use Strong's Concordance, access the original Hebrew or Greek Word and its meanings all in seconds. www.bible-discovery.com

If you have a Strong's, Young's, or any of several other large concordances, they are so heavy and cumbersome to use, and it takes ages to find what one is looking for. The Bible Gateway and Bible-Discovery are unbelievably quick, convenient, and easy to use.

Any time you might have a question about a time or event in history, or geographical material, the Internet can be a useful tool. Online encyclopaedias, historical details, maps etc., on every subject abound.

Of course we have to filter what we read there carefully to ensure that what they say does not conflict with the Scriptures, but only adds to our understanding of people, events, chronology and geography.

Beware of familiarity with your Bible

When we are familiar with any particular verse or passage in the Bible, there is a danger that we might read over something that is important.

Remember to pause and carefully ponder the words in verses familiar to you, think carefully about what we are reading. It is often the case that our previous associations with religious organisations may have resulted in our believing error, or at least being masked from seeing deeper or true understanding.

So it really does pay to read the verse or passage as if we had not read it before, thinking carefully about the words and their real meaning as we do.

As we do this, we can note any words that we do not fully understand and check them in a concordance or dictionary in order to get the true meaning in the original language. This is necessary because the translators often used secondary or even tertiary meanings of a word from the original text, and this may well obscure the actual or real meaning intended.

Be aware of the context

Many people use the Bible to support their own ideas and teachings. One way they either intentionally or unintentionally deceive is to take parts of the Word of God out of context. Using this ploy, they wrest or twist the scriptures to their own destruction, and to the confusion of others.

2 Peter 3:16 As also in all his epistles, speaking in them of these things; in which are some things hard to be understood, which they that are unlearned and unstable wrest, as they do also the other scriptures, unto their own destruction.

Be careful of using individual verses without checking to see if our understanding of the verse is confirmed by other passages in the Bible. What is the context of the verses surrounding the verse in question? Use the interrogative words who, what, when, where, etc., to help get the sense of the meaning.

Here is an instance of a text that many thousands of people are familiar with being used as a 'universal truth' that applies to everyone, but does it?

3 John 1:2 Beloved, I wish above all things that **thou** mayest prosper and be in health, even as thy soul prospereth.

Was it intended that we should use this inspired verse to think that God intends everyone to be prosperous and in good health all the time?

If we just look around us, clearly not! It seems more likely that this verse was intended as a personal greeting to an individual, for that is what it says.

Abundant health was not the case in the time of the Apostles as many around Christ were sick at times, and Paul mentions his own health problems, and also of those close to him.

Clearly health and prosperity are not universal, and is not the case in our world today, not even for well-meaning, sincere Christians! It is plain to see that God is allowing people everywhere on earth to experience the entire range of health and sickness, and also the extremes of poverty and wealth at this time in human history.

Failing to use context, and the plain words of the Bible, and indeed the evidence of the world around us, many thousands were taught to read over and even ignore the first verse of 3rd John. John was writing to an individual, Gaius.

3 John 1:1 The elder (John) unto (my friend) the wellbeloved Gaius, whom I love in the truth. 2 Beloved, I wish above all things that thou mayest prosper and be in health, even as thy soul prospereth.

John was wishing his friend 'all the best' so to speak. John was not intending to suggest that 'prosperity and health' was a promise from God to be claimed by all believers.

Introduction -- Essential Study Tools

Be aware of the chronology or the history of the time

In English, we have the simple single syllable word 'time'. Chronology is a four syllable word which sounds a bit daunting, but means the same thing.

When studying, as we read, be alert to catch any words which refer to 'time'. For instance: minute, morning, evening, day, week, month, harvest, year, before, now, then, after, and so on.

Then consider how any of these words fits in with the context, and to the larger picture in relation to the time frame that is being referred to, and also perhaps to the overall plan of God for His children.

None of the 'time' words in the Bible are in relation to the 'Gregorian Calendar' devised by Pope Gregory that is used in our current world.

All Biblical 'time' is in relation to the Solar/Lunar calendar. Bible 'days' are not midnight to midnight! They are sunset to sunset. All the words for 'time' have a direct relation to God's Calendar with the exception of the 'week'. The 'week' is not directly related to the month or the year. The number seven, and this seven day period 'week', and the Sabbath being made for man is one of God's 'mysteries'.

We cannot all be expert historians, but we can use books external to the Bible. For example, Josephus the Jewish very highly respected historian who wrote in 66 A.D., before the Bible was completed, whose works can shed a lot of light on the events and practices of the times. Just being aware of some of the history of the time we are reading about will help our understanding. So consider **when** what we are reading about occurred?

Commentaries can also be useful, but we need to be careful to evaluate what they say, and whether they are in accordance with the theme and truths of the Scriptures.

Introduction -- Essential Study Tools

Their authors are from many different denominations which have an extremely divergent or even a distorted view of many things, as they have many integrated pagan and heathen philosophies into their teachings, so we have to be alert.

Be aware of the geography

We can get a much better idea of the meaning of some scriptures by having a reasonable knowledge of the location of the events we are studying. So it pays to have some idea of the location of the action, the **where?**

So during study, be aware of any words which define the 'where': like the names of villages, towns, cities, and countries, rivers, mountains, seas, etc. It often helps to consult a map which shows the topography of the time. Most Bibles have such maps of time periods, also Bible dictionaries and commentaries can help in getting the 'feel' of the 'where'.

How far was it from the Tree of Crucifixion to the Curtain in the Temple? What was the distance from the source of the River Jordan at Mount Hermon to the Dead Sea? How far was Galilee from Jerusalem? What was it like there when Jesus was teaching his disciples? Being able to 'picture' the area in our minds helps to expand our understanding of events.

It can help to use the maps printed in the back of most Bibles, or we can scan the Internet to get maps we can print out of various eras in the past, and also maps that are current in our time. All these will help our appreciation of the area, events, and passages we are reading about.

Does this text or doctrine apply to Christian conduct in our era?

Some denominations quote verses from any part of the Bible regardless as to whether they are addressed to us in this era. Or whether, on the other hand, they are part of a system that has passed into history for now, like the rite of circumcision and the Temple sacrificial system, and Tithing for instance.

Many denominations cling onto selected parts of the Mosaic Law and claim that observing the letter of these Laws is essential for Salvation. They ignore the 'Progressive Revelation' given to us by Christ Jesus, that we are no longer under those physical Laws but now we are under the Spiritual Law of Love which is far more exacting than the physical laws were.

It is very important we understand clearly those Scriptures we are studying and know how they apply to our Christian life today, and those that do not.

Use interrogative words

One way to get more 'fish', is to bear in mind to employ the interrogative English words in mind as we study. There are six interrogative words in common use in English. They are:

who, what, where, when, why, and how.

If as we read, we ask ourselves to whom this was written? What is the text describing? Where did the event occur? When did this occur? Why is it important? And how does this apply to me, and whether indeed it does?

We need to be flexible in the use of this useful key. We certainly do not have to use it all the time, or for every word or verse. It is, however, a tool to pick up and use whenever it might be useful or needed.

The Bible uses repetition for emphasis

There are hundreds of examples in the Scriptures of two or more verses saying the exact same thing, or worded in a very similar way. Whenever Christ Jesus inspires repetition, it is to get our attention of how important the topic is. Here is an example:

Ezekiel 18:4 Behold, all souls are mine; as the soul of the father, so also the soul of the son is mine: the soul that sinneth, it shall die.

Ezekiel 18:20 The soul that sinneth, it shall die.

The meaning of these verses are ignored by millions, even perhaps billions who believe in the Immortality of the Soul, or in Reincarnation, both of which are Satanic notions.

Learning is a way of life

We are commanded to grow in grace and knowledge. We should be in a learning mode all our lives.

2 Peter 3:18 But grow in grace, and in the knowledge of our Lord and Saviour Jesus Christ. To him be glory both now and for ever. Amen.

Even without realising it, we 'teach' everyone we meet, often without saying a word! And we can learn from everyone we meet.

Proverbs 23:12 Apply thine heart unto instruction, and thine ears to the words of knowledge.

Proverbs 23:23 Buy the truth, and sell it not; also wisdom, and instruction, and understanding.

Proverbs 2:6 For the Lord giveth wisdom: out of his mouth cometh knowledge and understanding.

Proverbs 9:10 The fear of the Lord is the beginning of wisdom: and the knowledge of the holy is understanding.

Knowledge is what we know, facts: A switch can be used to turn the light on and off.

Understanding is how that knowledge applies to us, how it is so, and how it is to be applied. The light is powered by electricity from the power station through wires to our house. The light bulb offers resistance to the electric current which produces heat and light.

Introduction -- Essential Study Tools

Wisdom is the skill of the proper use of both knowledge and understanding. For instance: When or whether to turn the light on, and when or whether to turn it off!

There are seven points to learning:

1. We need a proper learning environment. Set up a comfortable area to study in. Make sure you have good light. Ensure the desk is at the right height for you, and that the chair is comfortable. Pen and paper at the ready, and the Internet available as a resource tool, we are ready to begin.

2. Nothing that we learn is unimportant, everything has its significance. We need not to be afraid of learning or think we cannot do it. Embrace it. Learning should be simple and it needs fearless application. And it should be mentally stimulating and emotionally satisfying.

3. We need to do our own personal study. Bible study is not the prerogative of ministers, otherwise we end up being entirely dependent upon them for our knowledge of the scriptures and of God. No father wants his children to be dependent upon others for what they know. A good father wants his children to learn for themselves. Our Heavenly Father certainly wants that for all His children.

4. Do not hide your lamp under a bushel. Christians are the light of the world. Be ready to give an answer to those who ask. And beware of casting pearls before 'swine', or sharing precious truths that Christ reveals to us personally to people whose minds are closed, who might turn and 'rend' you.

5. Be confident that you can learn. Christ has made Bible study the true key to personal development; to learning the truth about doctrines; to world history and chronology; and to related geography which are all

parts of what we need to lead a successful Christian and human life.

6. Set goals of how much time you want to spend and what you want to study. When you plan to work: Work your plan! Procrastination is the thief of time! Better a few minutes work, than putting it off for another day.

7. Make a practice of always to be learning new things. Use these practical tools contained in this introduction to help you to make the most effective use of your study time. Have an exciting and wonderful time!

Before you begin any period of study, be sure to ask Christ Jesus for His help, to have the right attitude, and to allow Him to guide your mind in humility and gratitude for all the understanding you gain as you study.

The first chapter of the book will cover the fundamentals of Scriptural knowledge.

CHAPTER 1
FUNDAMENTALS OF SCRIPTURAL KNOWLEDGE

The first and most important 'Key' to understanding the Bible and be able to grow in Grace and Knowledge before you even start is to ask God and Christ Jesus for Their help. You need the gifts of 'faith', 'open eyes' and 'open ears', and the help of the Holy Spirit, the Power of God, to understand the Bible and be convicted that it is indeed the Word of our Creator God.

Do not believe what any human being tells you what any section of the Bible means, ask Christ Jesus for His help.

Remember, Satan and his ministers can and do appear as 'angels of light'. Ministers of Churchianity do not have horns, they appear like 'good', sincere people. Indeed, they say that 'Jesus is the Christ', and claim to be doing God's work, but they are deceiving billions of people around the globe with a 'false' Gospel, exactly as Christ Jesus warned in Matthew 24.

Matthew 24:5 For many shall come in my name, saying, I am Christ; and shall deceive many.

Ministers will tell you that the Bible commands you to 'work out your own salvation', but is that really true?

Philippians 2:12 Wherefore, my beloved, as ye have always obeyed, not as in my presence only, but now much more in my absence, work out your own salvation with fear and trembling.

But even this often quoted verse is not actually a true representation of the thought Paul was teaching. Yes, we have to do the 'works' of reading and studying carefully, as well as all the other requirements of a Christian, but this quotation on its own is out of context and gives entirely the wrong impression of what we have to do.

It is not we who are working out our own salvation…

Philippians 2:13 For it is God which worketh in you both to will and to do of his good pleasure.

It is not we who can do the 'work' required, it is God, Christ Jesus who does the work, who through the flow of the Holy Spirit gives us the faith, and who opens our minds. It is essential that we understand this right from the start!

Remember: There is only one mediator between God and man, the Man Christ Jesus who is alive in Heaven.

1 Timothy 2:5 For there is one God, and one mediator between God and men, the man Christ Jesus;

Jesus, the ROCK said, "I will build my church (Greek: ecclesia – assembly, group)!" Christ said I will build My ecclesia, my group.

We certainly do not need religious people who claim to have the authority of Christ Jesus, and claim to come to you in His name, and by His authority to teach us, all in pursuit of their desire to control your mind.

John 2:27 But the anointing which ye have received of him abideth in you, **and ye need not that any man teach you:** but as the same anointing teacheth you of all things, and is truth, and is no lie, and even as it hath taught you, ye shall abide in him.

We most certainly do need the help of the Holy Spirit to open our minds.

John 16:13 Howbeit when he, the Spirit of truth, is come, he will guide you into all truth: for he shall not speak of himself; but whatsoever he shall hear, that shall he speak: and he will shew you things to come.

Note that the Holy Spirit is not a person, so the personal pronouns in this verse should not read 'he' but 'it'. This will be explained further in this book.

We need special information to enable us 'rightly to divide' God's Word.

Timothy 2:15 Study to shew thyself approved unto God, a workman that needeth not to be ashamed, rightly dividing the word of truth.

There are some other essential practical keys to study the Bible effectively, 'rightly to divide' God's Word, and gain real understanding. Because most people do not apply these important keys when they read the Bible, they usually a) do not understand what they read b) do not comprehend the real meaning and c) frequently get the message confused and end up misunderstanding or misrepresenting the scriptures.

For instance, most Christians have the notion that Christ spoke in parables to make the meaning clearer to the public. This is completely opposite to what Christ actually taught.

Matthew 13:10 And the disciples came, and said unto him, Why speakest thou unto them in parables? 11 He answered and said unto them, Because it is given unto you to know the mysteries of the kingdom of heaven, but to them it is not given.

The disciples did not understand the parables, but Christ explained the meaning to them; but Christ did not explain them to the general public.

Anyone who sincerely asks God and Christ for understanding in this era may receive the gifts of an open mind, of a humble heart, and the direct help of the Holy Spirit to enable them to understand the Holy Scriptures.

Matthew 13:34 All these things spake Jesus unto the multitude in parables; and without a parable spake he not unto them:

Christ here makes it very clear, that He spoke in parables "all these things", and "without a parable" he did not speak to them.

Matthew 13:35 That it might be fulfilled which was spoken by the prophet, saying, I will open my mouth in parables; I will utter things which have been kept secret from the foundation of the world.

Yahweh, God the Father and His Son Christ the Messiah had inspired the Old Testament prophets to explain this fact over and over again, that He would speak in parables to obscure the meaning, and secondly, He would reveal the way the Bible was written by God in a language that was simple in itself, but contained "secret" information. This "secret" information was not to be understood by anyone unless God opened their minds, their ears, and their eyes, and unless they had the help of the Holy Spirit.

People can read the words, the sentences, and they may understand what the words mean, but the real, true 'meaning' is hidden from them.

Why does God 'blind' people to the truth, and stop their ears from 'hearing' and understanding? This is the way God works with human beings, and it is His prerogative to do so. It must be the best way for our growth and development, all in His good time!

People do not always see this as 'fair'. Who are we to judge God as unfair?? As the Bible says, "Does the pot say to the potter why have you made me thus?" The earnest student of God's Word will come to appreciate a very different God from the counterfeit offered by thousands of so called 'Christian' sectarian churches.

Jesus dealt differently with His disciples than He did with the general public. When the disciples asked Him about the parables, He explained the meaning of the parables to them, yet they still did not always understand the deeper meaning.

Matthew 13:10 And the disciples came, and said unto him, Why speakest thou unto them in parables? 11 He answered and said unto them, Because it is given unto you to know the mysteries of the kingdom of heaven, but to them it is not given. 12 For whosoever hath, to him shall be given, and he shall have more abundance: but whosoever hath not, from him shall be taken away even that he hath. 13 Therefore speak I to them in parables: because they seeing see not; and hearing they hear not, neither do they understand. 14 And in them is fulfilled the prophecy of Esaias, which saith, By hearing ye shall hear, and shall not understand; and seeing ye shall see, and shall not perceive: 15 For this people's heart is waxed gross, and their ears are dull of hearing, and their eyes they have closed; lest at any time they should see with their eyes and hear with their ears, and should understand with their heart, and should be converted, and I should heal them.

Then Christ explained how blessed His disciples were (and we are!) to be given the insights He was sharing with them. They were learning things from Him that many Prophets (and sincere believers) had wanted to understand, but it had not been their time to have the clarity and the new information the disciples were receiving.

Matthew 13:16 But blessed are your eyes, for they see: and your ears, for they hear. 17 For verily I say unto you, That many Prophets and righteous men have desired to see those things which ye see, and have not seen them; and to hear those things which ye hear, and have not heard them.

Every word spoken by Christ while He was on earth was true. When the Pharisees questioned Him, He reminded them that the inspired scriptures cannot be broken.

John10:34 Jesus answered them, Is it not written in your law, I said, Ye are gods? 35 If he called them gods, unto whom the word of God came, and the scripture cannot be broken;

Only the wise will understand. And who are the wise? Those who have knowledge are those who deeply respect, love and 'fear' God.

Proverbs 1:7 The fear of the Lord is the beginning of knowledge: but fools despise Wisdom and instruction.

Proverbs 2:1 My son, if thou wilt receive my words, and hide my commandments with thee; 2 So that thou incline thine ear unto Wisdom, and apply thine heart to understanding; 3 Yea, if thou criest after knowledge, and liftest up thy voice for understanding; 4 If thou seekest her (Sophia - Wisdom) as silver, and searchest for her as for hid treasures; 5 Then shalt thou understand the fear of the Lord, and find the knowledge of God. 6 For the Lord giveth Wisdom: out of his mouth cometh knowledge and understanding. All the Knowledge, Understanding and Wisdom concerning what the Bible tells us about God's plan for humankind is a Spiritual gift. This information can only come through our being given the gift of the 'eyes to see' and the 'ears to hear'.

2 Timothy 1:9 Who hath saved us, and called us with an holy calling, not according to our works, but according to his own purpose and Grace, which was given us (as a free gift) in Christ Jesus before the world began,

Notice when this gift was given, before the world was created by God the Father and His Son Christ the Word.

Isaiah 6:8 Also I heard the voice of the Lord, saying, Whom shall I send, and who will go for us? Then said I, Here am I; send me. 9 And he said, Go, and tell this people, Hear ye indeed, but understand not; and see ye indeed, but perceive not. 10 Make the heart of this people fat, and make their ears heavy, and shut their eyes; lest they see with their eyes, and hear with their ears, and understand with their heart, and convert, and be healed.

Here is an important key to understanding the scriptures. The first time a word is used in prose, or the first time a subject is introduced in the Bible sets the key. For more understanding of the word or topic, then go to the last mention of that word or topic, and you have the 'alpha and the omega' or the 'A & Z' of it. Then you know where you have started, and you know what the conclusion of the matter is. Then one can select portions of scripture in between which shed more light on the subject.

For instance, in the beginning God said in Genesis, "Let us make man in our image". This "us" is a plural, but is talking about one God. One family of God, both male and female as is everything living. This concept is expanded in many parts of the Bible and could be a study subject on its own.

Isaiah 29:10 For the Lord hath poured out upon you the spirit of deep sleep, and hath closed your eyes: the Prophets and your rulers, the seers hath he covered. 11 And the vision of all is become unto you as the words of a book that is sealed, which men deliver to one that is learned, saying, Read this, I pray thee: and he saith, I cannot; for it is sealed: 12 And the book is delivered to him that is not learned, saying, Read this, I pray thee: and he saith, I am not learned.

Isaiah was talking to the top people. So it does not matter whether someone is well educated, a 'scholar', or not well educated, they will not understand the deep meaning of the scriptures because they are 'sealed' up until it is their time to know. Also in our era, 'sealed' for many others too, until the knowledge of the scriptures is increased at the time of the end.

Isaiah 29:13 Wherefore the Lord said, Forasmuch as this people draw near me with their mouth, and with their lips do honour me, but have removed their heart far from me, and their fear toward me is taught by the precept of men:

This is so true for the vast majority of people who think of themselves as Christian, or hold religious views. Most are controlled, guided, or rather mislead by false ministers and false prophets, who like the Pharisees of Christ's day, put their own ideas ahead of God's teachings in His Word.

Isaiah 29:14 Therefore, behold, I will proceed to do a marvellous (marvellous bad, not good!) work among this people, even a marvellous work and a wonder: for the wisdom of their wise men shall perish, and the understanding of their prudent men shall be hid. 15 Woe unto them that seek deep to hide their counsel from the Lord, and their works are in the dark, and they say, Who seeth us? and who knoweth us?

God sees all, but they, the religious people, do not really deeply believe in the One True God, nor do they respect His Word as the Truth. There is a veil over their eyes.

Isaiah 29:16 Surely your turning of things upside down shall be esteemed as the potter's clay: for shall the work say of him that made it, He made me not? or shall the thing framed say of him that framed it, He had no understanding? 17 Is it not yet a very little while, and Lebanon (Jerusalem) shall be turned into a fruitful field, and the fruitful field shall be esteemed as a forest?

The Temple was made from Cedars of Lebanon, and the use of the word Lebanon in this context means Jerusalem, not the country.

The religions of the present evil world have indeed turned everything precious of God's truths upside down, and inside out. Most reject the fact of Creation, and that they are actually children of God. Instead the majority now believe or accept blindly the ridiculous, insane theory of Darwin, that everything came from nothing!

As a result, some of the inhabitants of the world will have to learn the hard way. When? When Christ returns to reign.

Isaiah 24:17 Fear, and the pit, and the snare, are upon thee, O inhabitant of the earth. 18 And it shall come to pass, that he who fleeth from the noise of the fear shall fall into the pit; and he that cometh up out of the midst of the pit shall be taken in the snare: for the windows from on high are open, and the foundations of the earth do shake. 19 The earth is utterly broken down, the earth is clean dissolved, the earth is moved exceedingly. 20 The earth shall reel to and fro like a drunkard, and shall be removed like a cottage; and the transgression thereof shall be heavy upon it; and it shall fall, and not rise again. 21 And it shall come to pass in that day, that the Lord shall punish the host of the high ones (fallen angels) that are on high, and the (human) kings of the earth upon the earth. 22 And they shall be gathered together, as prisoners are gathered in the pit, and shall be shut up in the prison, and after many days shall they be visited. 23 Then the moon shall be confounded, and the sun ashamed, when the Lord of hosts shall reign in mount Zion, and in Jerusalem, and before his ancients gloriously.

There are some hard times coming for the inhabitants of this world prior to the Second Coming. But in the millennium Christ is going to remove the veil over everyone's eyes, and make a joyful feast for all people. Clearly this has not happened yet!

Isaiah 25:6 And in this mountain (His Government) shall the Lord of hosts make unto all people a feast of fat things, a feast of wines on the lees, of fat things full of marrow, of wines on the lees well refined. 7 And he will destroy in this mountain the face of the covering cast over all people, and the vail that is spread over all nations. 8 He will swallow up death in victory; and the Lord God will wipe away tears from off all faces; and the rebuke of his people shall he take away from off all the earth: for the Lord hath spoken it.

There is a wonderful time coming for the inhabitants of the Earth.

Acts 8:26-31 The story of the Ethiopian Eunuch teaches that we need some man (Jesus Christ, not a human!) to explain the meaning of the scriptures to us. We certainly can seek help from earnest students of the Bible, and share our new knowledge, but it has to be someone who has the Holy Spirit! Even then, we need to exercise great caution and pray we won't be deceived in any way.

Isaiah 53 foretells of the suffering and crucifixion of Christ in alarming detail. It was well known that it was the Jewish rulers and the priests who had instigated the crucifixion of Christ by the Roman officials.

Luke 24:19 And he said unto them, What things? And they said unto him, Concerning Jesus of Nazareth, which was a prophet mighty in deed and word before God and all the people: 20 And how the chief priests and our rulers delivered him to be condemned to death, and have crucified him.

Paul said that if the rulers had really known who Christ was, and the truth of the mystery, they would not have crucified Him.

Corinthians 2: 7 But we speak the wisdom of God in a **mystery, even the hidden wisdom,** which God ordained before the world unto our glory: 8 Which none of the princes of this world knew: for had they known it, they would not have crucified the Lord of glory. 9 But as it is written, Eye hath not seen, nor ear heard, neither have entered into the heart of man, the things which God hath prepared for them that love him.

This 'mystery', was the development of the Gospel which was revealed to Paul directly by Christ Jesus in or around 63 A.D., explaining the transition from the old way of looking at things to the new and more exciting 'good' news' about our future: The banishment of the enmity between humans under the law and God, by Christ's obedience, and Universal Salvation.

This is what some fundamental churches allude to, but never really explore, and they do not have any idea what they are missing! They keep Christ in the background as they insist on unnecessary obedience to some of the physical aspects of the old law. Some even illegally demand tithes from adherents and make their followers sin by paying them! Tithes were only ever collected by the Levites for the running and maintenance of the Temple. This 'bondage' even if only to some aspects of the law actually denies Christ's sacrifice, and the gift of His Spirit and Grace, and blocks people's understanding of Christ's magnified new spiritual Law of Love, and circumcision of the 'heart' (Deuteronomy 1:6) rather than the actual physical rite..

Galatians 2:16 Knowing that a man is not justified by the works of the law, but by the faith of Jesus Christ, even we have believed in Jesus Christ, that we might be justified by the faith of Christ, and not by the works of the law: for by the works of the law shall no flesh be justified. Verse

21 I do not frustrate the grace of God: for if righteousness come by the law, then Christ is dead in vain.

Those who put themselves back under any aspect of the Law, would have to keep it all. But this is not possible since there is no Temple, and no Priesthood. For instance, tithing of produce and animals was designed to provide those who operated the Temple with food and sustenance. When the Temple was destroyed, and the Priesthood was 'stood down' these laws were put into suspension. Ministers who insist on their parishioners tithing are making 'merchandise' of these hapless people.

2 Peter 2:1 But there were false prophets also among the people, even as there shall be false teachers among you, who privily shall bring in damnable heresies, **even denying the Lord that bought them,** and bring upon themselves swift destruction. 2 And many shall follow their pernicious ways; by reason of whom the way of truth shall be evil spoken of. 3 And through covetousness shall they with feigned words make merchandise of you: whose judgment now of a long time lingereth not, and their damnation slumbereth not.

So in attempting to practice parts of the Law to be 'obedient' to God, it means that they do not really believe that Christ changed the Law by bringing Faith and His Spirit, and the New Law of Love. So in truth, they are not really Christians at all!

Luke 6:46 And why call ye me, Lord, Lord, and do not the things which I say?

John 14:21 He that hath my commandments, and keepeth them, he it is that loveth me: and he that loveth me shall be loved of my Father, and I will love him, and will manifest myself to him.

Christ does not want Christians to be entangled in the old physical laws, but to keep His new Spiritual Laws with the help of the Holy Spirit.

We are still struggling with many aspects of the **'mystery, even the hidden wisdom',** but as it promises in Daniel, God is going to reveal more truths to His children as the end time approaches.

Daniel 12:4 But thou, O Daniel, shut up the words, and seal the book, even to the time of the end: many shall run to and fro, and knowledge (of the Book of Daniel) shall be increased… 9 And he said, Go thy way, Daniel: for the words are closed up and sealed till the time of the end.10 Many shall be purified, and made white, and tried; but the wicked shall do wickedly: and none of the wicked shall understand; but the wise shall understand.

John 16:13 Howbeit when he, the Spirit of truth (God's power) is come, he (it - God's Power) will guide you into all truth: for he (it) shall not speak of himself (itself); but whatsoever he (it) shall hear, that shall he (it) speak: and he (it) will shew you things to come.

Again, God's Holy Spirit is not an entity or a person. The Holy Spirit is the Power of God that He uses to perform His Works. The doctrine of the Trinity is a false teaching.

There is a coming restoration and expansion of Bible knowledge and Christianity before Christ returns. However, God does not pour it into our minds through a funnel, so we have to study!

Salvation is not by works, but there is still 'work' for a Christian to do, the work of using the gifts of Belief, Confidence, Faith, Repentance that He gives us as we study His Word.

Romans 11:4 But what saith the answer of God unto him? I have reserved to myself seven thousand men, who have not bowed the knee to the image of Baal. 5 Even so then at this present time also there is a remnant according to the election of grace.

Are there seven thousand 'reserved' by God in the world today who are given the gift of eyes to see? Who knows? Christ says 'few there be that find it'. Nobody can 'see' unless God removes the scales. Why does God blind? That is His prerogative, and we need to use His faith to trust that this is the best way for the development of His children at this time.

Seven thousand will become 144,000 of the Tribes of Israel who are sealed, plus an innumerable multitude more when Christ returns.

Romans 11:6 And if by Grace, then is it no more of works: otherwise Grace is no more Grace. But if it be of works, then it is no more Grace: otherwise work is no more work.

Grace is an amazing gift, as the song says, and all people will receive it in the end.

2 Corinthians 3:13 And not as Moses, which put a vail over his face, that the children of Israel could not stedfastly look to the end of that which is abolished: 14 But their minds were blinded: for until this day remaineth the same vail untaken away in the reading of the Old Testament; which vail is done away in Christ. 15 But even unto this day, when Moses is read, the vail is upon their heart.

People think they are worshipping God when they opt to put themselves under any part of the law of Moses in this era, but in fact they are ensuring the blinkers and blinders stay on! The whole of the Jewish people and their nation of Israel, as well as many 'Christian' denominations are still in bondage to their adherence to the Law which Christ came to fulfil.

How to study and rightly divide the Word of Truth.

Key No. 1 As stated at the beginning of this chapter, the vast majority of humans cannot understand parables and other key principles in the Bible because their eyes are blinded, and their ears cannot hear. We need to ask God and Christ for the help of the Holy Spirit.

Key No. 2 The information needed to understand any word, topic or teaching is rarely in one place in the scriptures, but clues to the complete meaning are usually scattered throughout the Bible, here a little and there a little.

We need to understand how the Bible is constructed and put together. Here is the next crucial key that we need. Many have preached this key without really understanding it, and they have not used it to help people study with purpose.

Instead many ministers have used the principle incorrectly, and have 'cherry picked' those scriptures from here and there which appear to support and give validity to the false teachings of their counterfeit gospel.

Isaiah 28:9 Whom shall he teach knowledge? and whom shall he make to understand doctrine? them that are weaned from the milk, and drawn from the breasts. 10 For precept must be upon precept, precept upon precept; line upon line, line upon line; here a little, and there a little: 11 For with stammering lips and another tongue (language) will he (God) speak to this people. 12 To whom he said, This is the rest wherewith ye may cause the weary to rest; and this is the refreshing: yet they would not hear. 13 But the word of the Lord was unto them precept upon precept, precept upon precept; line upon line, line upon line; here a little, and there a little; that they might go, and fall backward, and be broken, and snared, and taken.

Note the repetition for teaching and for emphasis. God really wanted those of Isaiah's time, and those who are open to His word now to understand this principle. Also note, that God speaks to His students with "stammering lips" (hesitantly? Needing our patience?), and in "another language", or in 'dark' sayings which only the Holy Spirit working in our minds can enable us to understand. Christ speaks to us using the Holy Spirit in terms of thoughts, ideas, concepts, knowledge and the understanding of God's thoughts for us.

Proverbs 1:6 To understand a proverb, and the interpretation; the words of the wise, and their dark sayings. 7 The fear of the Lord is the beginning of knowledge: but fools despise wisdom and instruction.

It is God's own language that we have to be familiar with, it is His method of teaching us. Precepts are built up from fragments, a line here and there.

Key No.3 Usually the first and the last mention of a word or topic show the start and conclusion of the topic, or the 'alpha' and the 'omega' of the subject. The other occurrences through the scriptures fill in additional information.

For instance, the word "Adam" is mentioned first in Genesis 2:19. Consulting a concordance we might come up with 31 other mentions of the word. The last mention is in Jude quoting Enoch regarding Christ's Second Advent and linking the word Adam to Him.

Corinthians 15:45 And so it is written, The first man Adam was made a living soul; the last Adam was made a quickening spirit.

One of the other references refers to Christ as the "last Adam", thus revealing more information for us. Other mentions put more detail into the subject.

The topic of 'baptism is mentioned in many places in the Bible. In the Old Testament it originally referred to 'washings', or 'cleansings'. So to track the meanings of 'baptisms' it would be good to start with the first references to 'washings' and check to the last mention of 'baptism'. This will help clear up the many apparent anomalies concerning the various 'baptisms'. Then we will learn that there is actually now only one baptism. Ephesians 4:5 One Lord, one faith, one baptism, which was performed for us by Christ as part of His Work of cleansing us when He was baptised by John the Baptist.

Key No. 4 Learn to recognise when the scripture is in straight 'prose', ordinary descriptive language, and when it is allegorical, figurative, or poetical. Those who do not have this key will find the Bible baffling, and think it is full of nonsensical things. The Bible is full of figures of speech common to the writers in their time, as indeed is the English language in common use today.

Figures of speech usually appear to be nonsense if taken literally. The phrase "out of sight, out of mind" simply means when something is not currently in our 'mind's eye' we are not thinking about it. One translation of this statement by a person not adequately educated in English interpreted this phrase as "invisible idiot". Out of sight = invisible, out of mind = insane!

This type of mistranslation can be the result when people who are not familiar with this important principle look superficially at the scriptures.

Timothy 2:15 Study to shew thyself approved unto God, a workman that needeth not to be ashamed, rightly dividing the word of truth.

Using these and other keys wisely, the earnest student will be more able 'rightly to divide the Word of God'.

1 Timothy 2:3 For this is good and acceptable in the sight of God our Saviour; 4 Who will have all men (all human beings) to be saved, and to come unto the knowledge

of the truth. 5 For there is one God, and one mediator between God and men, the man Christ Jesus;

The next chapter will expand on the need to be aware of timing of events as we study.

CHAPTER 2
PRINCIPLES OF CHRONOLOGY

The Bible is a book of history. There are three elements to history:

1. Events, both current at the time of writing, historical and prophetic in the future.
2. When, or what is the time frame in relation to other events.
3. Where, or the location, local, region, and world geography.
4. Who is writing, about whom.

Be aware of the chronology or the history of the time

In English, we have the simple single syllable word 'time'. Chronology is a four-syllable word which sounds a bit daunting, but means the same thing.

When studying, as we read, be alert to catch any words which refer to 'time'. For instance: minute, morning, evening, day, week, month, harvest, year, first, last, before, now, then, after, and so on.

Then consider how any of these words fits in with the context, and to the larger picture in relation to the time frame that is being referred to, and also perhaps to the overall plan of God for His children.

None of the 'time' words in the Bible are in relation to the Solar 'Gregorian Calendar' devised by Pope Gregory XIII in 1582 that is used in our current world.

All Biblical 'time' is in relation to the Solar/Lunar calendar, and all the words for 'time' in the Bible have a direct relation to God's Calendar with the exception of the 'week'. The 'week' is not directly related to the month or the year. The number seven, and this seven day period 'week', and the Sabbath being made for man is one of God's 'mysteries'.

Mark 1:14-15 Now after that John was put in prison, Jesus came into Galilee, preaching the gospel of the kingdom of

God, 15 And saying, The time is fulfilled, and the kingdom of God is at hand: repent ye, and believe the gospel.

The first thing mentioned as Jesus began to preach the gospel, He is marking the time frame, that it was when John the Baptist was put in prison. Also Christ is fulfilling prophecy from Isaiah that He would be preaching in Galilee.

Isaiah 9:1-2 Nevertheless the dimness shall not be such as was in her vexation, when at the first he lightly afflicted the land of Zebulun and the land of Naphtali, and afterward did more grievously afflict her by the way of the sea, beyond Jordan, in Galilee of the nations. 2 The people that walked in darkness have seen a great light: they that dwell in the land of the shadow of death, upon them hath the light shined.

The Olivet Prophecy in Matthew 24 was given just two days before Christ was crucified. Jesus said that the Temple would be destroyed and not one stone would be left upon another. The disciples asked "When"?

It is a good plan to be aware of adverbs and the other words listed above that emphasise timing: when, then, after, before, until and so on.

Then Christ lists the things which have to happen, wars, famine, pestilence, heavenly signs etc., in verses 4-31. Then to answer the question "when"? He says in verse 32-39:

Matthew 24:32 Now learn a parable of the fig tree; **When** his branch is yet tender, and putteth forth leaves, ye know that summer is nigh: 33 So likewise ye, **when** ye shall see all these things, know that it is near, even at the doors.

All these things include the possibility that all fleshly life on earth could be destroyed.

Matthew 24:22 And except those days should be shortened, there should no flesh be saved: but for the elect's sake those days shall be shortened.

Whenever the possibility of that event existed, and that time frame came to pass, it was not back then in Christ's time! But the destruction of all life on earth is certainly possible now with the formidable weapons that have been developed in our era.

Matthew 24:34 Verily I say unto you, This generation shall not pass, till all these things be fulfilled. 35 Heaven and earth shall pass away, but my words shall not pass away. 36 But of that day and hour knoweth no man, no, not the angels of heaven, but my Father only.

The phrase "this generation" has caused endless speculation. It could mean forty years, but there are different 'generations' lengths mentioned in the Bible. At the time of Christ, not even the angels knew the timing.

Matthew 24:37 But as the days of Noah were, so shall also the coming of the Son of man be. 38 For as in the days that were before the flood they were eating and drinking, marrying and giving in marriage, until the day that Noe entered into the ark, 39 And knew not until the flood came, and took them all away; so shall also the coming of the Son of man be.

Those drowned in the flood did not see it coming! What were they doing that God decided to kill everyone on earth apart from eight people? They were "eating, drinking and marrying and giving in marriage". People have always done these things, and there is nothing wrong in them. So why are they mentioned here in this context?

Could it be that just before the flood, the world's inhabitants were eating all the wrong things destroying their health; drinking to excess and getting drunk and committing foul acts; and were men marrying men and women marrying women like they are now? All of these abuses and excesses are a total abomination to God?

Is it unreasonable to guess that something really bad was going on with those people just before the flood? Of that there is not much doubt as God had decided to destroy them all for their behaviour. Jesus is saying the world's population is going to be behaving like that when He is about to come. People will think He delays His coming, or will not realise it is about to happen.

So chronology has always been a difficult subject to unravel. Chronology has been misused for aeons, with people setting dates, or alluding to them, and they have always been disappointed!

The disciples did not have the Holy Spirit at this time when Jesus was speaking to them, and they were still slow to understand, because having the Holy Spirit indwelling is a vital and crucial factor in our understanding God's Word and His plan.

How can you know that you have God's Holy Spirit? If we ask for, and invite the help of the Holy Spirit, we find then that we are not only open to new knowledge and understanding of the scriptures, but also begin to see things in a new "Light". When that "Light" in our minds is consistent with what we read in the entirety of the Holy Bible, it can only come from God.

A second check is when you find others around you are either 'not interested', or not open to new understanding, and may even be somewhat hostile to your 'strange' beliefs.

Perhaps criticism of your beliefs from those close to you might intensify, for as it says: Matthew 10:36 And a man's foes shall be they of his own household.

But Daniel said in 12:4 that (**the**) knowledge {of his prophecies} would increase at the time of the end, and it is beginning to happen right now!

Matthew 24:42 Watch therefore: for ye know not what hour your Lord doth come. 43 But know this, that if the goodman of the house had known in what watch the thief would come, he would have watched, and would not have suffered his house to be broken up. 44 Therefore be ye also ready: for in such an hour as ye think not the Son of man cometh.

Here Christ is being specific about chronology. We are warned by Christ to 'watch' world events. If you set a date you are wrong, it is pointless to do so. Christ is coming when you think not!

Matthew 24:48 But and if that evil servant shall say in his heart, My Lord delayeth his coming;

Another aspect of timing. Christ will not delay His coming. He will arrive exactly on schedule, God the Father's schedule.

Matthew 25:1 Then shall the kingdom of heaven be likened unto ten virgins, which took their lamps, and went forth to meet the bridegroom. 2 And five of them were wise, and five were foolish. 3 They that were foolish took their lamps, and took no oil with them: 4 But the wise took oil in their vessels with their lamps.

All ten virgins had 'oil', which is a type of the Holy Spirit, but only the wise took extra oil, realising that they could not know how long they were going to wait for the 'bridegroom'. A word to the wise! We can know the general time, but we cannot know the day or the hour.

Another chronological indication, but without any date.

The Second Coming could certainly happen on **a** day of Trumpets. Although that might sound logical, we cannot know! In Old Testament times, many King's reigns started then.

1 Corinthians 15:51 Behold, I shew you a mystery; We shall not all sleep, but we shall all be changed, 52 In a moment, in the twinkling of an eye, at the last trump: for the trumpet shall sound, and the dead shall be raised incorruptible, and we shall be changed.

Moses was used to create a calendar in Sinai. The Old Testament is for one group of people, and the New Testament is for another. Events, times, and peoples are different, but the whole plan of God is one coherent whole. Every piece of information we need is within the pages of the Bible. One day, it suggests that we might even have to ask Jews for new information!

In Genesis, God said, Genesis 1:3 "Let there be light". Light divides the day from the night that make up our 24-hour day.

God is Light. So His Creation of matter includes light.

Genesis 1:14 And God said, Let there be lights in the firmament of the heaven to divide the day from the night; and let them be for signs, and for days, and for seasons, and years. This is talking about a calendar.

So the sun and the moon and the stars were created for signs (information), about days, seasons and years. A year is almost exactly 365¼ days. The first man and woman were created on a Friday, probably in the Autumn part of the year. The Sabbath has no astronomical basis, but it was made for man. Nor indeed has the 'week' of seven days have a celestial basis. The number seven is one of God's mysteries.

In the Old Testament, the years, lifespans, and other year indications are counted from the 1st day of the 1st month, which is in the Autumn. That is until the time of the Exodus when God changed the basis of the calendar.

Exodus 12:1 And the Lord spake unto Moses and Aaron in the land of Egypt saying, 2 This month (Nisan – springing up, approximately our March/April) shall be unto you the beginning of months: it shall be the first month of the year to you.

This was the inauguration of the ecclesiastical calendar for God's people Israel from that time then and forward.

Note: This Chapter is focussed on Chronology. Dr. Martin spent decades studying this subject in relation to his archaeological work. He always said chronology was like a very complex jigsaw puzzle in the Bible, most difficult to unravel. The writing on this subject in this book is based on the fact that the compiler has not spent many years studying chronology, and also finds it very complex. Sometimes it requires more knowledge even to begin to decipher the information Dr. Martin gives in this part of his work, but hopefully what is included here will still provide the earnest student with a very useful 'key' to greater understanding.

Then the Passover was given to the children of Israel on the night before they departed from Egypt. Protected by God, and freed from the "sin" of Egypt by the blood of the Lamb, picturing Christ's sacrifice to come.

Exodus 12:3 Speak ye unto all the congregation of Israel, saying, In the tenth day of this month they shall take to them every man a lamb, according to the house of their fathers, a lamb for an house:

So prior to the Exodus years were calculated from Autumn to Autumn, and after the Exodus they were calculated from Spring to Spring. The years before the Exodus from Autumn to Autumn in the first six chapters of Genesis reveal some interesting secret clues about chronology. Everyone had the same official "birthday", the first of Tishri, the first month of the New Year.

Genesis 4:3 And in process of time it came to pass, that Cain brought of the fruit of the ground an offering unto the Lord.

The phrase "in the process of time" actually equals "the end of days", or the end of one year, and the beginning of the next. This then was Autumn time, and Cain and Abel were bringing the fruits of their labours to God.

In the book of Jude, he says that Enoch was a prophet.

Jude 1:14 And Enoch also, the seventh from Adam, prophesied of these, saying, Behold, the Lord cometh with ten thousands of his saints.

Enoch's son was called Methuselah, the longest living human being who lived 969 years, and he died. Methuselah name was given to him by his father who was a Prophet. His name means: "When he dies, it will be sent." What will be sent? The flood! (It always pays to take note of the actual meaning of the names of the prophets.)

Genesis 5 gives the length of time each of the generations from Adam lived. From this list, it is possible to calculate when the flood happened. It was in the year 1656 from Creation, or 2369 B.C.

Genesis 5:27 And all the days of Methuselah were nine hundred sixty and nine years, and he died. So Methuselah died, then the flood came.

Genesis 7:6 And Noah was six hundred years old when the flood of waters was upon the earth.

Birthdays were counted from the first of the year, so everyone had the same birthday! Our spiritual 'birthday' will be Trumpets, the 1st of Tishri.

Genesis 7:11 In the six hundredth year of Noah's life, in the second month, the seventeenth day of the month, the same day were all the fountains of the great deep broken up, and the windows of heaven were opened.

Note the precise historical record of the exact timing of this event.

The waters covered the earth, and it seems likely that water from the great fountains of the deep were added to by the melting of a band of ice around the Earth that was in the ionosphere at that time causing torrential rain.

The waters covered the earth for just over a year.

Genesis 8:13 And it came to pass in the six hundredth and first year (of Noah's life), in the first month, the first day of the month (and the 1st day of the year) (The Feast of Trumpets), the waters were dried up from off the earth: and Noah removed the covering of the ark, and looked, and, behold, the face of the ground was dry. 14 And in the second month, on the seven and twentieth day of the month, was the earth dried.

Again, note the precise historical record of the exact timing of this event.

The first day of the first month (Tishri) when the earth dried was the Day of Trumpets, in the Autumn.

The story of Joseph, taken from total disgrace in prison, and then set at the "right hand" of the Pharaoh in ONE DAY on the Day of Trumpets is also a type of what is going to happen to us at the time of our being changed or resurrected. We Christians shall go from the "prison" of physical life, or death, to Glory in one day.

We shall meet Christ in the air, and then actually find ourselves in Glory at the right hand of the Father. In a sense we who are true Christians are there now in allegory, in spiritual terms as we are "in Christ" who is in heaven at the right hand of the Father. (Colossians 3:1)

Genesis 41:1 And it came to pass at the end of two full years, that Pharaoh dreamed: and, behold, he stood by the river. 14 Then Pharaoh sent and called Joseph, and they brought him hastily out of the dungeon: and he shaved himself, and changed his raiment, and came in unto Pharaoh.

This happened on the first day of the new year, the day of Trumpets.

Genesis 41:39 And Pharaoh said unto Joseph, Forasmuch as God hath shewed thee all this, there is none so discreet and wise as thou art: 40 Thou shalt be over my house, and according unto thy word shall all my people be ruled: only in the throne will I be greater than thou. 41 And Pharaoh said unto Joseph, See, I have set thee over all the land of Egypt. 42 And Pharaoh took off his ring from his hand, and put it upon Joseph's hand, and arrayed him in vestures of fine linen, and put a gold chain about his neck;

From the depths of the dungeon in disgrace, to number two in the land of Egypt, the most powerful nation on Earth, *in one day*!

Also in the Minor Prophets, it says that the sins of Israel will be wiped out *in one day* at Christ's return.

Psalm 81:1 Sing aloud, blow up the trumpet on the new Moon.

Look at the important events recorded in the Bible that happened to the notables, they are usually on specific dates, which gives a new perspective to timing, and to chronology.

Genesis 15:12 And when the sun was going down, a deep sleep fell upon Abram; and, lo, an horror of great darkness fell upon him. 13 And he said unto Abram, Know of a surety that thy seed shall be a stranger in a land that is not theirs, and shall serve them; and they shall afflict them **four hundred years;** 14 And also that nation, whom they shall serve, will I judge: and afterward shall they come out with great substance.

Gen 17: Abraham was circumcised on the 14th Nisan and that day became the Passover. From that time, it was 430 years to the Exodus and that period ended on the same day of the year that it started.

Genesis 25:8 Then Abraham gave up the ghost, and died in a good old age, an old man, and full of years; and was gathered to his people.

Abraham did die in good old years, 400 years, this was not a rounded up figure, it worked out to the day when the land was apportioned

In Joshua 14, it explains how Joshua gave Caleb the son of Jephunneh his promised inheritance on the day he was 85 years old.

Joshua 14:6 Then the children of Judah came unto Joshua in Gilgal: and Caleb the son of Jephunneh the Kenezite said unto him, Thou knowest the thing that the LORD said unto Moses the man of God concerning me and thee in Kadeshbarnea. 7 Forty years old was I when Moses the servant of the LORD sent me from Kadeshbarnea to espy out the land; and I brought him word again as it was in mine heart. 8 Nevertheless my brethren that went up with me made the heart of the people melt: but I wholly followed the LORD my God. 9 And Moses sware on that day, saying, Surely the land whereon thy feet have trodden shall be thine inheritance, and thy children's for ever, because thou hast wholly followed the LORD my God. 10 And now, behold, the LORD hath kept me alive, as he said, these forty and five years, even since the LORD spake this word unto Moses, while the children of Israel wandered in the wilderness: and now, lo, I am this day fourscore and five years old. 11 As yet I am as strong this day as I was in the day that Moses sent me: as my strength was then, even so is my strength now, for war, both to go out, and to come in. 12 Now therefore give me this mountain, whereof the LORD spake in that day; for thou heardest in that day how the Anakims were there, and that the cities were great and fenced: if so be the LORD will be with me, then I shall be able to drive them out, as the LORD said. 13 And Joshua blessed him, and gave unto Caleb the son of Jephunneh Hebron for an inheritance.

God is watching over His planned chronological time periods precisely.

From the first Adam to the second "Adam", the Bible gives an 'idealised' chronology of the time that elapses between these two personalities, but we can discover some interesting things about the time frame. Like the genealogical tables which are 'idealised', and there are reasons for that.

The secret things belong to God, but the Holy Spirit does help us comprehend, and the veil will progressively come away and understanding will increase as we approach the time of the end.

From Creation to the flood, add up the years of the patriarchs from Adam to the flood, and Noah's age is given to the day, it comes to 1656 years. Go on from there from Adam to the 99th year of Abraham's life when he was circumcised, a very important event because that is when he became the father of the faithful, you come to 2107 years. What was Paul's teaching about in Galatians 6? It is all about circumcision, its importance initially, and its unimportance now we are no longer under the physical Law.

Then apply the 430 years after that of Genesis 14: Israel left Egypt on the 14th Nisan, the first Passover, (which is also the same day of the year that Christ was crucified).

The chronological patterns in the Bible are not immediately obvious, but on study, they reveal that God is meticulous about His timing, His times, His seasons, and His ages. Everything is precisely on time, and will continue to be so until "all is in all".

Not a lot of people would take any notice of the seemingly unimportant mentions of 'years', 'moons' or references to a calendar most people are not familiar with that are peppered through the text. Like the comment about Methusaleh's age and the flood, but they are all important clues.

Here in Psalms is mentioned the Feast of Trumpets.

Psalm 81:1 Sing aloud unto God our strength: make a joyful noise unto the God of Jacob. 2 Take a psalm, and bring hither the timbrel, the pleasant harp with the psaltery. 3 Blow up the trumpet in the new moon, in the time appointed, on our solemn feast day. 4 For this was a statute for Israel, and a law of the God of Jacob.

You cannot establish a complete chronology up to the time of David from the Patriarchs ages given in the Bible. However, there are chronological 'bridges' which help us link up the apparent 'gap' times.

1 Kings 6:1 States it is a 480 years period written out in Hebrew letters. This is accurate, it is not an error.

Paul addressed the men of Israel in Acts and under the inspiration of the Holy Spirit gave an interesting reference to this time as being 'about 450 years':

Acts 13:18 And about the time of forty years suffered he their manners in the wilderness. 19 And when he had destroyed seven nations in the land of Chanaan, he divided their land to them by lot. 20 And after that he gave unto them judges about the space of four hundred and fifty years, until Samuel the prophet. 21 And afterward they desired a king: and God gave unto them Saul the son of Cis, a man of the tribe of Benjamin, by the space of forty years. 22 And when he had removed him, he raised up unto them David to be their king; to whom also he gave their testimony, and said, I have found David the son of Jesse, a man after mine own heart, which shall fulfil all my will.

The 450 years does not include the time of Joshua.

Joshua 24:29 And it came to pass after these things, that Joshua the son of Nun, the servant of the Lord, died, being an hundred and ten years old.

Judges 2:8 And Joshua the son of Nun, the servant of the Lord, died, being an hundred and ten years old.

Remember, when the Bible repeats things, it is for emphasis, and can often be an essential clue to its importance.

When you take the 480 years down to the fourth year of Solomon, then you link up with the Exodus back to the time of Abraham's circumcision, and going back to the time of Noah and the flood, as we know that exact date, then all the way back to Adam himself.

Put them all together buttressed with some of the 'hidden' or 'secret' links given in the scripture, then you have a consistent and consecutive chronology down to the 4th year of Solomon. Now since Solomon had a forty year reign, to this must be added to the 36 years of Solomon's reign after the 4th year, to his death.

When we come to Solomon's death, we find that his son Rehoboam took over as king of Judah, in the South with its centre in Jerusalem, and plus the tribe of Levi and the tribe of Benjamin, and a portion of Simeon. Three years later the Kingdom of Israel split into two.

There were then 19 king's reigns from Rehoboam to Zedekiah who was the last king of Judah of the Davidic dynasty who ruled in Jerusalem. Zedekiah ruled in the time of Jeremiah and Ezekiel. In the 19th year of King Nebuchadnezzar of Babylon, Zedekiah was killed, the city of Jerusalem was destroyed, and the Temple was burnt to the ground. That ended the Davidic dynasty in Palestine.

The length of time those 19 kings ruled comes to 393 years, simple addition, whether you take the accounts in Kings or Chronicles, they are the same. Scholars today cannot believe that these 393 years is consistent or consecutive. They think there were some overlaps between the kings, but when you study carefully that is not the case.

These 393 must be added to the last 36 years of Solomon's reign from the 4th year when the Temple was started to when he died; then 480 years back to the Exodus; then

430 years back to the time of Abraham's circumcision, then 2107 back to the time of Adam's Creation. Put all these together and you have a consistent chronology all the way to the end of the Judaic Kingdom, and the 19th year of Nebuchadnezzar king of Babylon.

From there on you have to use a prophetical indication to stay with the Biblical chronology. It is the 70 year period which Jeremiah the Prophet said would exist of the Babylonian captivity, and with that 70 years added on to the whole scheme you can have again a consistent chronology all the way back to Adam.

In the last book of II Chronicles, and compare it with what is stated in the 1st chapter of Ezra, which in our version follows immediately after 2nd Chronicles, we find that the 70 years ends with Cyrus over Babylon.

From the 1st year of Cyrus, if we went to secular chronology it would not seem to agree with the Bible at all. Now we either have to believe the Bible, or say that it is an 'ideal' chronology based primarily on prophecy for teaching purposes, or we are going to have to say it is exactly correct and that it is the secular chronology that is wrong.

Although there are some indications in astronomical records that indicate secular chronology might be correct, we see all through the Bible that God has given us a most intricate and accurate chronology. When observing His precision in the Old and the New Testament over and over again in the Bible, it will be proved correct when we have a more complete understanding of the Bible. There are however, as Dr. Martin emphasised some scholastic problems to overcome, and that is true.

The difficulties are from the time of Cyrus as far as the Bible is concerned down to Alexander the Great because it is a difficult time. There are however 'bridges', one of which is the 70 weeks prophecy mentioned in Daniel 9. This seventy weeks leads right up to the Messiah.

Daniel was given this prophecy because he expected the 70 weeks of Jeremiah to end in his time, that the Kingdom of Judea would come back into existence, and indeed that the Kingdom of Heaven would emerge on the earth and the Messiah would be here.

But Daniel was given this vision and it was interpreted by Gabriel that this was not to be the case. There was to be another seventy weeks of years, and there is no doubt that this is what was meant. It has always been understood to be so by Biblical scholars, and the Bible supports it.

Seventy weeks means seventy weeks of years. Seventy weeks of seven days or a period of 490 years. From Cyrus 1,490 years onward we would find the Kingdom of God emerging on the earth, and the Messiah appearing as well.

However, this 70 weeks period is divided into three sections, or four divisions. 7 weeks to begin with or 49 years, followed by a period of 434 years or 62 weeks, put those together and you get 69 weeks, or 483 years which leads up to the Messiah appearing. There would then be one week of seven years left, and that was to be divided in half, 3½ on one side and 3½ on the other. People have wondered about the 70 weeks prophecy for years, it is difficult as we are not given all the chronological benchmarks or events that would make this clear.

These periods were 'cut out' of history, does this mean there were some gaps? These are still questions.

From the 1st year of Cyrus at the end of the 70 years captivity, which is clearly the Bible benchmark for the beginning of the 70 weeks; and go on down to the arrival of the Messiah 483 years, add that 483 from the Messiah back to the 1st of Cyrus; then the 70 years that Jeremiah said would elapse of the Babylonian captivity; plus the 393 years of the kings of Judah; plus the 36 years remaining of Solomon's reign, taking you back to the 4th year of Solomon' reign when he commenced building the

Temple; then 480 years back to the Exodus; 430 years back to the circumcision of Abraham covenant in his 99th year; then 2107 back to the creation of Adam, you will have an elapsed time from the 1st Adam to the 2nd 'Adam' of exactly 3999 full years as having passed as having been accomplished already. If that is the case, that means then, that means the Messiah would come onto the scene exactly at the beginning of year 4000.

To summarise:

!st year of Cyrus to the Messiah	483
70 years of captivity	70
Period of the Kings of Judah	393
Plus 36 years of Solomon's reign	36
Plus 480 years back to the Exodus	480
Plus back to Abraham's circumcision	430
Plus 2107 back to creation of Adam	2107
Total of 3999 years completed	3999
Messiah born at the beginning of year	4000

Dr. Martin felt that here was no doubt that Christ, was born on the first day of the seventh month, the month of Tishri, which then became known as the day of Trumpets, the first day of the new year. The Hebrew month of Tishri corresponds to September/October in the Gregorian Calendar.

There is however, another possibility to consider. It is that Christ the Lamb of God was born in the Springtime, March/April, which was the lambing period in Israel at that time. The shepherds who visited the baby in the manger were living in the fields at the time to watch over their lambing ewes. They would not have been living there in the winter time.

Isn't it interesting when you follow all the rules and the standards given in the scriptures, it comes to 3999. Does it mean when Jesus was 12 years old at His Bar Mitzvah, or when he was 20 years of age, or when He was 30 years of age and he commenced His ministry, or when He died on the tree of crucifixion, or when??? We are not told by Daniel. That is where one problem comes in which is why we cannot date Christ's Second Advent.

After that 4000 years, we now have 2000 more years that have elapsed, and maybe a few more, so we come to 6000, which when you add in the 1000 years of the millennium, we come to the 7000 years that seems to be the allotted time for mankind's period on this earth. If we take it to the time of His ministry or His death, we come to somewhere around 2028 – 2032 for the beginning of the Millennium. But who knows!!!! We do not, yet.

Chronology is a perplexing and difficult study, but it is certain that Christ Jesus has put all the information we need to know within the pages of His Word, and the time will come when He will reveal more to His servants.

Matthew 24:13 Watch therefore, for ye know neither the day nor the hour wherein the Son of man cometh. Verse 36 But of that day and hour knoweth no man, no, not the angels of heaven, but my Father only.

Mark 13:32 But of that day and that hour knoweth no man, no, not the angels which are in heaven, neither the Son, but the Father.

God is still watching over His chronological intentions and purposes precisely we can be sure! We can have faith in that!!

The next chapter will show the importance of geography, and to note where things happened according to the Biblical record.

CHAPTER 3

THE IMPORTANCE OF GEOGRAPHY IN THE BIBLE

Be aware of the geography

We need to look at each event in terms of where and when it occurred. It is essential that geographical as well as chronological facts are considered in order to arrive at a proper understanding of the scriptures.

We can get a much better idea of the meaning of some scriptures by having a reasonable knowledge of the location of the events we are studying. So it pays to have as clear an idea as possible of the location of the action, the **where?**

So during study, be aware of any words which define the 'where': like the names of villages, towns, cities, and countries, rivers, mountains, seas, etc. It often helps to consult a map which shows the topography of the time.

Most Bibles have such maps of time periods, also Bible dictionaries and commentaries can help in getting the 'feel' of the 'where' the action the passage describes was taking place, and where future prophesied events will actually occur.

For instance, knowing exactly where and when the crucifixion took place, and where and when the resurrection of Christ took place; and when and where Christ left from to ascend to heaven; and when and exactly where He will return to, will give us more clarity on the geography and chronology, and more insight into the scriptural record.

All the prophecies of the events of the Bible fit together perfectly. Doctrines including salvation become so much clearer and make more sense than ever before when we consider the 'when' and the 'where'.

The first proof of where the crucifixion took place is revealed by the record that there were two witnesses of the tearing of the temple curtain from the top to the bottom. The curtain was 80 feet high and 25 feet wide and very thick, and it hung up from a stone lintel 30 tons in weight.

So the curtain was eight storeys high and very thickly woven, about four inches thick, and it tore in half at the exact time of Christ's death. Since the Bible states that this occurrence was visible to at least two witnesses standing where Christ was crucified, the tree of crucifixion or cross had to be in line of sight of the Temple curtain. This was impossible from anywhere except the summit of the Mount of Olives to the East of the Temple.

From the West of the temple it would have been impossible. The tree of crucifixion had to be to the East of the temple for there to be a direct line of sight from the crucifixion site to the Temple. The Bible says that the Centurion who was standing by the tree saw the tearing of the Temple curtain happen.

Matthew 27:50 Jesus, when he had cried again with a loud voice, yielded up the ghost. 51 And, behold, the veil of the temple was rent in twain from the top to the bottom; and the earth did quake, and the rocks rent; 52 And the graves were opened; and many bodies of the saints which slept arose, 53 And came out of the graves after his resurrection, and went into the holy city, and appeared unto many. 54 Now when the Centurion, and they that were with him, watching Jesus, saw the earthquake, and those things that were done, they feared greatly, saying, Truly this was the Son of God.

Christ was buried only 180 yards away from the site of the cross. The timing or chronology of His death was also crucial. Christ was our Passover, and died to deliver us from the bondage and slavery of sin.

In the Temple area there were two other altars of incense outside the Holy Place. Another outside was the altar of the Red Heifer which was East of the temple, without, or outside the camp about two thirds of a mile away at Bethphage which was a place of assembly.

There was a square wall 2000 cubits, or about 3000 feet, away from the temple.

The site of the Church of the Holy Sepulchre and the garden tomb where most religious people believe it all happened are to the West of the Temple, but it is just not possible for that area to be correct because it could not be seen from the tree of crucifixion.

Hebrews 13:10 We have an altar, whereof they have no right to eat which serve the tabernacle. 11 For the bodies of those beasts, whose blood is brought into the sanctuary by the high priest for sin, are burned without the camp. 12 Wherefore Jesus also, that he might sanctify the people with his own blood, suffered **without the gate**.

Christ was killed outside the gate, outside the camp. He was forced to carry the patubulum or board plank cross piece. Christ could see and look at His Father's house as he suffered and died.

God's name is YHWH. The tetragrammaton YHWH was not allowed to be uttered by anyone in Israel, and not even the Priests. It was only allowed to be spoken by the High Priest and then only in the Holy of Holies once a year. It all centres on the day of Atonement, Yom Kippur, which atonement Christ was going to perform for us.

Because of Christ's sacrifice, and the tearing open of the curtain of the Temple, God was announcing that He was to become available to the whole world of His children, not just His people the Jews and Israel. Every human being was now to have direct access to God, and were to be allowed to say His name at any time.

Hebrews 13:13 Let us go forth therefore unto him without the camp, bearing his reproach. 14 For here have we no continuing city, but we seek one to come. 15 By him therefore let us offer the sacrifice of praise to God continually, that is, the fruit of our lips giving thanks to His name.

Part of our work as Christians now is to publicly proclaim and praise God's name continually. We do not have to use the tretragrammaton YHWH, or pronounce God's name in any particular way. We who have the Holy Spirit are in type and in Spirit currently in the Holy of Holies with Christ in the 'Heavenlies', and we can call him God, or the Father, or indeed 'Abba' or Dad!

Without the understanding of the geography and the chronology of the events of the crucifixion, proper clarity is not possible. Humankind wants to put God's headquarters ~~church~~ ekklesia on earth, but it is in Heaven.

Matthew 16:13 When Jesus came into the coasts of Caesarea Philippi, he asked his disciples, saying, Whom do men say that I the Son of man am? 14 And they said, Some say that thou art John the Baptist: some, Elias; and others, Jeremias, or one of the prophets. 15 Christ said to Peter, but whom say ye that I am? 16 And Simon Peter answered and said, Thou art the Christ, the Son of the living God.

Caesarea Phillippi was named after the Caesar. The disciples and the people were not really totally sure about who Christ was.

Matthew 16:17 And Jesus answered and said unto him, Blessed art thou, Simon Barjona (Bar=Son of, and Jona=Jonah): for flesh and blood hath not revealed it unto thee, but my Father which is in heaven.18 And I say also unto thee, That thou art Peter (Petros, a small pebble), and upon this Rock, (Petra, a mountain, meaning Christ the Rock) I (not Peter!) will build my ~~church~~ ekklesia; and the gates of hell shall not prevail against it.

1 Corinthians 10:4 And did all drink the same spiritual drink: for they drank of that spiritual Rock that followed them: and that Rock was Christ.

Christ, the Rock, is today building His Group, His '~~Church~~', His Ekklesia, His 'team'. Ekklesia is a feminine word, and a reminder that the group name of His Christians refers to the 'wife' of Christ.

Matthew 16:19 And I will give unto thee (to you Peter) the keys of the kingdom of heaven: and whatsoever thou (Peter) shalt bind on earth shall be bound in heaven: and whatsoever thou shalt loose on earth shall be loosed in heaven.

This statement that Christ made was addressed to Peter, and by inference, to His disciples. They were in charge of 'binding and loosing' in matters of administration of the new assembly or group of Christians. This was not addressed to the heads of any religious organisations, nor was it intended to be adopted by the Popes of Catholicism for centuries to come.

Then in Matthew 16 verse 20 Jesus said, "tell nobody who I am".

Only one Prophet in the Old Testament came from Galilee and that was Jonah. Jonah left from Joppa with a ticket to go to Tarshish or Spain, the completely opposite way to that which God had sent him.

During a storm caused by God, Jonah was cast overboard and the storm immediately abated, and he was swallowed by the specially prepared fish (NOT a wjhale!). Jonah 'died' for three days and three nights as he travelled in the Mediterranean. Jonah was spat out by the fish (whale) after 1000 miles journey Eastwards onto the shore of the Black Sea. The inhabitants there were worshippers of

Dagon the fish god, so they thought Jonah was a god. He preached to the Gentiles there who immediately repented.

Peter's father was named Jonah and it was in Joppa that Peter was first to preach to the Gentile Cornelius, and he repented. This in a sense is a mirror of what happened to Jonah.

This is another reason why we need to be familiar with the geography of events.

Joppa was on the coast at the foot of Mount Hermon which was snowcapped. Caesarea Philippi, named after the Roman Caesar, was southwest of Mount Hermon with a spring that becomes the source of the River Jordan. The source of the river Jordan is important in history it was a strategic place and will continue to be. The pagan gods were carved into the rock of Mount Hermon, but due to an earthquake many of them broke up as the rocks fell. In the area where all the gods were carved in Mount Hermon there were pebbles in the spring water which came out of a huge rock.

When Christ brought them there at the base of Mount Hermon, He was saying there is a time coming when all these gods will be totally destroyed.

Peter and the disciples did not think Christ was going to die. Jonah 'died' for three days and nights, and so would Christ, as He told the Pharisees, that the only sign He would give them was the sign given in the story of Jonah Matthew 16:21 From that time forth began Jesus to shew unto his disciples, how that he must go unto Jerusalem, and suffer many things of the elders and chief priests and scribes, and be killed, and be raised again the third day.

Matthew 16:28 Verily I say unto you, There be some standing here, which shall not taste of death, till they see the Son of man coming in his kingdom.

There are 'some standing here' shall not taste death until they see him 'coming' was referring to the **vision** six days later on the Mount of Transfiguration. It was only at this time Jesus began unfolding what would happen to Him.

Matthew 17:1 And after six days Jesus taketh Peter, James, and John his brother, and bringeth them up into an high mountain apart, 2 And was transfigured before them: and his face did shine as the sun, and his raiment was white as the light.

This was the Mount of Transfiguration. Christ's face shone like the sun, his raiment glowing white in his Glory

Then Moses and Elijah also appeared. How did the disciples know it was them? The Father gave them that information, and insights at that time. Be clear, it was all a vision, as Moses and Elijah were dead, and the Bible makes it clear that in reality the dead cannot appear.

Matthew 17:4 Then answered Peter, and said unto Jesus, Lord, it is good for us to be here: if thou wilt, let us make here three tabernacles; one for thee, and one for Moses, and one for Elias.

The three tabernacles, or booths related to the periods of the seven days of the Feast of Tabernacles representing the millennium, and the Last Great Day, all symbolic of the Kingdom of God.

Matthew 17:5 While he yet spake, behold, a bright cloud overshadowed them: and behold a voice (the voice of YHWH – God the Father) out of the cloud, which said, This is my beloved Son, in whom I am well pleased; hear ye him. 6 And when the disciples heard it, they fell on their face, and were sore afraid. 7 And Jesus came and touched them, and said, Arise, and be not afraid. 8 And when they had lifted up their eyes, they saw no man, save Jesus only. 9 And as they came down from the mountain, Jesus charged them, saying, Tell the **vision** to no man, until the Son of man be risen again from the dead.

So the Father comes down to Mount Hermon and speaks to six (the number of man) people, Peter, James, John, Christ, Moses and Elijah, God making the 7th. Seven is the special number of God.

From this information, and that in Nehemiah, we can actually date the timing of the transfiguration as it was at the time of building booths given in the Old Testament.

Nehemiah 8:13 And on the second day were gathered together the chief of the fathers of all the people, the priests, and the Levites, unto Ezra the scribe, even to understand the words of the law. 14 And they found written in the law which the LORD had commanded by Moses, that the children of Israel should dwell in booths in the feast of the seventh month: 15 And that they should publish and proclaim in all their cities, and in Jerusalem, saying, Go forth unto the mount, and fetch olive branches, and pine branches, and myrtle branches, and palm branches, and branches of thick trees, to make booths, as it is written. 16 So the people went forth, and brought them, and made themselves booths, every one upon the roof of his house, and in their courts, and in the courts of the house of God, and in the street of the water gate, and in the street of the gate of Ephraim. 17 And all the congregation of them that were come again out of the captivity made booths, and sat under the booths: for since the days of Jeshua the son of Nun unto that day had not the children of Israel done so. And there was very great gladness. 18 Also day by day, from the first day unto the last day, he read in the book of the law of God. And they kept the feast seven days; and on the eighth day was a solemn assembly, according unto the manner.

Many years had passed since the children of Israel had kept the Feast of Tabernacles. It was legal according to the Law, that the building of the booths could commence on the 1st of Tishri after the date of Trumpets. This was the start and end of the legal year when Kings were crowned and official annual events took place. It was also everyone's birthday when everyone's age advanced one year.

This was the date that Kings began to reign, and everyone had a birthday and advanced one year. In Matthew 17 verse five, the Father God, YHWH, comes to mount Herman and speaks to the six people. So there were six people plus the Father making seven. The Father then said, "this is my beloved son in whom I am well pleased".

Jesus said: Tell no man of this **vision**. What was the significance of the Mount Hermon area? In the book of Enoch, which is not part of the canon, was quoted by Jude, which was about the tradition of the Jews concerning the rebellion of (fallen) 'spirit sons of God' before the flood who 'morphed' as humans and inhabited women, which was in fact demon possession, and caused human women to marry and have children, some of whom became giants. (Genesis 6)

So when it speaks about 'marrying and giving in marriage' just before the flood, the people had become so wicked under the influence of the erring wicked spirits, that God decided to flood the Earth, and destroy all flesh from off the earth with the exception of eight people.

2 Peter 2:1 But there were false prophets also among the people, even as there shall be false teachers among you, who privily shall bring in damnable heresies, even denying the Lord that bought them, and bring upon themselves swift destruction.

Most of 'Churchianity' does not believe that this mention of false prophets has anything to do with them and their activities, but the whole of 2 Peter 2 is also written as a warning for our time.

2 Peter 2:2 And many shall follow their pernicious ways; by reason of whom the way of truth shall be evil spoken of. 3 And through covetousness (it is your money they are after)

shall they with feigned words (tithing is against the law!) make merchandise of you: whose judgment now of a long time lingereth not, and their damnation slumbereth not. 4 For if God spared not the angels that sinned, but cast them down to hell (tartaroo – the abyss) , and delivered them into chains of darkness, to be reserved unto judgment; 5 And spared not the old world, but saved Noah the eighth person, a preacher of righteousness, bringing in the flood upon the world of the ungodly;

In Greek mythology, Tartarus (/ˈtɑːrtərəs/; Ancient Greek: Τάρταρος, romanized: Tártaros) is the deep abyss that is used as a dungeon of torment and suffering for the wicked and as the prison for the Titans. The word is incorrectly translated as hell.

In coming to understand the Bible, always stay within the scriptures. It is one thing to use the quote from Enoch recorded in Jude, but we need to be cautious about using external writings unless they are aligned with what the Scriptures say. The Bible is the one and only standard we can utterly rely upon, provided that we have proper translations of the original texts to clarify the translations.

The River Jordan has the symbolism of salvation in it.

Matthew 3:13 Then cometh Jesus from Galilee to Jordan unto John, to be baptized of him.

Christ was baptised by John the Baptist in the Jordan which contained some fish, and the water is clear and symbolises cleansing. When Christ was baptised in the Jordan, in type so was every Christian who has repented, or will repent, the first step towards Salvation.

Colossians 2:10 And ye are complete in him, which is the head of all principality and power: 11 In whom also **ye are circumcised** with the circumcision made without hands, in putting off the body of the sins of the flesh by the circumcision of Christ: 12 **Buried** with him in baptism, wherein also ye are **risen** with him through the faith of the operation of God, who hath raised him from the dead. 13 And you, being dead in your sins and the uncircumcision of your flesh, hath he quickened together with him, having forgiven you all trespasses;

Christ's whole life was for us, and whatever He did, He did for us, and we were 'with Him' in type in everything He did. When He was circumcised, we were; baptised, we were; killed, we were; rose from the dead, we were!

There are some interesting facets of geography concerning the River Jordan. The River Jordan has its source in the region of Mount Hermon and finishes in the Dead Sea which is the location of the Lake of Fire, and this is a major key to understanding. From Mount Herman to Galilee is about 20 miles, and then on another 60 miles to the Dead Sea, the lowest place on Earth. The Sea of Galilee is 260 feet deep and contains an abundance of fish. By contrast the Dead Sea is so salty it cannot contain any fish.

When the Jordan reaches the Dead Sea the symbolism is of purging through fire. In the time of Strabo it was said that the fire of Sodom and Gomorrah was still burning in the Dead Sea. It is interesting to note that the English word Petroleum, is made up of Petra and Oleum and actually means 'rock oil'.

In the first century the Dead Sea gave off sulfur, asphalt, soot, smoke, gases and pitch intermittently. Volley in 1787 reports fiery activity in the Dead Sea, but nothing like that has happened in the last 200 years.

Gehenna and the fire that burned continuously outside Jerusalem was used by the inhabitants to dispose of all the rubbish from the city. It was in a valley, an abyss, which flows down around Jerusalem from the West to the East, and thence eventually to the Dead Sea. At the times of reconciliation and after Christ's return, the Dead Sea will become fresh water from the water flowing out of the split in the mountain, and fish will be able to live in it.

Another example of there being so much more within the scriptures than we sometimes realise is the story of when Christ came to the disciples and found that they had toiled all night and caught no fish at all. He told them to put the net on the other side of the boat and they drew it up with 153 fish in the net, straining it almost to breaking point. This miraculous event occurred after Christ's resurrection.

As we know each letter of the Hebrew alphabet has a numeric value. If you take the phrase Bene Elohim which means Children of God, referring to the disciples, and add up the numeric value of the letters in Hebrew, it comes to 153. The Word of God, our Elder Brother is truly amazing.

There is much yet to be discovered in terms of artifacts in the Holy Land. Perhaps one day soon there will be a great revival of archaeological research. Jeremiah was told to bury the Ark of the covenant in Jericho, East of Jordan. If they were ever to discover where the Cherubim were hidden by Jeremiah, this would constitute one of the greatest finds of all time. Perhaps that might occur at the time when the new Temple is being built in Jerusalem in the time of the end.

Geographical doctrinal note

Dr. Martin mentions in his lectures that a great deal of misunderstanding for many thousands of people has arisen because some denominations are teaching that the 'Lost Tribes of Israel' migrated to Europe, and thence to Britain, and subsequently to America. So they conclude that Britain is Ephraim, the United States is Manasseh, and that many of the countries of Europe are currently occupied by other of the Ten Tribes, like France being Reuben etc.

This misapplication of the Scriptures has been further compounded by ministers teaching that the 'end time' prophesied events that apply to the Jews and the Ten tribes therefore will directly affect specifically Britain,

America and Europe. This simply is not true and is a total distortion of what the Bible really teaches.

Dr. Martin confesses that he, himself, was taken in by these false teachings for many years until he came to appreciate the truth concerning the geography of the events preceding Christ's return. Dr. Martin points out, that even if these teachings concerning the peoples of G.B., U.S.A., and Europe do have any truth in them at all, the actual truth of the Bible record concerning land and geography would override any such man-made ideas.

The principles that makes a nonsense of those notions are clear. Firstly:

Acts 17:26 And hath made of one blood all nations of men for to dwell on all the face of the earth, and hath determined the times before appointed, and the bounds of their habitation;

God decided where His people would reside on Earth. When God gave land, and dominion over land to certain peoples, it was the LAND that God was gifting to them as an inheritance and referring to, not the people.

Certain people were given tracts of LAND for an inheritance and for their use, but that land had, and still has, a specific geographical location. The fact that peoples given those lands subsequently migrated to other parts of the world does not mean that the land they **now** live on was given to them by God, or is the subject of end time prophecies.

If anyone inherits a property in a certain country, and decides to migrate to another country, provided they do not sell the property, then the title remains theirs. Their title to that parcel of land does not transfer to the country they migrate to!

The Land of Promise given to Israel was the Holy Land, Palestine, and its boundaries are clearly defined geographically by Christ Jesus in the Bible. Jerusalem is the 'centre' of that land, and the events of the future 'end time' are focussed on that city, and upon the Middle East.

Further confusion is caused by some suggesting that the book of Daniel says there will arise Ten Nations at the end time, and that they will arise in Europe, which it does not say in Daniel. They further add to the confusion by saying that 'Babylon' is actually Rome. When Christ who inspired the writing of the Bible says Babylon, He means the Babylon of the Middle East, not Rome in Italy.

These ten nations that WILL arise are listed in Psalm 83. These nations were in place located in the Middle East at the time the Psalm was written. They will be in place again in the future in the Middle East where they were geographically located originally at the time when the end time prophecies regarding them begin to occur.

Psalm 83:1 Keep not thou silence, O God: hold not thy peace, and be not still, O God. 2 For, lo, thine enemies make a tumult: and they that hate thee have lifted up the head. 3 They have taken crafty counsel against thy people, and consulted against thy hidden ones. 4 They have said, Come, and let us cut them off from being a nation; that the name of Israel may be no more in remembrance. 5 For they have consulted together with one consent: they are confederate against thee:

This is clearly talking about the nations surrounding Israel who want to 'wipe Israel off the map'. Leaders of some Middle East countries have already made declarations according to news releases in the 21st century that this is what they want to do to Israel.

Here, listed in the Bible, are the ten nations that will 'surround' Israel at the end time with the intention of destroying Israel.

Psalm 83:6 The tabernacles of (1) Edom, and the (2) Ishmaelites; of (3) Moab, and the (4) Hagarenes; 7 (5) Gebal, and (6) Ammon, and (7) Amalek; the

(8) Philistines with the inhabitants of (9) Tyre; 8 (10) Assur also is joined with them: they have holpen the children of Lot. Selah.

These nations mentioned in the Psalm are all in and around the Middle East. The threat to erase Israel from being a nation will not come from Israel!

The European Union, or a 'Ten Nation' group have no intention of attempting to erase Israel from the map. However, Israel's hostile neighbours currently do espouse such a cause as prophesied. The turmoil and unrest in the Middle East continues to ferment, and many countries are getting more unstable year by year, and their hatred of Israel is increasing.

Matthew 24:42 Watch therefore: for e know not what hour your Lord doth come.

We as Christians are admonished to *watch*, and be aware of world events and to see how they might related to the prophetic indications in the Bible.

The next chapter will address the design and development of the Bible.

CHAPTER 4

DESIGN AND DEVELOPMENT OF THE HOLY BIBLE

When we consider any, and indeed virtually all translations of the 'complete' Bible of 66 books in the order we have them today, they do not compare with the early manuscripts either in the number of books nor the original order.

Every Bible in the world, hundreds or thousands of millions need very serious revision so they are aligned with the inspired original manuscripts.

How could this have happened? What is the consequence of their being in the wrong order? Confusion, and also the Truths and Plan of the book and its storyline are obscured

In the Book as we have it, the story flow is hidden from the reader; when the original order is restored the true story emerges.

Those who had canonised the Old Testament and the New Testament were directly inspired by Jesus Christ to put the complete Bible together. Canon means rule or standard.

Scholars have known that these facts are true, but have not acted on it.

If restored to the original order and structure, the centre of the Bible is the four Gospels and Acts. Christ's life, teaching, mission and Gospel is in the exact centre of the Holy Bible.

The Old Testament was canonised by Christ through Ezra who lived around 480-440 B.C., who worked with 120 Elders who ensured the accuracy of all the component parts.

The New Testament was canonised by Christ through Peter and Paul, and finally by John at the end of the 1st Century A.D.

Secular scholars suggest that the canonisation was actually performed later in the 3rd and 4th Centuries by churchmen. This does not agree with the Biblical statement that the task was given by the authority of Christ to His Prophets and Disciples who performed the work of canonisation under the direct inspiration of the Holy Spirit. Here is just one verse which indicates this.

Isaiah 8:16 Bind up the testimony, seal the law among my disciples. David, in Psalm 19 tells of the perfection in the motions of the heavens.

Psalm 19:1 The heavens declare the glory of God; and the firmament sheweth his handywork.

Looking at the heavens and the Earth, we see the incredible glory of God in the creation of the Universe, or rather what we can actually see of it.

Psalm19:2 Day unto day uttereth speech, and night unto night sheweth knowledge. 3 There is no speech nor language, where their voice is not heard.

We see the glory of the stars, but not only that, in what we observe, God is actually 'talking' to us and revealing knowledge to us if we only have the wit to see it.

Psalm19:4 Their line is gone out through all the earth, and their words to the end of the world. In them hath he set a tabernacle for the sun, 5 Which is as a bridegroom coming out of his chamber, and rejoiceth as a strong man to run a race. 6 His going forth is from the end of the heaven, and his circuit unto the ends of it: and there is nothing hid from the heat thereof.

The 'line' and the perfection of the architectural design of the heavens is 'talking' to us, and provides a 'tabernacle' or special place for the sun, which warms the whole earth each day as it rotates. The stability of the heavenly movements, more accurate than any clock man can create, reveals the perfect hand of God. Then the Psalmist compares the perfection of the heavens with the perfection of God's Law.

Psalm 19:7 The Law of the Lord is perfect, converting the soul: the testimony of the Lord is sure, making wise the simple. 8 The statutes of the Lord are right, rejoicing the heart: the commandment of the Lord is pure, enlightening the eyes. 9 The fear of the Lord is clean, enduring for ever: the judgments of the Lord are true and righteous altogether. 10 More to be desired are they than gold, yea, than much fine gold: sweeter also than honey and the honeycomb.

The inspired Psalmist, or rather actually Christ, is telling us that the Bible, the Law, the Statutes and the Commandments are perfect. The Bible is not just a book put together by men as they thought fit, but Master-crafted by the Creator of all things. It is tragic how few human beings actually believe that.

In Romans Paul quotes from Psalm 19:2-4, Romans 10:18 But I say, Have they not heard? Yes verily, their sound went into all the earth, and their words unto the ends of the world.

We are not talking about the nonsense of pagan or 'new age' astrology, but of pure astronomy. Our watches are set by the heavens. Even going back 2000 or more years, we can be accurate to seconds. With the ingenuity of astronomers and their ability to tell what was going on with the heavenly bodies thousands of years ago, and with modern equipment, they can project the patterns on a Planetarium screen for all to see, and we are confronted with the **evidence** that God's Universe is both orderly and timely.

The Word, or YHWH, the God of the Old Testament was Christ the Rock, and we need to know well all the many names of the Deity, and to be clear who is being referred to in each reference in the Bible. This is a study in itself.

Originally there were forty-nine or 7x7 books in the complete Bible which is the number of perfection. The Old Testament contains 22 books one for each of the 22 letters in the Hebrew alphabet. The New Testament has 27 books. Add the Old and the New together, 22 + 27= 49 (7x7) or absolute perfection.

There were three divisions in the Old Testament and four divisions in the New Testament which equals seven divisions again a perfect number.

Christ speaks of the three divisions of the Old Testament - The Law, the Prophets, and the Writings, eleven books which include the Psalms.

Luke 24:44 And he said unto them, These are the words which I spake unto you, while I was yet with you, that all things must be fulfilled, which were written in the Law of Moses, and in the Prophets, and in the Psalms, concerning me.

It is important to note that Christ's teachings of the New Law were given both before and after His resurrection.

THE HOLY BIBLE – GOD'S PERFECT STRUCTURE AND DESIGN

The Bible we have today has 66 books. The Old Testament contains 39 books. The New Testament contains 27 books. 39+27 = 66. Interesting that 6 is the number of man. This man-made structure and order obscures the perfection and completeness of the Holy Bible, God's Word to mankind.

In the 4th/5th century A.D., Saint Jerome, commissioned by Pope Damascus in 382, made up the Vulgate version in Latin. Jerome avoided the original order. He put the

Bible together in the Egyptian order as he thought fit. This confused the perfection and obscured the message of the Bible. This created chaos, so often the result of man's interference with the plan of God.

The Old Testament Canon was inspired by God, and arranged by Ezra in the 5th Century

B.C. originally consisted of 22 books, one for each letter of the Hebrew alphabet.

The New Testament 27 books were finally Canonised by John in the last decade of the first century A.D. after Christ had inspired him to write the book of Revelation.

Revelation is the 49th book, completing the numerical perfection of 7x7. The first five books of the Bible, Genesis, Exodus, Leviticus, Numbers, and Deuteronomy are known as the Law. The number 5 is the number of Law.

The 5 books, the New Testament Law, the Gospels and Acts form the exact centre of the Bible when all the books are in the original Divine Order as seen on this chart.

This chart designed by Gary E. Arvidson is copyright.

Copyright held at www.askelm.com © 1984
Ernest L. Martin.

The reader may copy this chart onto 8½x11 or A4 for personal study purposes.

CHRISTIANITY DIRECT FROM CHRIST - THE WORD OF GOD

THE HOLY BIBLE – GOD'S PERFECT STRUCTURE AND DESIGN

The Bible we have today has 66 books. The Old Testament contains 39 books. The New Testament contains 27 books. 39+27 = 66. This man-made structure and order obscures the perfection and completeness of the Holy Bible. God's Word to mankind. In the 4th/5th century A.D., Saint Jerome, commissioned by Pope Damasus in 382, made up the Vulgate version in Latin. Jerome avoided the original order. He put the Bible together in the Egyptian order as he thought fit. This confused the perfection and obscured the message of the Bible. This created chaos, so often the result of man's interference with the plan of God.

The Old Testament Canon was inspired by God, and arranged by Ezra in the 5th Century B.C. originally consisted of 22 books, one for each letter of the Hebrew alphabet. The New Testament 27 books were Canonized by John in the last decade of the first century A.D. after Jesus Christ had inspired him to write the book of Revelation. Revelation is the 49th book, completing the numerical perfection of 7x7. The first five books of the Bible, Genesis, Exodus, Leviticus, Numbers, and Deuteronomy are known as the Law. The number 5 is the number of Law. The 5 books, the New Testament Law, the Gospels and Acts form the exact centre of the Bible when all the books are in the Divine Order as seen on this chart.

Volume One		The Old Testament				New Testament PENTATEUCH					Volume Two		The New Testament	
3	Grand		Divisions			1	2	3	4	5	3	Grand		Divisions
						MATT	MARK	LUKE	JOHN	ACTS				
The Law	The Church (6 Books)		The State (11 Books)			Jewish	Jewish Gentile	Gentile	Universal	Universal	The Jew (1st Rank)	The Gentile (2nd Rank)		World Holocaust
GOD (5 Books)	2. PROPHETS		3. PSALMS			4. GOSPELS & ACTS (5 Books)					STATE (7 Books)	CHURCH (14 Books)		GOD (1 Book)
1. LAW	FORMER		WISDOM			Shaded = ON EARTH				IN HEAVEN Acts (Done in heaven)	5. GENERAL	6. PAUL		7. REVELATION
1. Genesis	1. Joshua, Judges		1. Psalms			Gospels (Christ on earth)								7. PROPHETIC
2. Exodus	2. Book of the Kingdoms		2. Proverbs								1. James	4. 7 CHURCHES		Revelation
3. Leviticus	LATTER		3. Job								2. I Peter	1. Rom.	The ABC's of Christian Doctrine	The Book of Sevens
4. Numbers	3. Isaiah		FESTIVAL				22 Books		22 Books		3. II Peter	2. I Cor.		
5. Deuteronomy	4. Jeremiah	MAJOR	4. Song	Passover							4. I John	3. II Cor.		
(The Old Testament Pentateuch is the beginning division of the Holy Scriptures. The following two divisions of the O.T. are subsidiary to the Law. The Prophets' divisions are superior to that of the Psalms (or Royal division) because the prophets were direct emissaries of God and were responsible for instructing and admonishing rulers and kings. The positioning shows authority of rank and teaching.)	5. Ezekiel		5. Ruth	Pentecost							5. II John	4. Gal	The XYZ's of Doctrine	Seven Churches
	MINOR		6. Lament.	Ab 10th				5			6. III John	5. Eph.		Seven Golden Candlesticks
	6. The Twelve		7. Eccl.	Tabernacles				New Testament Books			7. Jude	6. Phil.	8. I Thess.	Seven Stars
	1. Hosea		8. Esther	Purim				PENTATEUCH				7. Col	9. II Thess.	
	2. Joel	Assyrian						"THE FOUNDATION" (II Cor. 2:14)			(These seven epistles were plainly intended for the Jewish people. Their theme is non-doctrinal and is similar to Paul's doctrinal epistles. They are placed at first position to fulfill the principle "to the Jew first." (Romans 2:10). They are directed to Jewish Christians in general and not to specific churches. They were entitled by the "pillar" apostles with top rank over Paul.)	8. I Thess.	5. MILLENNIAL	Seven Spirits of God
	3. Amos	Period	RESTORATION									9. II Thess.	10. Hebrews	Seven Bowls
	4. Obadiah		9. Daniel										6. MINISTERIAL	Seven Seals
	5. Jonah	Babylonian	10. Ezra-Nehemiah										The Epistles for Professional Leaders	Seven Trumpets
	6. Micah	Period	11. Chronicles									11. I Tim.		Seven Thousand Men Israelite Jews
	7. Nahum											12. II Tim.		Seven Last Plagues
	8. Habakkuk		(This third division is the Royal (state or growth) exalted section and rank to the inferior or rank to the prophets of division two.)									13. Titus		Seven Golden Vials
	9. Zephaniah	Restoration										14. Phile.		Seven Mountains
	10. Haggai	Period												Seven Kings
	11. Zechariah													
	12. Malachi													
						1. The First Christian Principles — Gracie School (The central historical division of both Testaments)					II. High School	III. College		IV. Post Graduate Studies
Basic Law 6 Books +	Priests & Prophets 6 Books = 11 Books		Kings & Rulers + 11 Books = 22 Books			GOSPELS & ACTS (5) Books								(The Book of Revelation has all the mysteries of Israel in them being the final book of truth Testaments.)
						Ω LUKE A								
← 22 Books →						← 49 Books →						← 22 Books →		
← 24 Books →						(7 X 7)						← 24 Books →		

Chapter 4 - Design and Development of The Holy Bible

The five books of the Old Testament Law can be compared to the five books of the New Testament Law Pentateuch, Matthew, Mark, Luke, John, and Acts. The central book is Luke, the best source of N.T. history.

In the correct original order of the books of the New Testament, the New Law is followed by the fifth division of the Bible which is called the 'Universal Epistles'. This comprises James, I & II Peter, 1st, 2nd and 3rd John, and lastly Jude which equals seven epistles.

These are the prologue to Paul's fourteen books, the sixth division, which includes Hebrews although there is some doubt in the minds of 'scholars' as to whether Paul wrote Hebrews, Dr. Martin is certain that he did.

Christ through Paul wrote nine epistles to seven churches, Romans, I & II Corinthians, Galatians, Ephesians, Philippians, Colossians, I & II Thessalonians. Hebrews which is seen as the 'Millennial' book, then follow the 'Ministerial Epistles' 1st and 2nd Timothy, Titus, and Philemon. Fourteen Epistles in all.

The 7th division is the Book of Revelation.

The inspired order reveals so clearly the perfect structure of the New Testament, 5+7+14+1=27 books. The Bible, 22 of the O.T. plus 27 of the N.T. = 49 books or the perfect number of 49 books, with the life and story of Christ in the New Testament, and the 'Law of Love' being central to the whole Bible.

The proper order also reveals clearly the principle of 'Progressive Revelation' which runs as a thread throughout the whole Bible. God has first communicated with His fledgling children with the rigours of the O.T. Law which was the beginning of their serious 'Kindergarten' schooling.

In the N.T. Paul was growing in Grace and knowledge, and Peter and the other disciples were as well. This is how God always works, as He reveals in all His dealings with those He chooses to educate about His Plan for humankind. God does not just put a funnel to our heads and pour it all in at once. God teaches us by giving us 'Here a little and there a little, precept upon precept, precept upon precept, line upon line' over time. (Isaiah 28:10,13).

Those who quote even just one precept out of context and use it as their authority from God in their desire to control people with the principle are Satan's ministers. It is this malpractice and others which enslave people to men's organisations.

This is why Christ urges us not to listen to the doctrines or commandments of men, but to take part in our own education by studying and listening to what He has for us and continue to grow in Grace and knowledge.

Matthew 15:19 But in vain they do worship me, teaching for doctrines the commandments of men.

In the inspired order, then came the preparation of Christ's teaching of primary schooling in the Gospels and Acts. Then the secondary school of the 'General' Epistles. The first of Paul's letters began University Education in Romans, Corinthians and Galatians; followed by the advanced studies of the revelation of the 'Mystery' 63 A.D. recorded in Ephesians, Philippians, and Colossians, which gave the 'capstone' of the Gospel, which revealed the fact that we are to become God's actual children.

The Post Graduate teachings came with Christ's Book of Revelation written by John at the end of the 1st Century A.D. And canonised under inspiration as indeed are all the Books of the Bible.

The whole Bible is written in 'another tongue' which is God's own special way of communicating with His children. This 'other tongue' is not understood by the billions in the world at any given time, but only by those whose eyes, ears, and minds are specifically opened by Christ to receive

His message, when He decides the time is right for each individual.

God's 'other tongue' is not a spoken language, but the inspiration from God's mind to our human minds in terms of Knowledge, Understanding and Wisdom by concepts, ideas, clarity of thought, and the recognition of Truths.

There were 7000 who had not bowed the knee to Baal in the past.

Romans 11:4 But what saith the answer of God unto him? I have reserved to myself seven thousand men, who have not bowed the knee to the image of Baal. Christ said of the Truth, that there would be the 'few that find it'.

Matthew 7:14 Because strait is the gate, and narrow is the way, which leadeth unto life, and few there be that find it.

The 'few' who will make it into the first resurrection at Christ's return are undoubtedly also those who do not get entangled with the churches of this world, or 'defile themselves with women'. 'Women' in this context means 'church'.

Revelation 14:3 And they sung as it were a new song before the throne, and before the four beasts, and the elders: and no man could learn that song but the hundred and forty and four thousand, which were redeemed from the earth. 4 These are they which were not defiled with women; for they are virgins. These are they which follow the Lamb whithersoever he goeth. These were redeemed from among men, being the firstfruits unto God and to the Lamb. 5 And in their mouth was found no guile: for they are without fault before the throne of God.

Christians are able to stand faultless before the throne of God the Father because of Christ's perfect life, His sacrifice of dying for our sins, His being judged faultless by the Father, and His being able to present us to His Father faultless.

Historically, Judah and Israel had looked to joining up with other nations for their support and protection instead of relying on God who says:

Isaiah 8:12 Say ye not, A confederacy, to all them to whom this people shall say, A confederacy; neither fear ye their fear, nor be afraid. 13 Sanctify the Lord of hosts himself; and let him be your fear, and let him be your dread. *14 And he shall be for a sanctuary; but for a stone of stumbling and for a rock of offence to both the houses of Israel, for a gin and for a snare to the inhabitants of Jerusalem.* 15 And many among them shall stumble, and fall, and be broken, and be snared, and be taken.

This referred to Judah and Israel, and is important because it is quoted twice in the New Testament that God would be a stone of stumbling and a rock of offence to those who did not look to Him for protection and support.

Romans 9:33 As it is written, Behold, I lay in Sion a stumblingstone and rock of offence: and whosoever believeth on him shall not be ashamed.

1 Peter 2:8 And a stone of stumbling, and a rock of offence, even to them which stumble at the word, being disobedient: whereunto also they were appointed.

In this narrative, Isaiah suddenly refers to the need to secure the Scriptures, and he is talking about Canonisation. The Apostles certainly realized the importance and the relevance of Isaiah 8 in the 1st Century.

Isaiah 8:16 Bind up the testimony, seal the law among my disciples.

Christ was directly inspiring Isaiah when he was giving specific instruction for Canonisation and the disciples knew that. They knew that it was fast becoming necessary. God says through Isaiah, bind up and seal the law among whom? Among and by my disciples. Remember it is Christ who is inspiring Isaiah to write these words.

Isaiah 8:20 To the law and to the testimony: if they speak not according to this word, it is because there is no light in them.

Peter was the number one Apostle at that time.

This instruction from Christ for His Disciples to assemble the Bible applies today as much as when it was first written.

'Churchianity' and other religions of men have adapted and adopted pagan doctrines of demons and subtle forms of idolatry as the mainstay of their core beliefs. The largest 'church' (Check out CIRCE pronounced KIRKY) in the world has its own ideas of what should be included in their 'church' buildings and their doctrines.

2 Corinthians 11:14 And no marvel; for Satan himself is transformed into an angel of light. 15 Therefore it is no great thing if his ministers also be transformed as the ministers of righteousness; whose end shall be according to their works.

Some churches misuse the Law of God, continuing to insist on obedience to, and enforce the Old Testament physical laws of the schoolmaster which Christ replaced with the New Gospel of the Law of Faith and Love.

Galatians 3:24 Wherefore the law was our schoolmaster to bring us unto Christ, that we might be justified by faith. 25 But after that faith is come, we are no longer under a schoolmaster.

1 Timothy 4:1 Now the Spirit speaketh expressly, that in the latter times some shall depart from the faith, giving heed to seducing spirits, and doctrines of devils; 2 Speaking lies in hypocrisy; having their conscience seared with a hot iron; 3 Forbidding to marry, and commanding to abstain from meats, which God hath created to be received with thanksgiving of them which believe and know the truth.

Paul is describing the exact situation we have in the 21st Century. Teaching 'truths' which are lies, and even forbidding priests to marry; others promoting vegetarianism.

2 Timothy 3:13 But evil men and seducers shall wax worse and worse, deceiving, and being deceived.

2 Timothy 4:3 For the time will come when they will not endure sound doctrine; but after their own lusts shall they heap to themselves teachers, having itching ears; 4 And they shall turn away their ears from the truth, and shall be turned unto fables.

The fables of pagan activities like Saturnalia (Christmas), or worship of Ishtar (Easter), or celebration of wicked spirits (Halloween) are blatant idolatry. Also the fables of man's notions as to what the Bible teaches, like suggesting that when the Bible says Babylon it means Rome; or that the churches of Revelation were sequential through history rather than concurrent; or that the United Kingdom and America are Israel. These plausible fallacies have deceived many into believing what men teach, rather than relying on Christ to reveal His Truths.

Not long after Christ's ascension, in the 1st Century A.D., people claiming to be Christians began to allow and embrace many false doctrines, as the Apostles warn in the Scriptures.

Around 62-63 A.D., it had become apparent to the true Ekklesia that Christ was not going to return imminently. There was growing resistance to Apostolic authority in A.D. 66-67, and an insurrection was taking place among Christians. Peter, Paul with Luke, and John saw the need to keep Christ's teachings pure and safe from corruption. They were working with official inspired documents, but they could not stem the tide of rebellion against the true Gospel of Christ Jesus.

2 Peter 1:16 For we have not followed cunningly devised fables, when we made known unto you the power and

coming of our Lord Jesus Christ, but were eyewitnesses of his majesty.

Hundreds of years later in the 2nd, 3rd, and 4th Centuries A.D. various Councils of men, who had decidedly **not** been eyewitnesses to all that happened, came together with what clearly was seen as a body of literature that was "one piece". Their intention was to ratify the inclusion of many of these false doctrines, and further systematically corrupt the purity of the Scriptures. These 'cunningly devised fables', such as the doctrine of the 'Trinity', the Immortality of the Soul, the adoration of statues of Mary, still form much of the body of belief of the main denominations of 'Churchianity' to this day.

So is it likely, as most 'scholars' believe, that the Living Christ allowed those Councils of spiritually perverted men to finalise the Canonisation of the New Testament? Christ certainly did allow them to pollute His Book with a certain amount of distorted error as part of His 'blinding' of the world. But the Canonisation? Absolutely not! It is clear when we examine the Scriptures carefully, that it was Christ's own disciples and Apostles who Canonised and sealed up the Word into a complete work.

So when people question how one can be sure that any writings give an accurate account of what Christ taught, we have scriptural evidence that He made sure that the Canon was in the hands only of those who had known Him personally and were eyewitnesses of all He did.

The original manuscripts had to be written by those who had been actual eyewitnesses and were there to hear all of Christ's preaching and teachings in Judea, Jerusalem, Berea, Samaria, and Galilee. Only His Apostles could do this, especially in an era of insurrections and distortions of the true Gospel similar to those we have in our time. The Canon had to be secure from adulteration. Under Christ's inspiration John completed the task in Ephesus around 96 A.D.

2 Peter 1:3 According as his divine power hath given unto us all things that pertain unto life and godliness, through the knowledge of him that hath called us to glory and virtue: 4 Whereby are given unto us exceeding great and precious promises: that by these ye might be partakers of the divine nature, (the scriptures and yourselves) having escaped the corruption that is in the world through lust.

2 Peter 1:15 Moreover I will endeavour that ye may be able after my decease to have these things always in remembrance.16 For we have not followed cunningly devised fables, when we made known unto you the power and coming of our Lord Jesus Christ, but were **eyewitnesses** of His Majesty.

The select few were there on the Mount of Transfiguration and saw the vision. Matthew chapters 16 and 17 tell the whole marvellous story.

2 Peter 1:17 For He received from God the Father honour and glory, when there came such a voice to him from the excellent glory, "This is my beloved Son, in whom I am well pleased." 18 And this voice which came from heaven we heard, when we were with him in the holy mount. 19 We have also a more sure word of prophecy; whereunto ye do well that ye take heed, as unto a light that shineth in a dark place, until the day dawn, and the day star arise in your hearts:

Peter is emphasising that no part of the official scriptures is the subject of private interpretation, and that 'light', God's Word was shining by God's Power in the dark and murky place of this world, protecting the 'more sure word of prophecy', and would continue to do so "until the day dawn" when Christ returns.

2 Peter 1:20 Knowing this first, that no prophecy of the scripture is of any private interpretation. 21 For the

prophecy came not in old time by the will of man: but holy men of God spake as they were moved by the Holy Ghost.

How can we be sure that any writings included in the Bible are an accurate account of events and facts? In 44-45 A.D., only Peter and John were still alive, and were concerned about this. The Manuscripts had to be written only by those who had been eyewitnesses of all of Christ's preaching, teaching and works in Jerusalem, Judea, Berea, Samaria, and Galilee.

Peter is making it clear that he did have the authority directly from Christ to do what he was doing with the Word of Christ. Only Christ's Apostles were authorised to be involved with the Canon. Especially as it was during an era of fables, distortions, insurrections, with pretenders like Simon Magus who were conspiring against the purity of the true Gospel, as many others have done through the centuries, and continue to do to this day.

Acts 8:9 But there was a certain man, called Simon, which beforetime in the same city used sorcery, and bewitched the people of Samaria, giving out that himself was some great one:

Simon the sorcerer may have been baptised, but his next action showed that he certainly was not under the guidance of the Holy Spirit.

Acts 8:17 Then laid they their hands on them, and they received the Holy Ghost.18 And when Simon saw that through laying on of the apostles' hands the Holy Ghost was given, he offered them money, 19 Saying, Give me also this power, that on whomsoever I lay hands, he may receive the Holy Ghost.

He had to learn that becoming a Christian is by invitation of Christ and is certainly not to be bought. Paying for indulgences and forgiveness was a feature of the Catholic church in the later centuries A.D.

The truth had to be free from any form of adulteration, and it was John, humanly the brother of our Lord who finalised the Canon of the New Testament in A.D. 96. The Bible we have, despite its many so-called 'errors', was assembled under the watchful eye of Christ.

Work has been done to produce a current translation from the original texts, and in the proper order as accurately as it is possible to do. In fact such a version is now available. When this fact becomes better known, and studied by those who are given the 'eyes to see', knowledge of the true Gospel will begin to spread throughout the Earth as prophesied.

Regrettably many of the 'top scholars' do not believe that Peter wrote II Peter, or that John wrote Revelation, and they believe that the books 'just came together' of themselves. For instance many say or suggest that::

1. "Surely you are not so naïve to believe that Peter wrote 1st and 2nd Peter, and that John wrote 1st, 2nd, and 3rd John and the book of Revelation?"

2. Virtually all 'scholars' think that the N.T. Canon was put together in the 2nd Century, but there is no historical evidence of this.

3. 'Scholars' are not at all concerned about the chaos that has resulted from Saint Jerome who lived 347 – 420 A.D. Pope Damascus commissioned him to produce the Latin Vulgate.

Jerome started by revising the Gospels, using the Greek manuscripts available. This he did because of the vast differences he found in the Latin versions, as there were as many Latin versions as there were original manuscripts. About the same time, he started revising the Old Testament by using the Septuagint which was a Greek version of the Old Testament.

It is said that Jerome had 'visitations' from 'angels' who guided him in his work. Jerome's completed work was called the 'Vulgate' because he used the common or vulgar language of early medieval times. He jumbled up the books in the order he thought fit which resulted in chaos and confusion, and the proper theme of the Bible became obscured. The Vulgate Latin Bible was completed in 400 A.D.

1. Ecclesiastical Scholars are not at all interested in the order of the books being restored, as they do not appreciate or understand why this is so important.

Until these, and other false notions are set straight, and the Bible is given the respect it deserves, the world will blunder on in sublime ignorance of the Majesty of the Holy Scriptures as we should have them now.

We can be very thankful that Christ has inspired some of His Ekklesia to perform the massive task of 'cleaning' up the translations and correcting the order of the books directly from the original manuscripts so that we can have a 'more sure Word of Prophecy' at this crucial time in world history.

The next chapter will look at Prophecy which is History written in advance.

CHAPTER 5
PROPHECY – & CHRIST'S MARRIAGES

The Bible is made up of two themes, history and prophecy. We look forward to the fulfilment of the promises given to us. Nobody has received or inherited them yet, but that time is coming.

Acts 15:18 Known unto God are all his works from the beginning of the world.

This verse is a proof of God, as He is the only One who knows the beginning from the end of all things. 1 Corinthians 15 is also a proof of God's power and the historical fact of Christ's death and resurrection.

1 Corinthians 15:3 For I delivered unto you first of all that which I also received, how that Christ died for our sins according to the scriptures; 4 And that he was buried, and that he rose again the third day according to the scriptures: 5 And that he was seen of Cephas (Peter), then of the twelve: 6 After that, he was seen of above five hundred brethren at once; of whom the greater part remain unto this present, but some are fallen asleep (have died). 7 After that, he was seen of James; then of all the apostles. 8 And last of all he was seen of me (Paul) also, as of one born out of due time. 9 For I am the least of the apostles, that am not meet to be called an apostle, because I persecuted the ~~church~~ ekklesia of God.

The Apostles were inspired by Christ to preach the **concrete evidence** as witnessed by so many of the reality and fact of the death and resurrection of our Saviour. There was **rock solid evidence** of these events, as there were so many hundreds of witnesses at the time.

Acts 2:**2** Until the day in which he was taken up, after that he through the Holy Ghost had given commandments unto the apostles whom he had chosen: 3 To whom also he shewed himself alive after his passion **by many infallible**

proofs, being seen of them forty days, and speaking of the things pertaining to the kingdom of God:

They were also inspired to preach the Gospel of Salvation for all, not just for the Jews and the fact that His resurrection would be the certain foundation of our future resurrection also, and those later after the Millennium, and the White Throne Judgement.

1 Thessalonians 4:13 But I would not have you to be ignorant, brethren, concerning them which are asleep, that ye sorrow not, even as others which have no hope. 14 For if we believe that Jesus died and rose again, even so them also which sleep in Jesus will God bring with him. 15 For this we say unto you by the Word of the Lord, that we which are alive and remain unto the coming of the Lord shall not prevent (precede) them which are asleep. 16 For the Lord himself shall descend from heaven with a shout, with the voice of the archangel, and with the trump of God: and the dead in Christ shall rise first: 17 Then we which are alive and remain shall be caught up together with them in the clouds, to meet the Lord in the air: and so shall we ever be with the Lord. 18 Wherefore comfort one another with these words.

Notice that the dead in Christ will rise first, although this is a fact, there will only be a split second between the resurrection of the dead who have been dead for years, hundreds or even thousands of years, and those who are alive at the time of Christ's return who will be caught up into the clouds to join that throng to begin our eternal lives in and with Christ.

Revelation 21:1 And I saw a new heaven and a new earth: for the first heaven and the first earth were passed away; and there was no more sea. 2 And I John saw the holy city, new Jerusalem, coming down from God out of heaven, prepared as a bride adorned for her husband. 3 And I heard a great voice out of heaven saying, Behold, the tabernacle of God is with men, and he will dwell with them, and they shall be his people, and God himself shall be with them, and be their God. 4 And God shall wipe away all tears from their eyes; and there shall be no more death, neither sorrow, nor crying, neither shall there be any more pain: for the former things are passed away. 5 And he that sat upon the throne said, Behold, I make all things new. And he said unto me, Write: for these words are true and faithful. 6 And he said unto me, It is done. I am Alpha and Omega, the beginning and the end. I will give unto him that is athirst of the fountain of the water of life freely. 7 He that overcometh shall inherit all things; and I will be his God, and he shall be my son (and daughters).

The Earth is destined to become the permanent 'footstool' of God and His Son, their headquarters from which the Universe will be ruled by them together with those who have been given the gift of Eternal Life to reign with them for ever.

Revelation 21:22 And I saw no temple therein: for the Lord God Almighty and the Lamb are the temple of it. 23 And the city had no need of the sun, neither of the moon, to shine in it: for the glory of God did lighten it, and the Lamb is the light thereof. 24 And the nations of them which are saved shall walk in the light of it: and the kings of the earth do bring their glory and honour into it. 25 And the gates of it shall not be shut at all by day: for there shall be no night there. 26 And they shall bring the glory and honour of the nations (Gentiles) into it. 27 And there shall in no wise enter into it any thing that defileth, neither whatsoever worketh abomination, or maketh a lie: but they which are written in the Lamb's book of life.

Many things are thought to have happened according to the Scriptures, and indeed they have, and many also have a future fulfilment. Isaiah 13 and 14 depict some such events, as also in Jeremiah 52. Babylon is to rise again to become a world power before the Second Advent, and then to be finally destroyed again.

Ezekiel calls Jerusalem the centre of the Earth at the time in the future when once again David will reign as King over God's people and His human children in the Millennium.

Ezekiel 37:24 And David my servant shall be king over them; and they all shall have one shepherd: they shall also walk in my judgments, and observe my statutes, and do them. 25 And they shall dwell in the land that I have given unto Jacob my servant, wherein your fathers have dwelt; and they shall dwell therein, even they, and their children, and their children's children for ever: and my servant David shall be their prince for ever. 26 Moreover I will make a covenant of peace with them; it shall be an everlasting covenant with them: and I will place them, and multiply them, and will set my sanctuary in the midst of them for evermore. 27 My tabernacle (dwelling place) also shall be with them: yea, I will be their God, and they shall be my people. 28 And the heathen shall know that I the Lord do sanctify Israel, when my sanctuary shall be in the midst of them for evermore.

But before this happens, a false Kingdom will suddenly appear, one that looks just like the Kingdom of God, that seems to have all the credentials, even setting up and enforcing the rule of God's Laws, the Sabbaths, Holy Days, Dietary Laws, etc., and will last for three and a half years.

Matthew 24:15 When ye therefore shall see the abomination of desolation, spoken of by Daniel the prophet, stand in the holy place, (whoso readeth, let him understand:)

Prophecies of Ezekiel indicate that a new Nebuchadnezzar will arise and so will ten kings or nations in the region of Mesopotamia, the Euphrates and Egypt, not in Europe as some suggest. A new world order will begin to be established in the area of Iraq and Iran, and other Middle

East kingdoms. Jerusalem is still the centre of the world of the Bible.

Everything future will centre around that geographical location. The country of Israel with its population of Israelites, Jews, and Arabs and all nations who live there will continue to be the focus of attention in world news.

Many religious groups believe and teach that Russia will invade Palestine before Christ's returns. Russia will not invade Palestine or Israel before the establishment of the Kingdom of God. Gog and Magog or Meshech are not Russia or Moscow. The events of Ezekiel 38 do not happen until the end of the Millennium. Check out in that chapter, verses 8-16, they will invade when Israelies are living at peace in unwalled villages which is unlikely to happen in our era.

A new Elijah will arise as it is prophesied in Malachi.

Malachi 4:5 Behold, I will send you Elijah the prophet before the coming of the great and dreadful day of the Lord

Matthew 17:10 And his disciples asked him, saying, Why then say the scribes that Elias must first come? 11 And Jesus answered and said unto them, Elias truly shall first come, and restore all things.

The two witnesses, types of Moses and Elijah, as Priests will be witnessing to the world during the time of the Tribulation.

Revelation 11:3 And I will give power unto my two witnesses, and they shall prophesy a thousand two hundred and threescore days, (3½ years) clothed in sackcloth.

The two witnesses will not wear the garb of religious hierarchy, or the 'fish' (Dagon the fish god) hats of that bishops and others wear now..

When the Beast and the False Prophet ascend to power, there will have to be a Temple for them to usurp the position of standing in the Holy Place, and defiling the Temple.

The new Temple will be built on Mount Moriah, on the Mount of Olives, near the Dome of the Rock, perhaps only a hundred meters North. It will be a very beautiful building built over the very spot where Abraham was willing to sacrifice Isaac.

Nowhere near the Western wall they worship now, which was part of an old castle, not the Temple. There would be a worldwide uprising of Moslems if the Dome of the Rock was demolished, and would cause universal Jihad.

We, members of Christ's Ecclesia, are not and will not be involved with the Temple when it is built, as we are **now in type,** *spiritually speaking* at the right hand of the Father in Heaven in His Holy Temple in Heaven.

Ephesians 2: 4 But God, who is rich in mercy, for his great love wherewith he loved us, 5 Even when we were dead in sins, hath quickened us together with Christ, (by grace ye are saved;) 6 And hath raised us up together, and made us sit together in heavenly places in Christ Jesus:

This false Kingdom will mimic the Kingdom of God so well that it will deceive almost all the inhabitants of the Earth into believing that Christ has arrived. Only the Ekklesia will not be fooled, and some will go through the Tribulation and be killed, but the Corporate Body of Christ will not die, they will be protected.

How can true Christians know absolutely that this personage in the Temple is not the real Christ?

1. The first person to sit in the future Temple will NOT be Christ.
2. If I have a human body, the person sitting in the Temple is NOT Christ.

3. If I have not been resurrected from the dead, it is NOT Christ.

4. If I have not been caught up into the clouds with Christ, it is NOT Christ.

There needs to be no doubt whatsoever in our minds. No matter how much it might seem that Christ has come, He has NOT come if we are still human.

There will be no second born in the Kingdom, only First-born, those who are in Christ and will partake of His rank of being the First-born Son of God.

1 Timothy 2:3 For this is good and acceptable in the sight of God our Saviour; 4 Who will have **all** men (and women!) to be saved, and to come unto the knowledge of the truth. 5 For there is one God, and one mediator between God and men, the man Christ Jesus; 6 Who gave himself a ransom for all, to be testified in due time.

God has Willed that ALL people will be saved, and therefore that is what will eventually happen, all in their order, each at the time appointed for them by God.

The Tree of Life is an Almond Tree, as was Aaron's Rod that budded. It is the first tree to blossom, and produce the show of new life. Christ was sacrificed on that type of Tree which represented Life.

Things in the Bible are couched in symbolic terms, but they are also tangible and real at the same time. As we study, we need to search out the meaning of symbolic words and symbols and the reality they depict.

Our being part of the Body of Christ is a mystery. The Lord's Supper taking of the wine and the bread were symbolic of His blood and His body. They were symbolic yes, but we can also in reality *in type* be a part of the life to come on the same Almond Tree, the Christ was crucified on, and was afterward resurrected.

Why are Human Beings on this Earth? To become part of God, His human children are to become joint heirs with Christ in His Body, which is the Ekklesia.

Romans 8:17 And if children, then heirs; heirs of God, and joint-heirs with Christ; if so be that we suffer with him, that we may be also glorified together.

We are all heirs of the Will of God, and we will inherit Glory according to the terms of that Will which is clearly explained in God's Word.

It takes billions of years for light to travel from one side of the Milky Way to the other. The enormity of the Universe is well beyond the imagination of a human mind. There is one resurrection but there are different glories.

1 Corinthians 15:40 There are also celestial bodies, and bodies terrestrial: but the glory of the celestial is one, and the glory of the terrestrial is another. 41There is one glory of the sun, and another glory of the moon, and another glory of the stars: for one star differeth from another star in glory.

As the stars and planets are all different, we will have individuality in the Kingdom. Salvation depends upon Christ, and our future position will depend to a degree upon our 'works', gold and silver; or hay and wood and stubble. Examples of decreasing value.

We need to make our foundation secure, and our Foundation is Christ, and the durability and the quality of our part of the 'building' depends somewhat on what we do with our talents.

This 'labour' is absolutely nothing to do with the 'works' of the Law, but it is about the parable of the talents, where Christ was very clear that He expects us to be productive with the talents He has given us.

Matthew 25:14 For the kingdom of heaven is as a man travelling into a far country, who called his own servants, and delivered unto them his goods. 15 And unto one he gave five talents, to another two, and to another one; to every man according to his several ability; and straightway took his journey. 16 Then he that had received the five talents went and traded with the same, and made them other five talents. 17 And likewise he that had received two, he also gained other two. 18 But he that had received one went and digged in the earth, and hid his lord's money. 19 After a long time the lord of those servants cometh, and reckoneth with them. 20 And so he that had received five talents came and brought other five talents, saying, Lord, thou deliveredst unto me five talents: behold, I have gained beside them five talents more. 21 His lord said unto him, Well done, thou good and faithful servant: thou hast been faithful over a few things, I will make thee ruler over many things: enter thou into the joy of thy lord. 22 He also that had received two talents came and said, Lord, thou deliveredst unto me two talents: behold, I have gained two other talents beside them. 23 His lord said unto him, Well done, good and faithful servant; thou hast been faithful over a few things, I will make thee ruler over many things: enter thou into the joy of thy lord. 24 Then he which had received the one talent came and said, Lord, I knew thee that thou art an hard man, reaping where thou hast not sown, and gathering where thou hast not strawed: 25 And I was afraid, and went and hid thy talent in the earth: lo, there thou hast that is thine. 26 His lord answered and said unto him, Thou wicked and slothful servant, thou knewest that I reap where I sowed not, and gather where I have not strawed: 27 Thou oughtest therefore to have put my money to the exchangers, and then at my coming I should have received mine own with usury (interest). 28 Take therefore the talent from him, and give it unto him which hath ten talents. 29 For unto every one that hath shall be given, and he shall have abundance: but from him that hath not shall be taken away even that which he hath. 30 And cast ye the unprofitable servant into outer darkness: there shall be weeping and gnashing of teeth.

Heavenly rewards, yes, and terrestrial rewards and gifts on Earth, yes!! The reward for those who respond to and use daily the gifts and talents given to them by Christ will be in the first resurrection, and will have a position in the Kingdom of God ruling with Christ in the Millennium.

Those who neglect to use their gifts may have to wait until the second resurrection at the end of the millennium to inherit eternal life.

1 Corinthians 3:7 So then neither is he that planteth any thing, neither he that watereth; but God that giveth the increase. 8 Now he that planteth and he that watereth are one: and every man shall receive his own reward according to his own labour. 9 For we are labourers together with God: ye are God's husbandry, ye are God's building. 10 According to the grace of God which is given unto me, as a wise masterbuilder, I have laid the foundation, and another buildeth thereon. But let every man take heed how he buildeth thereupon. 11 For other foundation can no man lay than that is laid, which is Jesus Christ. 12 Now if any man build upon this foundation gold, silver, precious stones, wood, hay, stubble; 13 Every man's work shall be made manifest: for the day shall declare it, because it shall be revealed by fire; and the fire shall try every man's work of what sort it is. 14 If any man's work abide which he hath built thereupon, he shall receive a reward. 15 If any man's work shall be burned, he shall suffer loss: but he himself shall be saved; yet so as by fire. 16 Know ye not that ye are the temple of God, and that the Spirit of God dwelleth in you?

Those in Christ who have put their abilities and talents to good use. Those who have studied earnestly the Word of God, those who have really lived the Christian way of love towards others, will be in the Kingdom of God.

Those who have neglected to use their talents will miss out on this reward for living a productive life, and have to wait until a later time for Salvation.

CHRIST'S MARRIAGES

In the Old Testament it tells of how Christ 'married' Israel, and then divorced them because of their physical and spiritual adultery with 'other gods'.

The Prophets make it very clear that Israel, the 'wife' of YHWH, throughout history consistently committed idolatry both physically and spiritually by worshipping other gods in ways which were both heinous and ungodly.

Isaiah 50:1 Thus saith the Lord, Where is the bill of your mother's divorcement, whom I have put away? Or which of my creditors is it to whom I have sold you? Behold, for your iniquities have ye sold yourselves, and for your transgressions is your mother put away.

Jeremiah 3:8 And I saw, when for all the causes whereby backsliding Israel committed adultery I had put her away, and given her a bill of divorce; yet her treacherous sister Judah feared not, but went and played the harlot also.

How did Judah and Israel play the harlot? They allowed themselves to mix and marry with the heathen and pagan peoples around them. They also partook of their idolatries, and joined in their activities with heinous acts involving sexual depravity, murdering their own children and offering them to other gods. **This did not happen at just one time in history, but repeatedly throughout their generations, and of course to this time in the 21st Century.**

Hosea 1:9 Then said God, Call his name Loammi: for ye are not my people, and I will not be your God.

We can only imagine the distress and pain that YHWH went through when He had to say: I am not your God, and you are not my people. God indeed does have feelings, and He has gone through pain and suffering like all parents do as their children are nurtured into adulthood.

Hosea the Prophet was instructed by God to take a wife of whoredoms, a prostitute, to make the point very clearly that Israel and Judah had committed adultery against God countless times over thousands of years.

Hebrews 8:8 For **finding fault with them**, he saith, Behold, the days come, saith the Lord, when I will make a new covenant with the house of Israel and with the house of Judah: 9 Not according to the covenant that I made with their fathers in the day when I took them by the hand to lead them out of the land of Egypt; because they continued not in my covenant, and I regarded them not, saith the Lord.

When Christ returns, He will again 'marry' Israel. This will occur after a suitable period of giving Israel time to come to realise the absolute grossness of their former behaviour towards their Creator and their rejection of Him as their Saviour, and completely repent in dust and ashes.

After Christ's return, Israelites and 'Jews', whether descendants of Judah or not, will have to come to realise that they have a lot to deal with, change and repent of, as both they and their forebears throughout history consistently rejected God and His loving attempts to deal with them as His wife. Also some who eventually said:

Matthew 27:25 Then answered **all the people** (not just Jews), and said, His blood be on us, and on our children.

Orthodox 'Jews' will need to come to realise that their public religious lives are obnoxious to God. That bobbing and mumbling hour after hour in public is exactly what Christ was talking about when He said:

Matthew 6:5 And when thou prayest, thou shalt not be as the hypocrites are: for they love to pray standing in the synagogues and in the corners of the streets, that they may be seen of men. Verily I say unto you, They have their reward. 6 But thou, when thou prayest, enter into thy closet, and when thou hast shut thy door, pray to thy Father which is in secret; and thy Father which seeth in secret shall reward thee openly. 7 But when ye pray, use not vain repetitions, as the heathen do: for they think that they shall be heard for their much speaking.

Matthew 23:5 But all their works they do for to be seen of men: they make broad their phylacteries, and enlarge the borders of their garments,

The strange garb that is worn by those in Jerusalem to this day, the black robes and the black hats identify the religious Jews to all. The Kippah, is the little circle of cloth that can be worn conveniently under a street hat. It is still the practice of many Orthodox Jewish men to wear a head covering throughout the day, not just during prayer. Even the Prime Minister of Israel has appeared on newscasts wearing one for all to see.

One tradition holds that a Jewish man should not walk more than four cubits in any direction with an uncovered head. They wear their hair with side curls which is supposed by some to be an indication of piety and spirituality. Their traditions and their other traditional beliefs embodied in the Talmud, and of course their denial of Christ as the Messiah, are still part of what separates them from true Christianity.

Zechariah 13:4 And it shall come to pass in that day, that the (false) prophets shall be ashamed every one of his vision, when he hath prophesied; neither shall they wear a rough garment to deceive:

The orthodox Jews wear garments that represent piety to most people, but they are not following Christ or His Holy Bible, they regard the 'doctrines of men', and their precious traditions they get from Talmudic sources as more important.

Matthew 15:9 But in vain they do worship me, teaching for doctrines the commandments of men.

Christ was totally disparaging about the religious leaders of the day, and His Word is equally clear about how He feels about the religious leaders who claim to be Christian now in our era.

Matthew 15:14 Let them alone: they be blind leaders of the blind. And if the blind lead the blind, both shall fall into the ditch.

It is an awesome responsibility to teach others, more especially if what they are teaching is a false Gospel.

2 Peter 2:1 But there were false prophets also among the people, even as there shall be false teachers among you, who privily shall bring in damnable heresies, even denying the Lord that bought them, and bring upon themselves swift destruction.

Jews deny the Lord that bought them, and so do those who call themselves Christians and deny the sacrifice of Christ by continuing in vain partial, pathetic attempts to keep parts of the old Law.

2 Corinthians 3:14 But their minds were blinded: for until this day remaineth the same vail untaken away in the reading of the Old Testament; which vail is done away in Christ. 15 But even unto this day, when Moses is read, the vail is upon their heart.

Of course it is not wrong to read and learn an almost infinite number of lessons by studying the ancient law. But to attempt to live by those physical Laws, which is a totally impossible task for any human being, while ignoring the sacrifice of Christ and His introduction of His New Law of Love at such a cost, is a horrible crime, the sin of self-righteousness.

Of course we should do our utmost to live within the Law of Love, and avoid sin as much as we are able, constantly being aware of the need for the help of the Holy Spirit, and the continual flow of forgiveness from Christ our Master.

We also need to avoid like the plague being involved in any way shape or form with pagan idolatrous festivals like Christmas, Easter, and Halloween, knowing that God the Father and Christ hate them. These activities are almost universally celebrated by huge numbers of those who call themselves Christians, not thinking for one moment that they are doing anything wrong.

Jeremiah 10:2 Thus saith the Lord, Learn not the way of the heathen, and be not dismayed at the signs of heaven; for the heathen are dismayed at them. 3 For the customs of the people are vain: for one cutteth a tree out of the forest, the work of the hands of the workman, with the axe. 4 They deck it with silver and with gold; they fasten it with nails and with hammers, that it move not.

Is that a clear description of a Christmas tree? Is it clear that God is telling us not to do it? Absolutely.

Isaiah 1:12 When ye come to appear before me (YHWH), who hath required this at your hand, to tread my courts? 13 Bring no more vain oblations; incense is an abomination unto me; the new moons and sabbaths, the calling of assemblies, I cannot away with; it is iniquity, even the solemn meeting. 14 **Your** new moons and **your** appointed feasts my soul hateth: they are a trouble unto me; I am weary to bear them.

Any form of worship that has the trappings of, or are in any way associated with the ways of the heathen offends God.

Hebrews 6:4 For it is impossible for those who were once enlightened, and have tasted of the heavenly gift, and were made partakers of the Holy ~~Ghost~~ Spirit, 5 And have tasted the good word of God, and the powers of the world to come, 6 If they shall fall away, to renew them again unto repentance; seeing they crucify to themselves the Son of God afresh, and put him to an open shame.

That is a frightening warning from the writer of Hebrews, writing under the inspiration of the Holy Spirit for our admonition today.

Matthew 23:13 But woe unto you, scribes and Pharisees, hypocrites! for ye shut up the kingdom of heaven against men: for ye neither go in yourselves, neither suffer ye them that are entering to go in. 14 Woe unto you, scribes and Pharisees, hypocrites! for ye devour widows' houses, and for a pretence make long prayer: therefore ye shall receive the greater damnation.

The West wall in Jerusalem is one place where they still practice their public prayers. It is not a part of the old Temple but of a Roman fort!

Matthew 23:15 Woe unto you, scribes and Pharisees, hypocrites! for ye compass sea and land to make one proselyte, and when he is made, ye make him twofold more the child of hell than yourselves.

It is really horrifying to realise that even the most sincere religious people who teach false ideas, doctrines and gospels to their adherents, are making them a 'twofold child of hell' by getting them to believe in their incorrect version of Christianity.

Jeremiah 5:31 The prophets (priests, preachers, ministers) prophesy falsely, and the priests bear rule by their means; and my people **love** to have it so: and what will ye do in the end thereof?

People say in their deceived state how good it is to know the Lord! But do they? No!

Christ 'married' Israel, the people that He had chosen to represent His way of life and living. But the children of Israel continuously committed both physical and spiritual adultery with other false gods of sticks, and stones, images, statues, relics, and with heinous practices, many that were based on immoral sex and violence, so Christ divorced them.

But eventually in due time, Christ will once again take Israel and Judah to Himself, once again call them His people, and marry them.

Hosea 1:9 Then said God, Call his name Loammi: for ye are not my people, and I will not be your God. 10 Yet the number of the children of Israel shall be as the sand of the sea, which cannot be measured nor numbered; and it shall come to pass, that in the place where it was said unto them, Ye are not my people, there it shall be said unto them, Ye are the sons of the living God.

Marriage is a sacred sacrament designed by God to represent our relationship with Him. That wonderful symbolism is now being dragged through the mire by those who flaunt their sexual orientation and preference for single sex 'marriages'.

Genesis 2:24 Therefore shall a man leave his father and his mother, and shall cleave unto his wife: and they shall be one flesh.

A husband and wife are 'one flesh', and in order for God's children to be 'one' with Christ, in due time He will 'marry' them all.

Matthew 19:5 And said, For this cause shall a man leave father and mother, and shall cleave to his wife: and they twain shall be one flesh? 6 Wherefore they are no more twain, but one flesh. What therefore God hath joined together, let not man put asunder.

Originally it was only Israel including the Jews that had an intimate relationship with YHWH, or Christ, and the possibility of Salvation, until Christ divorced them. God then opened the door to the Gentiles who were 'grafted' in and also became heirs of the promises of Grace and Life. Romans chapter eleven explains this.

Romans 11:13 For I speak to you Gentiles, inasmuch as I am the apostle of the Gentiles, I magnify mine office: 14 If by any means I may provoke to emulation them which are my flesh, and might save some of them. 15 For if the casting away of them be the reconciling of the world, what shall the receiving of them be, but life from the dead? 16 For if the firstfruit be holy, the lump is also holy: and if the root be holy, so are the branches. 17 And if some of the branches be broken off, and thou, being a wild olive tree, wert grafted in among them, and with them partakest of the root and fatness of the olive tree; 18 Boast not against the branches. But if thou boast, thou bearest not the root, but the root thee. 19 Thou wilt say then, The branches were broken off, that I might be grafted in. 20 Well; because of unbelief they were broken off, and thou standest by faith. Be not highminded, but fear: 21 For if God spared not the natural branches, take heed lest he also spare not thee. 22 Behold therefore the goodness and severity of God: on them which fell, severity; but toward thee, goodness, if thou continue in his goodness: otherwise thou also shalt be cut off. 23 And they also, if they abide not still in unbelief, shall be grafted in: for God is able to graft them in again. 24 For if thou wert cut out of the olive tree which is wild by nature, and wert grafted contrary to nature into a good olive tree: how much more shall these, which be the natural branches, be grafted into their own olive tree? 25 For I would not, brethren, that ye should be ignorant of this mystery, lest ye should be wise in your own conceits; that blindness in part is happened to Israel, **until** the fulness of the Gentiles be come in. 26 And so all Israel shall be saved: as it is written, There shall come out of Sion the Deliverer, and shall turn away ungodliness from Jacob (Israel):

Then Paul explains to the Ephesians who were Gentiles, that due to Christ's life, His circumcision, all Gentiles are now seen by God as circumcised in heart, and as such are no longer 'strangers'.

Ephesians 2:11 Wherefore remember, that ye being in time past Gentiles in the flesh, who are called Uncircumcision by that which is called the Circumcision in the flesh made by hands; 12 That at that time ye (Gentiles) were without Christ, being aliens from the commonwealth of Israel, and strangers from the covenants of promise, having no hope, and without God in the world: 13 But now in Christ Jesus ye who sometimes were far off are made nigh by the blood of Christ. 14 For he is our peace, who hath made both one, and hath broken down the middle wall (refers to the curtain in the Temple which split in two at the time of Christ's death) of partition between us; 15 Having abolished in his flesh the enmity, even the law of commandments contained in ordinances; for to make in himself of twain one new man, so making peace; 16 And that he might reconcile both unto God in one body by the cross, having slain the enmity thereby: 17 And came and preached peace to you which were afar off, and to them that were nigh. 18 For through him we both have access by one Spirit unto the Father. 19 Now therefore ye are no more strangers and foreigners, but fellowcitizens with the saints, and of the household of God; 20 And are built upon the foundation of the apostles and prophets, Jesus Christ himself being the chief corner stone; 21 In whom all the building fitly framed together groweth unto an holy temple in the Lord: 22 In whom ye also are builded together for an habitation of God through the Spirit.

'Israel', that is all the descendants of the twelve tribes of Jacob whose name was changed to Israel, are still 'blinded' to the truth. They will have to wait until the 'fulness of the Gentiles be come in' before they will be given the opportunity to enter the New Covenant that Christ has prepared for His currently divorced 'wife' after He returns in Glory to take over the Earth.

But Christ is 'married' now, not to Israel, but *in type* to His Ekklesia, His group that he has been building since He made the announcement to His disciples that He would.

Matthew 16:18 And I say also unto thee, That thou art Peter, (a tiny pebble!) and upon this Rock (Me, the Rock that guided Israel in the wilderness) I will build my ~~church~~ ekklesia; and the gates of hell shall not prevail against it.

How misunderstood that statement of Christ has been over the centuries, perverted by the suggestion that Christ would put the building of his 'church' into the hands of mere men!

The Restoration of all things is coming. Christ has only been married to one wife at any one time. Once we become resurrected and fully in Him, in the Millennium He will once again 'marry' physical Israel, and be their 'husband'.

Revelation 19:6 And I heard as it were the voice of a great multitude, and as the voice of many waters, and as the voice of mighty thunderings, saying, Alleluia: for the Lord God omnipotent reigneth. 7 Let us be glad and rejoice, and give honour to him: for the marriage of the Lamb is come, and his wife hath made herself ready. 8 And to her was granted that she should be arrayed in fine linen, clean and white: for the fine linen is the righteousness of saints. 9 And he saith unto me, Write, Blessed are they which are called unto the marriage supper of the Lamb. And he saith unto me, These are the true sayings of God.

Christians can live with true joy in their hearts with the absolute assurance that we have a glorious future up ahead of us married to Christ Jesus, ruling in the Kingdom of God.

The next chapter discusses Biblical Archaeology.

CHAPTER 6
BIBLICAL HISTORY & ARCHAEOLOGY

Note: The dates given in this chapter are intended as a guide, and should not be regarded as absolutely accurate. They are sufficiently accurate to form a useful broad brush picture, yet very useful view of the history of human beings. Due to the difficulties in the exact interpretation of the chronology of the Bible or archaeological artefacts, dates may need to be revised as our understanding of history improves in the light of more research.

It is essential to be aware of what is going on in the Middle East, with especial regard to any archaeological activity, and whether the discoveries fit in with the Scriptures.

Archaeologists do not always have respect for the historical accuracy of the Holy Bible. They tend to look at what the Bible says in connection with what they are working on to see if it fits their understanding, and if not they pronounce the Bible inaccurate. It seems that they feel that their 'take' on any find is the authority, but indeed it is the other way around, the Bible is **the** authority.

There are many thousands of 'tels', or mounds all over the Middle East. History shows that the practice over centuries was to build new cities over ones which had decayed. They used the stones as foundations and the building materials in new construction.

There are millions of tablets and other written material buried under many layers in the historical sites.

There are also millions of pieces of material with written information which have been ignored and 'buried' in the archives of museums that have never been researched. We need to be aware of what peoples of the past, who lived at different times actually wrote of their lifestyle, politics, and religions, and the events of the time.

Due to lack of trained expertise, funding, local and professional politics, and religious bias, little is being explored in our era.

The Bible IS the standard. It was written by YHWH, our Creator, Lord, and Master. The Bible covers seven major historic (idealised) periods.

1st 4000 B.C. - 2344 B.C.

The first 1656 years of man on earth before the flood.

2nd 2344 B.C. - 1491 B.C.

The Flood and the Patriarchal period from Noah to the Exodus. Genesis and Job throw light on that, Egypt was at the peak of its power, then crashed after the plagues and the death of the firstborn.

3rd 1491 B.C. - 1067 B.C.

Israel wandering 40 years in the Sinai desert until they all died, then the 400 year period of the 'Dark Ages' from Joshua to the time of David and Solomon which was a type of millennium then Palestine went into a steady decline. Israel and the Jews were taken into captivity and Jerusalem and the Temple were destroyed.

4th 1067 B.C. - 3 B.C. The first year of Cyrus 536 B.C. to Christ's birth.

5th 2 B.C. - 96 A.D. Then Christ came, from the revelation of the mystery in 63 AD to the end of the 1st Century A.D., 40 years of very hazy information.

6th 96 A.D. - 2nd Advent

7th Post Millennium – Eternity

These periods should be taken as 'idealised', but this does not mean they are not a realistic representation of an overview of history.

OVERVIEW OF HISTORY FROM ADAM TO ETERNITY
1st 4000 B.C. - 2344 B.C.

Reformation of the earth and the creation of Adam and Eve - Flood

There were 1656 A.M. Years (**A.M.** = After Man) from the creation of Adam until the flood came.

Genesis 2:17 But of the tree of the knowledge of good and evil, thou shalt not eat of it: for in the day that thou eatest thereof thou shalt surely die.

Genesis 5:5 And all the days that Adam lived were nine hundred and thirty years: and he died.

Adam died within the 'day', God's day which is as a thousand years.

2 Peter 3:8 But, beloved, be not ignorant of this one thing, that one day is with the Lord as a thousand years, and a thousand years as one day.

687 A.M.

Methusaleh was born. His name meant 'when he dies, it will come' referring to the flood) lived for 969 years, the longest of any man recorded in the Bible.

1056 A.M. Noah was born

Genesis 5:29 And he called his name Noah, saying, This same shall comfort us concerning our work and toil of our hands, because of the ground which the Lord hath cursed.

Genesis 6:5 And God saw that the wickedness of man was great in the earth, and that every imagination of the thoughts of his heart was only evil continually. 6 And it repented the Lord that he had made man on the earth, and it grieved him at his heart. 7 And the Lord said, I will destroy man whom I have created from the face of the earth; both man, and beast, and the creeping thing, and the fowls of the air; for it repenteth me that I have made them.

Genesis 6: 8 But Noah found grace in the eyes of the Lord. 9 These are the generations of Noah: Noah was a just man and perfect in his generations, and Noah walked with God.

1650 A.M.

At the end of the pre-flood era, men and women were working to limited way with metals, they had musical instruments, but the structure of society was primitive, and wild idolatrous and immoral practices abounded. So bad was human behaviour, to the extent that God 'repented' or was sorry that He had made man. But of course He had a Master Plan which had been devised since before the world began.

1656 A.M.

Methuselah died in the year when the flood came in 1656 A.M. Or approximately 2369

B.C. Christ the second Adam came almost exactly 4000 years after the first Adam.

Genesis 5:25 And all the days of Methuselah were nine hundred sixty and nine years: and he died.

Thanks to Noah being 'just', 'walking with God', and being 'perfect in his generations' Who. This meant that Noah had not indulged in improper inbreeding practices, which had been going on between humans and wicked spirits. God allowed eight people, Noah and his wife and children and their wives to be saved from the flood. Every other person was drowned.

Genesis 7:6 And Noah was six hundred years old when the flood of waters was upon the earth.

At that time there were 'bands' of ice around the earth high up in the atmosphere similar to those visible around some planets now. These bands caused very different climactic conditions on the earth.

As the earth rotated, there would be periods of darkness or semi-darkness even during the times when the Sun would be shining onto the earth. It was these ice bands that melted and fell as rain onto the earth at the time of the flood. There is an indication of this in Job 38 when God is asking Job, where were you when I created the earth?

Job 38:8 Or who shut up the sea with doors, when it brake forth, as if it had issued out of the womb? 9 When I made the cloud the garment thereof, and thick darkness a swaddlingband for it,

It was God who contained the seas, and the clouds and the thick darkness caused by the 'swaddlingband' around the earth.

Job 38:10 And brake up for it my decreed place, and set bars and doors, 11 And said, Hitherto shalt thou come, but no further: and here shall thy proud waves be stayed?

And God who broke up those 'swaddlingbands' for His purpose of flooding the earth, and He made the Moon to cause the tides, but prevents the waves from coming any further than they do. Sceptics think it all just happens as a result of evolution. Sacrilege!

2nd 2344 B.C. (or 1656 A.M.) - 1491 B.C.

The Flood occurred 1656 years (2369 B.C.) after the creation of Adam and Eve. The Patriarchal period was from Noah to the Exodus. Genesis and Job throw light on that, Egypt at the peak of its power, then which crashed after the ten plagues and the death of the firstborn.

Noah, whose name means 'comfort' was ordered by God to construct the Ark, a truly enormous boat, in which He would cause all that breathed upon the earth to enter in before the waters covered the earth.

Genesis 7:4 For yet seven days, and I will cause it to rain upon the earth forty days and forty nights; and every living substance that I have made will I destroy from off the face of the earth. 5 And Noah did according unto all that the Lord commanded him. 6 And Noah was six hundred years old when the flood of waters was upon the earth. 7 And Noah went in, and his sons, and his wife, and his sons' wives with him, into the ark, because of the waters of the flood.

The fact that Noah was six hundred years old when the flood of waters was upon the earth gives an important benchmark when anyone is attempting to study the chronology of the Bible.

Genesis 7:15 And they went in unto Noah into the ark, two and two of all flesh, wherein is the breath of life. 16 And they that went in, went in male and female of all flesh, as God had commanded him: **and the Lord shut him in**. 17 And the flood was forty days upon the earth; and the waters increased, and bare up the ark, and it was lift up above the earth.

Note that God, (Christ) (Not Noah as in the film!) shut the door of the Ark just before the rains came, preventing any others from entering in. Note also, that this narrative was written under the direct inspiration of Christ, the YHWH of the Old Testament, so it is not a spurious tale, but the truth.

Genesis 7:4 For yet seven days, and I will cause it to rain upon the earth forty days and forty nights; and every living substance that I have made will I destroy from off the face of the earth.

Genesis 8 gives another exact benchmark date.

Genesis 8:13 And it came to pass in the six hundredth and first year, in the first month, the first day of the month, the waters were dried up from off the earth: and Noah removed the covering of the ark, and looked, and, behold, the face of the ground was dry. 14 And in the second month, on the seven and twentieth day of the month, was the earth dried.

Genesis 8:20 And Noah builded an altar unto the Lord; and took of every clean beast, and of every clean fowl, and offered burnt offerings on the altar.

When God actually pronounced meats to be 'clean and unclean' for the benefit of all humankind is not recorded in the Bible, but clearly the distinction existed shortly after Adam and Eve were created because of the offerings of the Cain and Abel scenario.

It is important to note that God had ordained that animals would be 'clean' and 'unclean' long before the flood. Abel's sacrifice was acceptable to God, but Cain's was not, and it does not say why in the Bible. And here after the deliverance of the flood, Noah, walking with God, builds an altar and sacrifices 'clean' animals and birds to God.

Because of ignorance of the Scriptures, people call the laws of 'clean & unclean' meats, 'Jewish'. If this date of Noah's sacrifice is taken as being around 2344 B.C. and it is realised that Judah (Yehudah) was born in approximately 1739 B.C., about six hundred years after the flood, then to call the food laws 'Jewish' does not make any sense at all. They were God's Laws of beneficial nutrition.

Because of the sin of Adam and Eve, God had cursed the ground of the earth.

Genesis 3:17 And unto Adam he said, Because thou hast hearkened unto the voice of thy wife, and hast eaten of the tree, of which I commanded thee, saying, Thou shalt not eat of it: cursed is the ground for thy sake; in sorrow shalt thou eat of it all the days of thy life;

At this time God removed the curse that had been on the ground of the earth since the sin of Adam and Eve. And God also gives a promise that seedtime and harvest and the seasons will never cease as long as the earth exists.

Genesis 8:21 And the Lord smelled a sweet savour; and the Lord said in his heart, I will not again curse the ground any more for man's sake; for the imagination of man's heart is evil from his youth; neither will I again smite any more every thing living, as I have done. 22 While the earth remaineth, seedtime and harvest, and cold and heat, and summer and winter, and day and night shall not cease.

During those years before the flood, no rain fell on the earth. The weather patterns were completely different.

Genesis 2:5 And every plant of the field before it was in the earth, and every herb of the field before it grew: for the Lord God had not caused it to rain upon the earth, and there was not a man to till the ground. 6 But there went up a mist from the earth, and watered the whole face of the ground.

God also now makes the promise to His children that the earth will never again be flooded, and appoints the rainbow as His sign of that promise.

Scientists are prone to scoff, saying that the rainbow is a natural event, which it is. But God says we can take it as a sign that He will not flood the Earth again.

Genesis 9:8 And God spake unto Noah, and to his sons with him, saying, 9 And I, behold, I establish my covenant with you, and with your seed after you; 10 And with every living creature that is with you, of the fowl, of the cattle, and of every beast of the earth with you; from all that go out of the ark, to every beast of the earth. 11 And I will establish my covenant with you, neither shall all flesh be cut off any more by the waters of a flood; neither shall there any more be a flood to destroy the earth. 12 And God said, This is the token of the covenant which I make between me and you and every living creature that is with you, for perpetual generations: 13 I do set my bow in the cloud, and it shall be for a token of a covenant between me and the earth. 14 And it shall come to pass, when I bring a cloud over the earth, that the bow shall be seen in the cloud: 15 And I will remember my covenant, which is between me and you and every living creature of all flesh; and the waters shall no more become a flood to destroy all flesh. 16 And the bow shall be in the cloud; and I will look upon it, that I may remember the everlasting covenant between God and every living creature of all flesh that is upon the earth. 17 And God said unto Noah, This is the token of the covenant, which I have established between me and all flesh that is upon the earth.

People can sneer at this promise made to humankind, and say that a rainbow is just a natural phenomenon of white light being broken into the spectrum by droplets of rain. That fact is true, but without this inspired revelation we would not know that it is also a perpetual sign of an absolute promise to us from God that there will never again a flood to destroy all flesh.

The flood happened, Christ says so, many times in His Word. It was a time for new beginnings. The earth was cursed before the flood because of sin, but that this curse was now lifted, and God also made promises to humans that the climate would change and provide seasons, and that the earth would never again be flooded.

THE BIRTH OF NATIONS:

This historic period is that of the beginning of the birth of the nations after the flood, the Patriarchal period, post Exodus, until the time of David and Solomon and the building of the Temple.

After the flood in 2344 B.C. there were only eight people on earth, and it would clearly take some time, and many generations before there would be a substantial number of people on the planet.

2327 B.C.

Noah: Got drunk two nights in a row, and his daughters who feared Noah's line would end instead of trusting God, they had sex with Noah. Then Ham took advantage of Noah being drunk, and emasculated him, and as a result Noah lost his ability to have more children.

Genesis 9:23 And Shem and Japheth took a garment, and laid it upon both their shoulders, and went backward, and covered the nakedness of their father; and their faces were backward, and they saw not their father's nakedness. 24 And Noah awoke from his wine, and knew what his younger son (Ham) had done unto him. 25 And he said, Cursed be Canaan; a servant of servants shall he be unto his brethren.

Canaan was the fourth son of Ham, so it was appropriate that God selected him to receive the punishment because of his father's sin.

Abraham: Lied to the Pharaoh of Egypt telling him that his wife was his sister. The Pharaoh did not appreciate this as the potential was to get him in trouble with God.

Genesis 12:18 And Pharaoh called Abram and said, What is this that thou hast done unto me? why didst thou not tell me that she was thy wife? 19 Why saidst thou, She is my sister? so I might have taken her to me to wife: now therefore behold thy wife, take her, and go thy way. 20 And Pharaoh commanded his men concerning him: and they sent him away, and his wife, and all that he had.

1900 B.C.

In Genesis 12 it speaks of Abraham going down to Egypt and the whole nation knew he was there. This was around 1921 B.C. about 400 years after the flood and there still would not have been a large population on earth.

Genesis 13:1 And Abram went up out of Egypt, he, and his wife, and all that he had, and Lot with him, into the south.

Then Abraham and Lot went to live in Canaan, but strife developed between the herdsmen of Abram and Lot.

Genesis 13:8 And Abram said unto Lot, Let there be no strife, I pray thee, between me and thee, and between my herdmen and thy herdmen; for we be brethren. 9 Is not the whole land before thee? separate thyself, I pray thee, from me: if thou wilt take the left hand, then I will go to the right; or if thou depart to the right hand, then I will go to the left.

So Abraham gave Lot the choice as to where he would live. He chose the plains, where the cities of Sodom and Gomorrah were. Abraham went to live in the land of Canaan.

Genesis 1318 Then Abram removed his tent, and came and dwelt in the plain of Mamre, which is in Hebron, and built there an altar unto the Lord.

Lot was living on the plain, and four 'kings' came and took him away. These 'kings' were probably family or tribal chiefs, as by that time the nations were still not really developed to any real size.

Abraham took 318 people as an army to rescue Lot, defeated those who had taken him away, and delivered him and his family.

Not long later, the situation in Sodom and Gomorrah had deteriorated to the point where **everyone** in those cities was involved with homosexual immoral activities. The account says that **all** the men of Sodom surrounded Lot's house, and demanded that he bring out the 'men', who were actually angels, so that they could 'know them' (meaning sexually), as it says in the KJV. So for all the men of the city to assemble, there was still a relatively small population.

Abraham and Sarah were childless, but God promised that they would not only have a child, but his descendants would be like the sand of the sea. So through the miraculous intervention of God, Isaac was born.

Genesis 21:5 And Abraham was an hundred years old, when his son Isaac was born unto him.

Abraham was willing to sacrifice Isaac to God, and it was this test that proved his obedience to God, who accepted him as righteous.

In his old age, Abraham did not want Isaac to take a wife from the Canaanites (who were idolatrous pagans), so he commissioned his servant to go to Mesopotamia to find her.

When he arrived in the area the servant asked God for a sign to help him to find the right wife for Isaac. The sign he asked for would be that as women came down to the well to get water, the one who not only willingly gave him to drink but offered to draw water for his ten camels as well. This would represent a most unusual attitude of willing service. Even before he had he finished praying, a woman came to draw water, not just any woman but a relative of Abraham.

Genesis 24:15 And it came to pass, before he had done speaking, that, behold, Rebekah came out, who was born to Bethuel, son of Milcah, the wife of Nahor, Abraham's brother, with her pitcher upon her shoulder.

16 And the damsel was very fair to look upon, a virgin, neither had any man known her: and she went down to the well, and filled her pitcher, and came up. 17 And the servant ran to meet her, and said, Let me, I pray thee, drink a little water of thy pitcher. 18 And she said, Drink, my lord: and she hasted, and let down her pitcher upon her hand, and gave him drink. 19 And when she had done giving him drink, she said, I will draw water for thy camels also, until they have done drinking. 20 And she hasted, and emptied her pitcher into the trough, and ran again unto the well to draw water, and drew for all his camels.

Genesis 24:28 And the damsel ran, and told them of her mother's house these things. 29 And Rebekah had a brother, and his name was Laban: and Laban ran out unto the man, unto the well.

The narrative goes on to tell the wonderful story of just how God so miraculously provided Isaac with a beautiful wife Rebekah.

Rebekah was barren, and Isaac entreated God that she might have a child. Then follows the very important historical fact that Rebekah bore twins who were Jacob and Esau who were destined to play a vital part in the development of God's plan for Israel.

Even with those who God selected to work with through history were afflicted with deceitful ways, sometimes over most important issues that would have consequences for thousands of years to come.

1897 B.C.

Isaac was born.

1872 B.C.

Abraham showed that he was willing to sacrifice Isaac, but God provided the ram instead.

Genesis 22:1 And it came to pass after these things, that God did tempt Abraham, and said unto him, Abraham: and he said, Behold, here I am. 2 And he said, Take now thy son, thine only son Isaac, whom thou lovest, and get thee into the land of Moriah; and offer him there for a burnt offering upon one of the mountains which I will tell thee of. 3And Abraham rose up early in the morning, and saddled his ass, and took two of his young men with him, and Isaac his son, and clave the wood for the burnt offering, and rose up, and went unto the place of which God had told him.

Notice Abraham rose up early in the morning, he was hastening to obey God even over such a horrendous test.

Genesis 22:13 And Abraham lifted up his eyes, and looked, and behold behind him a ram caught in a thicket by his horns: and Abraham went and took the ram, and offered him up for a burnt offering in the stead of his son.

1838 B.C.

Jacob and Esau are born.

Genesis 25:19 And these are the generations of Isaac, Abraham's son: Abraham begat Isaac: 20 And Isaac was forty years old when he took Rebekah to wife, the daughter of Bethuel the Syrian of Padanaram, the sister to Laban the Syrian. 21 And Isaac intreated the Lord for his wife, because she was barren: and the Lord was intreated of him, and Rebekah his wife conceived. 22 And the children struggled together within her; and she said, If it be so, why am I thus? And she went to enquire of the Lord. 23 And the Lord said unto her, Two nations are in thy womb, and two manner of people shall be separated from thy bowels; and the one people shall be stronger than the other people; and the elder shall serve the younger. 24 And when her days to be delivered were fulfilled, behold, there were twins in her womb. 25 And the first came out red, all over like an hairy garment; and they called his name Esau. 26 And after that came his brother out, and his hand took hold on Esau's heel; and his name was called Jacob: and Isaac was threescore years old when she bare them.

Genesis 25:26 And after that came his brother out, and his hand took hold on Esau's heel; and his name was called Jacob: and Isaac was threescore years old when she bare them.

Genesis 25:27 And the boys grew: and Esau was a cunning hunter, a man of the field; and Jacob was a plain man, dwelling in tents. 28 And Isaac loved Esau, because he did eat of his venison: but Rebekah loved Jacob. 29 And Jacob sod pottage: and Esau came from the field, and he was faint: 30 And Esau said to Jacob, Feed me, I pray thee, with that same red pottage; for I am faint: therefore was his name called Edom. 31 And Jacob said, Sell me this day thy birthright. 32 And Esau said, Behold, I am at the point to die: and what profit shall this birthright do to me? 33 And Jacob said, Swear to me this day; and he sware unto him: and he sold his birthright unto Jacob. 34 Then Jacob gave Esau bread and pottage of lentiles; and he did eat and drink, and rose up, and went his way: thus Esau despised his birthright.

When Isaac was old, and his eyes were dim, he called Esau to him and told him to go out hunting to kill a deer and come back and prepare his favourite savoury meat dish for him.

1805 B.C.

Jacob bought Esau's Birthright for a bowl of soup, then conspired with his Mother to cheat Esau out of his blessing from Isaac.

Isaac's wife Rebekah overheard the request, and immediately summoned Jacob, and told him to prepare the food for his father. Then by trickery and deceit managed to deceive Isaac into thinking that Jacob was Esau, and Isaac unaware of the switch, gave Jacob the blessing, the birthright which should have gone to the elder Esau. As quoted above, Esau had 'sold' his birthright to Jacob some time before for a bowl of soup because he was so hungry after being out hunting. In this way Esau despised the value of his birthright.

Jacob had served Laban for two periods of seven years in order to be allowed to marry his daughters. Laban married Jacob off to Leah by deceit, and Jacob was willing to work another seven years to have Rachel as his wife. When serious ill-will developed between Laban and his family and Jacob and his family,

Genesis 31:1 And he heard the words of Laban's sons, saying, Jacob hath taken away all that was our father's; and of that which was our father's hath he gotten all this glory. 2 And Jacob beheld the countenance of Laban, and, behold, it was not toward him as before. 3 And the Lord said unto Jacob, Return unto the land of thy fathers, and to thy kindred; and I will be with thee. ...

1739 B.C.

Over time, there had been serious friction between Jacob and Esau, so much so that Jacob was fearful for his life as Esau approached with 400 men.

Genesis 32: 6 And the messengers returned to Jacob, saying, We came to thy brother Esau, and also he cometh to meet thee, and four hundred men with him.

The awful warring situation in the country called Israel in our era between the 'Jews' and the 'Palestinians' is actually friction between the descendants of two twin brothers which makes it totally tragic. It may be that the majority of those living in Palestine are Edomites as well as descendants of Jacob!

1729 B.C.

Joseph is thrown down into a pit by his brothers.

Genesis 37: 23 And it came to pass, when Joseph was come unto his brethren, that they stript Joseph out of his coat, his coat of many colours that was on him; 24 And they took him, and cast him into a pit: and the pit was empty, there was no water in it.

Genesis 37:28 Then there passed by Midianites merchantmen; and they drew and lifted up Joseph out of the pit, and sold Joseph to the Ishmeelites for twenty pieces of silver: and they brought Joseph into Egypt.

1729 B.C. Joseph is made chief of the household of a high official of the Pharaoh.

Genesis 39:1 And Joseph was brought down to Egypt; and Potiphar, an officer of Pharaoh, captain of the guard, an Egyptian, bought him of the hands of the Ishmeelites, which had brought him down thither. 2 And the Lord was with Joseph, and he was a prosperous man; and he was in the house of his master the Egyptian. 3 And his master saw that the Lord was with him, and that the Lord made all that he did to prosper in his hand. 4 And Joseph found grace in his sight, and he served him: and he made him overseer over his house, and all that he had he put into his hand.

1721 B.C.

Joseph's master was an official of the Pharaoh. His master's wife lusted after Joseph, and was determined to have him.

Genesis 39:7 And it came to pass after these things, that his master's wife cast her eyes upon Joseph; and she said, Lie with me. 8 But he refused, and said unto his master's wife, Behold, my master wotteth not what is with me in the house, and he hath committed all that he hath to my hand; 9 There is none greater in this house than I; neither hath he kept back any thing from me but thee, because thou art his wife: how then can I do this great wickedness, and sin against God?

Potiphar's wife proceeded to vent her wrath because Joseph had refused her.

Genesis 39:10 And it came to pass, as she spake to Joseph day by day, that he hearkened not unto her, to lie by her, or to be with her. 11 And it came to pass about this time, that Joseph went into the house to do his business; and there was none of the men of the house there within. 12 And she caught him by his garment, saying, Lie with me: and he left his garment in her hand, and fled, and got him out. 13 And it came to pass, when she saw that he had left his garment in her hand, and was fled forth, 14 That she called unto the men of her house, and spake unto them, saying, See, he hath brought in an Hebrew unto us to mock us; he came in unto me to lie with me, and I cried with a loud voice: 15 And it came to pass, when he heard that I lifted up my voice and cried, that he left his garment with me, and fled, and got him out.

Potiphar's wife cried out to her husband's servants and told them that Joseph had tried to rape her.

Genesis 39:16 And she laid up his garment by her, until his lord came home. 17 And she spake unto him according to these words, saying, The Hebrew servant, which thou hast brought unto us, came in unto me to mock me: 18 And it came to pass, as I lifted up my voice and cried, that he left his garment with me, and fled out. 19 And it came to pass, when his master heard the words of his wife, which she spake unto him, saying, After this manner did thy servant to me; that his wrath was kindled. 20 And Joseph's master took him, and put him into the prison, a place where the king's prisoners were bound: and he was there in the prison.

1721 B.C.

God's law forbids bearing false witness against anyone, it is a terrible crime often with dreadful consequences. But God was looking after Joseph's interests.

Genesis 39:21 But the Lord was with Joseph, and shewed him mercy, and gave him favour in the sight of the keeper of the prison.

1715 B.C.

Pharaoh has a dream which none of his 'wise' men can interpret, but finally Joseph is brought out of prison and tells the Pharaoh the meaning of the seven lean and seven fat cattle. As a result, Pharaoh promotes Joseph to be second only to the Pharaoh over the whole land of Egypt.

In this sense, Joseph is a type of Christ, being taken from prison and in one day sitting at the right hand of the Pharaoh, as happened to Christ after His abasement, suffering and death, who after His resurrection ascended to the Right Hand of the Father in Heaven in one day.

Genesis 41:39 And Pharaoh said unto Joseph, Forasmuch as God hath shewed thee all this, there is none so discreet and wise as thou art: 40 Thou shalt be over my house, and according unto thy word shall all my people be ruled: only in the throne will I be greater than thou. 41 And Pharaoh said unto Joseph, See, I have set thee over all the land of Egypt. 42 And Pharaoh took off his ring from his hand, and put it upon Joseph's hand, and arrayed him in vestures of fine linen, and put a gold chain about his neck; 43 And he made him to ride in the second chariot which he had; and they cried before him, Bow the knee: and he made him ruler over all the land of Egypt. 44 And Pharaoh said unto Joseph, I am Pharaoh, and without thee shall no man lift up his hand or foot in all the land of Egypt. 45 And Pharaoh called Joseph's name Zaphnathpaaneah; and he gave him to wife Asenath the daughter of Potipherah priest of On. And Joseph went out over all the land of Egypt.

46 And Joseph was thirty years old when he stood before Pharaoh king of Egypt. And Joseph went out from the presence of Pharaoh, and went throughout all the land of Egypt.

Joseph rose to a position of immense power in the 18th Century B.C., and at that time the population began to explode as the exponential doubling curve began to take effect.

Joseph was also involved in the development of the Pyramids, and other great buildings and infrastructure.

Egypt was a very civilised place, the people were highly educated, sophisticated, had extensive libraries, amazing knowledge of the heavens and astronomy, and technical knowledge of architecture. The pyramids were built in the time of Joseph's rule next to the Pharaoh, and his administration of the seven good years.

Then exactly as God had revealed to Joseph concerning the forthcoming famine all over the world and in Egypt, Joseph had stored up vast quantities food in the good years.

Genesis 41:56 And the famine was over all the face of the earth: and Joseph opened all the storehouses, and sold unto the Egyptians; and the famine waxed sore in the land of Egypt. 57 And all countries came into Egypt to Joseph for to buy corn; because that the famine was so sore in all lands.

Genesis 42:1 Now when Jacob saw that there was corn in Egypt, Jacob said unto his sons, Why do ye look one upon another? 2 And he said, Behold, I have heard that there is corn in Egypt: get you down thither, and buy for us from thence; that we may live, and not die. 3 And Joseph's ten brethren went down to buy corn in Egypt.

Then follows the story how Joseph engineers the situation where Jacob who had been grieving all those years since he had been shown Joseph's coat of many colours covered in blood, and was convinced that he was dead, Jacob and his twelve sons including Benjamin are brought into Egypt.

Genesis 45:25 And they went up out of Egypt, and came into the land of Canaan unto Jacob their father, 26 And told him, saying, Joseph is yet alive, and he is governor over all the land of Egypt. And Jacob's heart fainted, for he believed them not. 27 And they told him all the words of Joseph, which he had said unto them: and when he saw the wagons which Joseph had sent to carry him, the spirit of Jacob their father revived: 28 And Israel said, It is enough; Joseph my son is yet alive: I will go and see him before I die.

1705 B.C.

Jacob and his family go down to Egypt, and are there for the next 215 years. The children of Israel prospered greatly and quickly grew in number until…

Genesis 46:1 And Israel took his journey with all that he had, and came to Beersheba, and offered sacrifices unto the God of his father Isaac. 2 And God spake unto Israel in the visions of the night, and said, Jacob, Jacob. And he said, Here am I. 3 And he said, I am God, the God of thy father: fear not to go down into Egypt; for I will there make of thee a great nation: 4 I will go down with thee into Egypt; and I will also surely bring thee up again: and Joseph shall put his hand upon thine eyes. 5 And Jacob rose up from Beersheba: and the sons of Israel carried Jacob their father, and their little ones, and their wives, in the wagons which Pharaoh had sent to carry him. 6 And they took their cattle, and their goods, which they had gotten in the land of Canaan, and came into Egypt, Jacob, and all his seed with him: 7 His sons, and his sons' sons with him, his daughters, and his sons' daughters, and all his seed brought he with him into Egypt.

Genesis 47:5 And Pharaoh spake unto Joseph, saying, Thy father and thy brethren are come unto thee: 6 The land of Egypt is before thee; in the best of the land make thy father and brethren to dwell; in the land of Goshen let them dwell: and if thou knowest any men of activity among them, then make them rulers over my cattle.

1634 B.C.

Joseph dies.

Exodus 1:5 And all the souls that came out of the loins of Jacob were seventy souls: for Joseph was in Egypt already. 6 And Joseph died, and all his brethren, and all that generation. 7 And the children of Israel were fruitful, and increased abundantly, and multiplied, and waxed exceeding mighty; and the land was filled with them.

1588 B.C.

Now there was a new Pharaoh or king over Egypt who had no experience of Joseph or what he had done for the country.

Exodus 1:8 Now there arose up a new king over Egypt, which knew not Joseph. 9 And he said unto his people, Behold, the people of the children of Israel are more and mightier than we: 10 Come on, let us deal wisely with them; lest they multiply, and it come to pass, that, when there falleth out any war, they join also unto our enemies, and fight against us, and so get them up out of the land. 11 Therefore they did set over them taskmasters to afflict them with their burdens. And they built for Pharaoh treasure cities, Pithom and Raamses. 12 But the more they afflicted them, the more they multiplied and grew. And they were grieved because of the children of Israel. 13 And the Egyptians made the children of Israel to serve with rigour: 14 And they made their lives bitter with hard bondage, in morter, and in brick, and in all manner of service in the field: all their service, wherein they made them serve, was with rigour.

By this time the Children of Israel had grown to number 600,000 men plus their wives and families, and the Pharaoh had taken severe steps to reduce the birthrate.

1573 B.C.

Moses is born to a Levite (priestly) couple, and is saved miraculously by God from the effects of the law issued by the Pharaoh that all male Hebrew children born in Egypt should be slain at birth. This law was issued as the Israelites were getting too many and too strong for the Pharoah's liking.

So Moses' mother put him in a basket lined with pitch and tar to make it waterproof.

Exodus 2:2 And there went a man of the house of Levi, and took to wife a daughter of Levi. 2 And the woman conceived, and bare a son: and when she saw him that he was a goodly child, she hid him three months. 3 And when she could not longer hide him, she took for him an ark of bulrushes, and daubed it with slime and with pitch, and put the child therein; and she laid it in the flags by the river's brink. 4 And his sister stood afar off, to wit what would be done to him.

Exodus 2:5 And the daughter of Pharaoh came down to wash herself at the river; and her maidens walked along by the river's side; and when she saw the ark among the flags, she sent her maid to fetch it. 6 And when she had opened it, she saw the child: and, behold, the babe wept. And she had compassion on him, and said, This is one of the Hebrews' children.

Pharaoh's daughter plucks Moses out of the river and brings him up in the Pharaoh's court as her own. As a result, Moses received the best possible education in the arts and sciences while living in the most advanced civilisation in the world. This prepared him for the exacting work he would do during his life. Moses was responsible for making adjustments to the Hebrew Calendar during the period of the wanderings in the Sinai Desert. When the Spring and Autumn official days were changed.

1533 B.C.

Moses then murders an Egyptian who is beating an Israelite, he flees and goes to live in Midian.

1490 B.C.

The end of 215 years children of Israel were in Egypt. God appears to Moses in the burning bush, and gives him his commission to lead the Israelites out of Egypt.

3rd 1491 B.C. - 1067 B.C.

Israel wandered 40 years in the Sinai desert until they all died. Then ensued the 400 year period of the 'Dark Ages' from Joshua to the time of David and Solomon, which was a type of millennium, then Palestine went into a steady decline. Israel and the Jews were taken into captivity and Jerusalem and the Temple were destroyed.

Exodus 3:11 And Moses said unto God, Who am I, that I should go unto Pharaoh, and that I should bring forth the children of Israel out of Egypt?

Exodus 12:1 And the Lord spake unto Moses and Aaron in the land of Egypt saying, 2 This month shall be unto you the beginning of months: it shall be the first month of the year to you.

Prior to the Exodus, years were counted from Spring to Spring, and the Passover was in the Spring. After the Exodus, the official year was taken from the 1st of Tishri, and everyone had the same birthday, and all kings and official reigns began and ended in the Autumn. Christ was born on the Feast of Trumpets on the 1st Tishri, 2-3 B.C. So when it talks in Genesis about the birth of Cain and Abel being "in the process of time" in the King James, the Hebrew actually means "in the end of days, meaning the end of the official year for counting purposes.

This establishment of Day of Trumpets is mentioned in the Psalms.

Psalm 81:3 Blow up the trumpet in the new moon, in the time appointed, on our solemn feast day. 4 For this was a statute for Israel, and a law of the God of Jacob. This he ordained in Joseph for a testimony, when he went out through the land of Egypt: where I heard a language that I understood not.

1491 B.C.

The beginning of the plagues on Egypt and the Exodus.

By the time that the Children of Israel left Egypt they had grown in numbers. There were armed men of Israel 600,000 plus women and children, so the number who went through the Red Sea numbered a total population of around 2 million. Hard to imagine, but true.

Exodus 14:8 And the Lord hardened the heart of Pharaoh king of Egypt, and he pursued after the children of Israel: and the children of Israel went out with an high hand.

Taking much wealth with them, gold, jewellery, and other valuable things no doubt rejoicing, but not for long.

Exodus 14:9 But the Egyptians pursued after them, all the horses and chariots of Pharaoh, and his horsemen, and his army, and overtook them encamping by the sea, beside Pihahiroth, before Baalzephon. 10 And when Pharaoh drew nigh, the children of Israel lifted up their eyes, and, behold, the Egyptians marched after them; and they were sore afraid: and the children of Israel cried out unto the Lord. 11 And they said unto Moses, Because there were no graves in Egypt, hast thou taken us away to die in the wilderness? Wherefore hast thou dealt thus with us, to carry us forth out of Egypt? 12 Is not this the word that we did tell thee in Egypt, saying, Let us alone, that we may serve the Egyptians? For it had been better for us to serve the Egyptians, than that we should die in the wilderness.

The children of Israel had for ever been guilty of complaining to Moses for all their hardships, never looking past Moses to see that God had a hand in everything they did. So patient Moses as always tells them to trust God that He will deliver them,

Exodus 14:13 And Moses said unto the people, Fear ye not, stand still, and see the salvation of the Lord, which he will shew to you to day: for the Egyptians whom ye have seen to day, ye shall see them again no more for ever 14 The Lord shall fight for you, and ye shall hold your peace.

Moses told them to be quiet, but inside him also was in an attitude of complaining to God, so God said to Moses:

Exodus 14:15 And the Lord said unto Moses, Wherefore criest thou unto me? speak unto the children of Israel, that they go forward: 16 But lift thou up thy rod, and stretch out thine hand over the sea, and divide it: and the children of Israel shall go on dry ground through the midst of the sea.

Exodus 14:21 And Moses stretched out his hand over the sea; and the Lord caused the sea to go back by a strong east wind all that night, and made the sea dry land, and the waters were divided. 22 And the children of Israel went into the midst of the sea upon the dry ground: and the waters were a wall unto them on their right hand, and on their left.

So the children of Israel went through the sea dry shod, witnessing the incredible miracle of the power of the Almighty God.

Exodus 14:29 But the children of Israel walked upon dry land in the midst of the sea; and the waters were a wall unto them on their right hand, and on their left. 30 Thus the Lord saved Israel that day out of the hand of the Egyptians; and Israel saw the Egyptians dead upon the sea shore. 31 And Israel saw that great work which the Lord did upon the Egyptians: and the people feared the Lord, and believed the Lord, and his servant Moses.

Yes, the children of Israel saw and experienced the miraculous deliverance God provided for them, and feared the Lord, and believed Moses. But for how long? How long did they remember this event and continue to fear God and respect Moses? Not long at all, less than three days!

Exodus 15:22 So Moses brought Israel from the Red sea, and they went out into the wilderness of Shur; and they went three days in the wilderness, and found no water. 23 And when they came to Marah, they could not drink of the waters of Marah, for they were bitter: therefore the name of it was called Marah. 24 And the people murmured against Moses, saying, What shall we drink? 25 And he cried unto the Lord; and the Lord shewed him a tree, which when he had cast into the waters, the waters were made sweet:

there he made for them a statute and an ordinance, and there he proved them.

The Children of Israel continued in the desert for about six weeks, and once again fell into a murmuring attitude against Moses and against God. They were supposed to be preparing to enter the Promised Land.

<u>1490 B.C.</u>

God said, send out men to search out the land of Canaan.

Numbers 13:1 3 And the Lord spake unto Moses, saying, 2 Send thou men, that they may search the land of Canaan, which I give unto the children of Israel: of every tribe of their fathers shall ye send a man, every one a ruler among them. 3 And Moses by the commandment of the Lord sent them from the wilderness of Paran: all those men were heads of the children of Israel. So one leading man was chosen from each of the tribes of Israel to go and spy out the land.

Numbers 13:17 And Moses sent them to spy out the land of Canaan, and said unto them, Get you up this way southward, and go up into the mountain: 18 And see the land, what it is, and the people that dwelleth therein, whether they be strong or weak, few or many; 19 And what the land is that they dwell in, whether it be good or bad; and what cities they be that they dwell in, whether in tents, or in strong holds; 20 And what the land is, whether it be fat or lean, whether there be wood therein, or not. And be ye of good courage, and bring of the fruit of the land. Now the time was the time of the firstripe grapes.

Numbers 13:23 And they came unto the brook of Eshcol, and cut down from thence a branch with one cluster of grapes, and they bare it between two upon a staff; and they brought of the pomegranates, and of the figs. 24 The place was called the brook Eshcol, because of the cluster of grapes which the children of Israel cut down from thence. 25 And they returned from searching of the land after forty days. 26 And they went and came to Moses, and to Aaron, and to all the congregation of the children of Israel, unto the wilderness of Paran, to Kadesh; and brought back word unto them, and unto all the congregation, and shewed them the fruit of the land. 27 And they told him, and said, We came unto the land whither thou sentest us, and surely it floweth with milk and honey; and this is the fruit of it.

They spent 40 days exploring, and found indeed that the land was 'flowing with milk and honey' as promised by God, with bunches of grapes that took two men to carry them! But those that were sent to search out the land were not willing to trust God to help them conquer the land.

Numbers 13:28 Nevertheless the people be strong that dwell in the land, and the cities are walled, and very great: and moreover we saw the children of Anak there. 29 The Amalekites dwell in the land of the south: and the Hittites, and the Jebusites, and the Amorites, dwell in the mountains: and the Canaanites dwell by the sea, and by the coast of Jordan. 30 And Caleb stilled the people before Moses, and said, Let us go up at once, and possess it; for we are well able to overcome it. 31 But the men that went up with him said, We be not able to go up against the people; for they are stronger than we. 32 And **they brought up an evil report of the land which they had searched unto the children of Israel,** saying, The land, through which we have gone to search it, is a land that eateth up the inhabitants thereof; and all the people that we saw in it are men of a great stature. 33 And there we saw the giants, the sons of Anak, which come of the giants: and we were in our own sight as grasshoppers, and so we were in their sight.

So once again the children of Israel rebelled against God's appointed servants, and therefore against God, because they were fearful and refused to go into the Promised Land.

Numbers 14:14 And all the congregation lifted up their voice, and cried; and the people wept that night. 2 And all the children of Israel murmured against Moses and against Aaron: and the whole congregation said unto them, Would God that we had died in the land of Egypt! or would God we had died in this wilderness! 3 And wherefore hath the Lord brought us unto this land, to fall by the sword, that our wives and our children should be a prey? were it not better for us to return into Egypt? 4 And they said one to another, Let us make a captain, and let us return into Egypt. 5 Then Moses and Aaron fell on their faces before all the assembly of the congregation of the children of Israel.

The leaders, Joshua and Caleb, the only two survivors of the original Israelites which came out of Egypt were devastated.

Numbers 14:6 And Joshua the son of Nun, and Caleb the son of Jephunneh, which were of them that searched the land, rent their clothes: 7 And they spake unto all the company of the children of Israel, saying, The land, which we passed through to search it, is an exceeding good land. 8 If the Lord delight in us, then he will bring us into this land, and give it us; a land which floweth with milk and honey. 9 Only rebel not ye against the Lord, neither fear ye the people of the land; for they are bread for us: their defence is departed from them, and the Lord is with us: fear them not. 10 But all the congregation bade stone them with stones. And the glory of the Lord appeared in the tabernacle of the congregation before all the children of Israel. 11 And the Lord said unto Moses, How long will this people provoke me? and how long will it be ere they believe me, for all the signs which I have shewed among them? 12 I will smite them with the pestilence, and disinherit them, and will make of thee a greater nation and mightier than they.

Once again Moses, Aaron, Joshua and Caleb were in fear of their lives, being threatened with stoning, which is a terrible way to die. God wanted to destroy them all, but Moses pleaded for the lives of the tribes of Israel. But God had had enough of their rebellion, and decided they would all die in the desert and only their descendants would enter the Promised Land.

The children of Israel had left Egypt in a state of total devastation, after the plagues, and especially the last one when God's 'angel of death' killed all the firstborn of the land. The land of Egypt was in absolute chaos from which it did not recover for four hundred years.

At the time of the Exodus, when the 600,000 men of Israel plus their families came out of Egypt under Moses, they were some of the most skilled professional architects, builders, designers, stone masons, carpenters and joiners in the world. They had been involved with the building of the Pyramids and many other of the magnificent buildings of Egypt, canal systems and other marvels.

Had they gone into the promised land of Canaan at that time, it would not have taken them very long to recreate the type of civilisation they had left behind in Egypt. But because they refused to go into the land, and did not trust God to take care of them and empower them to overcome the Canaanites, and due to their horrendous idolatrous activities and their rebellion against God at every turn, God became very angry with them.

The result should be an object lesson to everyone who reads the Biblical record to see what God eventually might do when a people persists in disobeying Him.

Their punishment was to wander in the Sinai desert for 40 years until all but two had died. It was their children that would go into the Promised Land. But during that forty years, the children of Israel lost all the knowledge they had in Egypt. During that time they lost all their professional and artisan skills completely. When their children finally entered the Promised Land they were an ignorant, nomadic people of around two million, totally incapable of building up a new civilisation. This is why during the next four hundred years the Israelites remained in Palestine in a type of 'dark ages'.

Exodus 16:1 And they took their journey from Elim, and all the congregation of the children of Israel came unto the wilderness of Sin, which is between Elim and Sinai, on the fifteenth day of the second month after their departing out of the land of Egypt. 2 And the whole congregation of the children of Israel murmured against Moses and Aaron in the wilderness: 3 And the children of Israel said unto them, Would to God we had died by the hand of the Lord in the land of Egypt, when we sat by the flesh pots, and when we did eat bread to the full; for ye have brought us forth into this wilderness, to kill this whole assembly with hunger.

What the children of Israel did not realise was that they were testing God's patience to the absolute limit. But God in His mercy provided them with flesh in the form of Quails, and Manna from heaven, and had provided water too.

Exodus 16:33 And Moses said unto Aaron, Take a pot, and put an omer full of manna therein, and lay it up before the Lord, to be kept for your generations. 34 As the Lord commanded Moses, so Aaron laid it up before the Testimony, to be kept.

This was the pot of Manna that was to be kept in the Tabernacle and later in the Temple for a continuous testimony to God's lovingly providing for Israel.

As they travelled, they once again had no water, and they immediately turned on Moses who then feared for his life!

Exodus 17:3 And the people thirsted there for water; and the people murmured against Moses, and said, Wherefore is this that thou hast brought us up out of Egypt, to kill us and our children and our cattle with thirst? 4 And Moses cried unto the Lord, saying, What shall I do unto this people? they be almost ready to stone me.

And once again, God heard Moses' prayer, and provided water. Not long after this an army of Amalakites came after Israel.

Exodus 17:8 Then came Amalek, and fought with Israel in Rephidim.

Once again, God came to their rescue and delivered them miraculously, but Moses had to keep his hands high for Israel to win the battle.

Exodus 19:19 In the third month, when the children of Israel were gone forth out of the land of Egypt, the same day came they into the wilderness of Sinai.

So after three months, God is preparing to give the children of Israel His Covenant and the ten commandments. So He reminds them how He has taken care of them.

Exodus 19:4 Ye have seen what I did unto the Egyptians, and how I bare you on eagles' wings, and brought you unto myself. 5 Now therefore, if ye will obey my voice indeed, and keep my covenant, then ye shall be a peculiar treasure unto me above all people: for all the earth is mine: 6 And ye shall be unto me a kingdom of priests, and an holy nation.

These are the words which thou shalt speak unto the children of Israel. 7 And Moses came and called for the elders of the people, and laid before their faces all these words which the Lord commanded him. 8 And all the people answered together, and said, All that the Lord hath spoken we will do. And Moses returned the words of the people unto the Lord.

Once again the children of Israel are moved to comply, but again not for long. Despite all the evidence they had witnessed of God's power, they chose to forget that, and demand of Aaron to make gods for them to worship.

Idolatry is the worst sin, and in the case of Israel, it overlay their lack of appreciation for all God had done for them at every turn.

Exodus 32:1 And when the people saw that Moses delayed to come down out of the mount, the people gathered themselves together unto Aaron, and said unto him, Up, make us gods, which shall go before us; for as for this Moses, the man that brought us up out of the land of Egypt, we wot not what is become of him. 2 And Aaron said unto them, Break off the golden earrings, which are in the ears of your wives, of your sons, and of your daughters, and bring them unto me. 3 And all the people brake off the golden earrings which were in their ears, and brought them unto Aaron. 4 And he received them at their hand, and fashioned it with a graving tool, after he had made it a molten calf: and they said, These be thy gods, O Israel, which brought thee up out of the land of Egypt. 5 And when Aaron saw it, he built an altar before it; and Aaron made proclamation, and said, To morrow is a feast to the Lord.

Here is the prime example of using objects as a focus to worship God, which He expressly forbids, as nothing physical can remotely represent the glory of God. Many churches in our era are full of such paraphernalia.

1451 B.C.

At the end of the forty years, their punishment in the Sinai Desert was because the children of Israel refused to go into the Promised Land.

Exodus 16:35 And the children of Israel did eat manna forty years, until they came to a land inhabited; they did eat manna, until they came unto the borders of the land of Canaan.

1451 B.C.

Moses blessed Joshua, and then died. Joshua was full of the Spirit of the Lord, and wisdom.

Joshua 1:1 Now after the death of Moses the servant of the Lord it came to pass, that the Lord spake unto Joshua the son of Nun, Moses' minister, saying, 2 Moses my servant is dead; now therefore arise, go over this Jordan, thou, and all this people, unto the land which I do give to them, even to the children of Israel. 3 Every place that the sole of your foot shall tread upon, that have I given unto you, as I said unto Moses. 4 From the wilderness and this Lebanon even unto the great river, the river Euphrates, all the land of the Hittites, and unto the great sea toward the going down of the sun, shall be your coast.

Notice the expansion of the territory that God was giving to the Israelites, it was now to include from the wilderness, to Lebanon in the North of Palestine, to the Euphrates, and all the land from the Euphrates to the coast of the Mediterranean. So they were given much more land.

Israel met the Amalekites – God once again deliverer the Children of Israel. With help, Moses kept his arms and hands high, so they won the battle.

B.C. 1397

Once again, Israel had lost sight of Yahweh and His love for them.

The whole world went into a deep dark age of economic depression for 400 years until David came on the scene.

End verse of the book of Judges.

Judges 21:25 In those days there was no king in Israel: every man did that which was right in his own eyes.

This is the way of the entire world's population in our era. Nobody respects government, so we really live in an age of anarchy.

1074 B.C.

Israel had God, Christ, their Creator watching over them and giving them support whenever they were in an obedient frame of mind which was not very often! As usual they were grumbling and dissatisfied, and wanted to be like all the other nations around them and have a human king to look to.

This is really one of the saddest stories in the history of Israel. The results of their actions at this time in their past are still affecting them in this era.

1 Samuel 8:8 And it came to pass, when Samuel was old, that he made his sons judges over Israel. 2 Now the name of his firstborn was Joel; and the name of his second, Abiah: they were judges in Beersheba. 3 And his sons walked not in his ways, but turned aside after lucre, and took bribes, and perverted judgment.

Samuel had lost control of his own children, had not kept them in line, and had allowed them the freedom to pursue money and pervert judgement. Again typical of our era.

1 Samuel 8:4 Then all the elders of Israel gathered themselves together, and came to Samuel unto Ramah, 5 And said unto him, Behold, thou art old, and thy sons walk not in thy ways: now make us a king to judge us like all the nations. 6 But the thing displeased Samuel, when they said, Give us a king to judge us. And Samuel prayed unto the Lord.

Now Samuel is allowing himself to be pressured by the 'Elders' who are demanding a human king, and prays to the Lord about it.

1 Samuel 8:7 And the Lord (Christ Jesus) said unto Samuel, Hearken unto the voice of the people in all that they say unto thee: for they have not rejected thee, but they have rejected me, that I should not reign over them. 8 According to all the works which they have done since the day that I brought them up out of Egypt even unto this day, wherewith they have forsaken me, and served other gods, so do they also unto thee.

This was a moment of enormous historical importance. God tells Samuel, yes, give them what they want, but I will tell you what the result of having human kings will be. The Lord gave to them, but he warned that a human king would **TAKE** from them in every aspect of their lives, and so it is unto this day!! So God tells Samuel what it is going to be like under a human king, and so Samuel tells all the people what God has told him:

1 Samuel 8:9 Now therefore hearken unto their voice: howbeit yet protest solemnly unto them, and shew them the manner of the king that shall reign over them. 10 And Samuel told all the words of the Lord unto the people that asked of him a king.

Here is fair warning from Christ to His people of the consequences of their choice to reject Him, but of course they do not listen, they just want their own way. *A human King (or Government) will always TAKE from you.*

1 Samuel 8:11 And he (Samuel, repeats what God, Christ had) said, This will be the manner of the king that shall reign over you: He will **TAKE** your sons, and appoint them for himself, for his chariots, and to be his horsemen; and some shall run before his chariots.

12 And he will appoint him captains over thousands, and captains over fifties; and will set them to ear his ground, and to reap his harvest, and to make his instruments of war, and instruments of his chariots. 13 And he will **TAKE** your daughters to be confectionaries, and to be cooks, and to be bakers. 14 And he will **TAKE** your fields, and your vineyards, and your oliveyards, even the best of them, and give them to his servants. 15 And he will **TAKE** the tenth of your seed, and of your vineyards, and give to his officers, and to his servants. 16 And he will **TAKE** your menservants, and your maidservants, and your goodliest young men, and your asses, and put them to his work. 17 He will **TAKE** the tenth of your sheep: and ye shall be his

servants.18 And ye shall cry out in that day because of your king which ye shall have chosen you; and the Lord will not hear you in that day.

Despite all these very serious warnings Israel refused to listen.

Samuel 8:19 Nevertheless the people refused to obey the voice of Samuel; and they said, Nay; but we will have a king over us; 20 that we also may be like all the nations; and that our king may judge us, and go out before us, and fight our battles. 21 And Samuel heard all the words of the people, and he rehearsed them in the ears of the Lord. 22 And the Lord said to Samuel, Hearken unto their voice, and make them a king.

So God, Christ said to Samuel, 'Listen to the people, and give them what they want.' And Samuel said unto the men of Israel, Go ye every man unto his city.

It was not long however, that God regretted that he had allowed His children this 'freedom' to choose to have a king. Saul was the chosen one, and he very quickly descended into idolatry of the worst kind and rejoiced in it.

1074 B.C.

Saul was made king over Israel. He and his son Jonathan began to get the tribes of Israel together to form a united nation.

1 Samuel 11:15 And all the people went to Gilgal; and there they made Saul king before the Lord in Gilgal; and there they sacrificed sacrifices of peace offerings before the Lord; and there Saul and all the men of Israel rejoiced greatly.

And God regretted ever making Saul king.

1 Samuel 15:35 And Samuel came no more to see Saul until the day of his death: nevertheless Samuel mourned

for Saul: and the Lord repented (was truly sorry) that he had made Saul king over Israel.

1073 B.C. What we find now during the 400 years after the Exodus from Joshua to the time of David, Israel and Palestine had been in a low state of barbarism and ignorance which applied also to Egypt, and to Babylon and Assyria of which there is no mention in the Bible concerning that time. This was indeed a 'dark age' period.

The Bible IS the standard, it was written by Christ, and its historical details are correct, and it is the authority.

1 Samuel 13:19 Now there was no smith found throughout all the land of Israel: for the Philistines said, Lest the Hebrews make them swords or spears: 20 But all the Israelites went down to the Philistines, to sharpen every man his share, and his coulter, and his axe, and his mattock. 21 Yet they had a file for the mattocks, and for the coulters, and for the forks, and for the axes, and to sharpen the goads.

So at the end of the 400 year period after the Exodus, there were no qualified blacksmiths in the whole of Israel. They had a few simple tools like files, but to get their ploughs, axes and other tools made, they had to go to the Philistines, but now the Philistines were coming to war with Israel. None of the people of Israel had any weapons, nor had they been able to work with metals at all. Only King Saul and Jonathan had weapons.

1 Samuel 13: 22 So it came to pass in the day of battle, that there was neither sword nor spear found in the hand of any of the people that were with Saul and Jonathan: but with Saul and with Jonathan his son was there found.

The Philistines on the coast are mentioned and the indication is that their state of civilisation there was superior to that of Israel and Palestine in that period. Even at the end of this 400 year period, the time of King Saul and Jonathan, when David was beginning to get the tribes of

Israel together, and unifying the land, Israel and Palestine were still in an age of primitive barbarism. If archaeological finds appear to contradict this, it is because they are being incorrectly dated and interpreted.

This indicates the low state of civilisation that Israel was in. They had lost all their skills in the 40 years of wandering in the Sinai desert, and even 440 years after the Exodus they were still in a state of appalling ignorance, and in a 'dark age' indeed.

This is an object lesson to all who ignore God's instructions, and throw His wishes for our best in His face. Because the children of Israel failed to trust that God would protect them as they went into the land, they all died in the Sinai desert, and although their children finally went into the land of Canaan, they remained in a low, uncivilised state of ignorance for the next 400 years until prosperity finally came when Solomon's reign began.

Remember, when the children of Israel came out of Egypt in the Exodus, they were among the most expert and skilled architects, builders, stone masons, carpenters, and artisans of all kinds in the whole world. They had been involved in constructing the marvels of Egypt during the 215 years they were there, including the pyramids, and other wonders of ancient Egypt.

However they left Egypt's civilisation in a state of ruin due to the ten plagues, and especially with the effect of the death of all their firstborn.

Even though they had witnessed so many miracles of deliverance and protection God had given them, within a few weeks they made the golden calf, committed idolatry in a big way, turned on Moses and refused to go into the land of Canaan because they were afraid of the Canaanites instead of trusting God to deliver them safely. They could have easily built themselves a greater civilisation than they had had in Egypt in a few decades, but their lack of trust in God resulted in them spending 40 years in the desert, during which time, they lost all their knowledge and skills.

Any artefacts that show 'primitiveness' can therefore be dated to this time period if we use the Bible as the standard.

1073 B.C.

The battle of Michmash

1 Samuel 13:23 And the garrison of the Philistines went out to the passage of Michmash.

Michmash was 7 miles North of Jerusalem, and in 1 Samuel 14 it tells how God intervened in the battle and caused a great earthquake, so they won the battle.

Anyone who wants to destroy a civilisation and a culture simply keeps moving them.

Here is an example of 1day=1year. During the 40 years wandering in the Sinai Desert, Israel lost all their expertise in every area, became ignorant nomads, no skills were maintained or passed on to the children, there was no means to do so, or to use them. They wore the same shoes until they died.

They lived only on Manna and the water that gushed out of the Tabernacle. They moved from place to place until every last one of them died except two, Joshua and Caleb.

God was seriously angry with Israel. When they left Egypt dark ages fell onto that country and Palestine for 400 years.

1 Samuel 13:19 In Saul's time, Israel was still in a low state evidenced by the fact that there was no smith in Israel to work with metals, they had to get help from the Philistines. There were no weapons of iron in the land apart from the King and his son.

4th 1067 B.C. - 3 B.C.

The period of David, Solomon, then first year of Cyrus to Christ's birth.

1067 B.C. David was anointed by the Lord, and the Spirit of the Lord departed from Saul.

1 Samuel 16:13 Then Samuel took the horn of oil, and anointed him in the midst of his brethren: and the Spirit of the Lord came upon David from that day forward. So Samuel rose up, and went to Ramah. 14 But the Spirit of the Lord departed from Saul, and an evil spirit from the Lord troubled him.

Another example of how the Lord uses evil to forward His purposes.

1067 B.C. David slays Goliath. As time went on David united the North and the South, got an army together to defend Israel, obeyed God, and prosperity began to return.

1067 B.C. Solomon anointed by Zadok and becomes King of Israel.

1 Kings 1:39 And Zadok the priest took an horn of oil out of the tabernacle, and anointed Solomon. And they blew the trumpet; and all the people said, God save king Solomon.

1015 B.C.

David dies. When David died, under Solomon, Israel enjoyed a period of vast prosperity and archaeological sophistication began. Solomon built the Temple in Jerusalem, and for the next 40 years Israel enjoyed a type of Messianic and Millennial reign. Israel became the top nation in the entire world which recognised this and many kings and Cleopatra came to witness for themselves the vast wealth and prosperity of Solomon's kingdom.

Israel became the top nation in the world enjoying unprecedented wealth, prosperity and global renown for 40 years, and in a sense Israel had some control politically and financially over Egypt, Babylon, and Assyria.

So when archaeologists look at Egyptian, Babylonian, and Hittite artefact of this period, the evidence should reflect the prosperity of the era. This is exactly what they will find if they accept the authority of the Scriptures.

When further exploration of 'tels' (piles of old rubbish in the main) in the Middle East is undertaken, it will certainly help to fill in more details to supplement the gaps in the Biblical record.

1 Chronicles 29:26 Thus David the son of Jesse reigned over all Israel. 27 And the time that he reigned over Israel was forty years; seven years reigned he in Hebron, and thirty and three years reigned he in Jerusalem.

28 And he died in a good old age, full of days, riches, and honour: and Solomon his son reigned in his stead.

From the end of David's reign, who was a type of the Messiah to come, and 'out of his loins' came Christ humanly speaking through Mary.

1014 B.C.

Solomon to build Temple

2 Chronicles 2:1 And Solomon determined to build an house for the name of the Lord, and an house for his kingdom.

1011 B.C.

Solomon begins to build the Temple

992 B.C.

Queen of Sheba visits Solomon

2 Chronicles 9:19 And when the queen of Sheba heard of the fame of Solomon, she came to prove Solomon with hard questions at Jerusalem, with a very great company, and camels that bare spices, and gold in abundance, and precious stones: and when she was come to Solomon, she communed with him of all that was in her heart.

975 B.C.

Solomon reigned 40 years.

1 Kings 11:42 And the time that Solomon reigned in Jerusalem over all Israel was forty years. 43 And Solomon slept with his fathers, and was buried in the city of David his father: and Rehoboam his son reigned in his stead.

It is fascinating that 'scholars' say that they can find no evidence that Solomon lived, or that the Queen of Sheba visited him in all his human glory and wealth. We can be sure that he did live, because God's Word in both the Old Testament and the New mention him. There are 274 mentions of Solomon in the Bible and ten of them are in the New testament. But of course, most 'scholars' have little respect for the Bible.

After Solomon's reign, Israel broke into two nations. Any break up causes decline. However for the next 320 years there was fairly good prosperity, but nothing like there was under Solomon. Rehoboam taxed the people excessively. The ten tribes headed by Ephraim made their capital in the North, and Judah, Benjamin, Simeon and Levi took over the South with the capital in Jerusalem.

971 B.C.

As explained above, secular historians and archaeologists say that there was no such person as King Shishak, as there is no record of him in any of their finds. The reason for that is the word 'Shishak' is a cipher.

Much like children in school make up a 'code' or 'cipher' by using the alphabet back to front to spell words, this word Shishak is a cipher. The Hebrew letters BBL (remember there are no vowels written in Hebrew) when equated to the Hebrew alphabet in ever, becomes SSK, or Shishak. Shishak is cipher for the King of Babylon, who removes the Temple treasures.

2 Chronicles 12:9 So Shishak king of Egypt came up against Jerusalem, and took away the treasures of the house of the Lord, and the treasures of the king's house;

he took all: he carried away also the shields of gold which Solomon had made.

772 B.C.

The Assyrians conquered the Northern Tribes and carried them away to Assyria. From this point on, there would be two kingdoms of Hebrews: in the North - Israel, and in the South - Judah. The Israelites had formed their capital in the city of Samaria. From the time of Israel's captivity, they became 'lost' to the world to all intents and purposes. The Judaeans kept their capital in Jerusalem. These kingdoms remained separate states for over two hundred years. The history of the both kingdoms is a litany of ineffective, disobedient, and corrupt kings.

608 B.C.

Jerusalem and the Temple were destroyed by the King Nebuchadnezzar of Babylon, and the Judaeans were taken captive to Babylon for a period of 70 years. Although this period is disputed by many historians, this is inspired scripture written by Christ, so is correct.

Daniel 11:1 In the third year of the reign of Jehoiakim king of Judah came Nebuchadnezzar king of Babylon unto Jerusalem, and besieged it. 2 And the Lord gave Jehoiakim king of Judah into his hand, with part of the vessels of the house of God: which he carried into the land of Shinar to the house of his god; and he brought the vessels into the treasure house of his god.

605 B.C.

Nebuchadnezzar has a dream of World domination, one government, one God and one religion, Daniel interprets it. Thus is born the concept of World Government.

Daniel 2:1 And in the second year of the reign of Nebuchadnezzar dreamed dreams, wherewith his spirit was troubled, and his sleep brake from him.

He could not remember the dream and none of his astrologers could tell him what the dream was. But God was with Daniel and he told Nebuchadnezzar what he had dreamed and the king knew it was right.

Daniel 2:31 Thou, O king, sawest, and behold a great image. This great image, whose brightness was excellent, stood before thee; and the form thereof was terrible. 32 This image's head was of fine gold, his breast and his arms of silver, his belly and his thighs of brass, 33 His legs of iron, his feet part of iron and part of clay. 34 Thou sawest till that a stone was cut out without hands, which smote the image upon his feet that were of iron and clay, and brake them to pieces. 35 Then was the iron, the clay, the brass, the silver, and the gold, broken to pieces together, and became like the chaff of the summer threshingfloors; and the wind carried them away, that no place was found for them: and the stone that smote the image became a great mountain (government), and filled the whole earth.

Christ at His return, will destroy all human governments as He sets up the Kingdom of God.

The Head of Gold was Babylon, then Silver was Medo-Persia, then Iron was Greco- Macedonian Empire, then the fourth of Iron mixed with clay shows the deterioration of worldly governments domination through the ages.

Daniel 2:36 This is the dream; and we (God and I) will tell the interpretation thereof before the king. 37 Thou, O king, art a king of kings: for the God of heaven hath given thee a kingdom, power, and strength, and glory. 38 And wheresoever the children of men dwell, the beasts of the field and the fowls of the heaven hath he given into thine hand, and hath made thee ruler over them all. Thou art this head of gold. 39 And after thee shall arise another kingdom inferior to thee, and another third kingdom of brass, which shall bear rule over all the earth. 40 And the fourth kingdom shall be strong as iron: forasmuch as iron breaketh in pieces and subdueth all things: and as iron that breaketh all these, shall it break in pieces and bruise. 41 And whereas thou sawest the feet and toes, part of potters' clay, and part of iron, the kingdom shall be divided; but there shall be in it of the strength of the iron, forasmuch as thou sawest the iron mixed with miry clay. 42 And as the toes of the feet were part of iron, and part of clay, so the kingdom shall be partly strong, and partly broken. 43 And whereas thou sawest iron mixed with miry clay, they shall mingle themselves with the seed of men: but they shall not cleave one to another, even as iron is not mixed with clay. 44 And in the days of these kings shall the God of heaven set up a kingdom, which shall never be destroyed: and the kingdom shall not be left to other people, but it shall break in pieces and consume all these kingdoms, and it shall stand for ever. 45 Forasmuch as thou sawest that the stone was cut out of the mountain without hands, and that it brake in pieces the iron, the brass, the clay, the silver, and the gold; the great God hath made known to the king what shall come to pass hereafter: and the dream is certain, and the interpretation thereof sure.

Nebuchadnezzar progressively came to know the true God during his reign, as God was using him to set up the Babylonish, or confused type of government which would dominate the world until the second coming of Christ.

Daniel 2:47 The king answered unto Daniel, and said, Of a truth it is, that your God is a God of gods, and a Lord of kings, and a revealer of secrets, seeing thou couldest reveal this secret.

Many religious people interpret the fourth kingdom of iron and miry clay as being Rome, the Catholic Church, and a Germany dominated Europe to precede Christ's Second Coming, but nowhere does the Bible suggest this.

When the Bible says Babylon, it means Babylon not Rome! The fourth kingdom and the ten kings will also arise in the future in the same area of Babylon and the Middle East, as God has always focussed on that area of the world.

Babylon means confusion which certainly describes human governments to this day in the 21st Century. The confusion will continue until Christ returns and smashes all the kingdoms of this world into fine dust, and sets up His Kingdom of God.

538 B.C.

Cyrus proclamation ordering the rebuilding of the Temple

The Jews under Zerubbabel and Joshua the High Priest returned from the Medo Persian captivity in 586 B.C. to Jerusalem bearing the proclamation from Cyrus authorising them to rebuild the Temple.

Ezra 1:1 Now in the first year of Cyrus king of Persia, that the word of the Lord by the mouth of Jeremiah might be fulfilled, the Lord stirred up the spirit of Cyrus king of Persia, that he made a proclamation throughout all his kingdom, and put it also in writing, saying, 2 Thus saith Cyrus king of Persia, The Lord God of heaven hath given me all the kingdoms of the earth; and he hath charged me to build him an house at Jerusalem, which is in Judah.

But as usual, Judah and the High Priest failed to start work on the Temple as instructed, but instead they typically built themselves some rather superior residences. So God says, "Consider your ways!" Judah were complaining about the lack blessings, and God said in effect, what did you expect? After nearly 19 years, you are not building My House (the Temple) but your own!

Haggai 1:1 In the second year of Darius the king, in the sixth month, in the first day of the month, came the word of the Lord by Haggai the prophet unto Zerubbabel the son of Shealtiel, governor of Judah, and to Joshua the son of Josedech, the high priest, saying, 2 Thus speaketh the Lord of hosts, saying, This people say, The time is not come, the time that the Lord's house should be built. 3 Then came the word of the Lord by Haggai the prophet, saying, 'Is it time for you, O ye, to dwell in your cieled houses, and this house lie waste? 5 Now therefore thus saith the Lord of hosts; Consider your ways.'

The first year of Cyrus to Christ's birth. Seventy weeks means seventy weeks of years. Seventy weeks of seven days or a period of 490 years. From Cyrus 490 years onward we would find the Kingdom of God emerging on the earth, and the Messiah appearing as well.

The 70 weeks prophecy in Daniel is divided into three sections, or four divisions. 7 weeks to begin with or 49 years, followed by a period of 434 years or 62 weeks, put those together and you get 69 weeks, or 483 years which leads up to the Messiah appearing.

There would then be one week of seven years left, and that was to be divided in half, 3½ on one side and 3½ on the other. People have wondered about the 70 weeks prophecy for years, it is difficult as we are not given all the chronological benchmarks or events that would make this clear. These periods were 'cut out' of history, does this mean there were some gaps? These are still questions.

446 B.C.

Nehemiah. The whole story of the Bible tells us that when people obey God, blessings follow; when they fail to obey God, there are no blessings, and even what they do have is taken away. Christ told us of this principle.

Matthew 25:29 For unto every one that hath shall be given, and he shall have abundance: but from him that hath not shall be taken even that which he hath.

Palestine has always been the key area, and Jerusalem its centre, the focus of God's attention. The Bible is the key to history, and to the future of the world.

By the 8th Century B.C. Israel were in captivity with the Assyrians. Then 130 years later in 586 B.C., Israel went into captivity by Nebuchadnezzar. The Temple, Jerusalem, and the cities of Palestine were destroyed completely.

For the next 70 years, every mound excavated for this period showed the destruction. Professor Allbright, Israeli head of research reviewed the time of the Babylonian captivity and found every tell or mound showed destruction just as Jeremiah and Ezekiel had prophesied. The nation's artefacts for the same period including those from Egypt mentioning Pharaoh Hophra show the same. Before this time, especially from before the 9th Century B.C., chronology is very difficult to unravel. After that there is more related evidence to go on.

There are also important astronomical evidences written down which can be checked with the information and data we have available to us in this era.

Virtually no historians accept that the Babylonian captivity was of 70 years duration, most would say around 50 years. Is God telling the truth in the Bible, or are the historians right? No contest! There is a need for extensive historical investigation to find more written evidence of this period.

Joshua to Saul was 400 years of a dark age – historians say it was prosperous! The design of pottery was clearly different in different eras, like 1930's cars were different from those made in 2000 not difficult to tell apart!

Before the 9th Century, it is very difficult for archaeologists to piece together the chronology but from the 8th Century B.C., on the decree of Cyrus in 538-515 B.C., and his decree to rebuild the Temple.

Part of the reason for this is the fact that in the 6th Century B.C., Nebuchadnezzar destroyed all the historical records he could get his hands on.

Then there is a gap until Alexander the Great who came on the scene in 332 B.C., From Daniel the mid-6th C to mid-4th C, there is not enough information to go on.

Prior to the 9th B.C., all archaeology is based on Egypt, and due to the Egyptian habit of extending periods of Egyptian history by naming all the dynasties in succession when many were concurrent as shown in Velikowsky's Ages in Chaos, the timing is all wrong.

Egyptian historian Manetho about 305-285 B.C. made up 31 dynasties, the first after the flood. He lists them all as successive, but many were concurrent leading to an 'expanded' history which is blithely accepted by many.

Velikowsky, who wrote 'Ages in Chaos' was more Bible based and his story of concurrent Pharoahs is more likely. Archaeologists have a 400 year mismatch with the Bible and vice versa, but of course they think they are right and the Bible is wrong.

The Biblical history should be the standard, not the other way around, and is correct in every detail as it was written by God (Christ) the Word.

The Bible shows in a few places that there were several kingdoms in Egypt, kingdom against kingdom,

Jeremiah 46:25 The Lord of hosts, the God of Israel, saith; Behold, I will punish the multitude of No, and Pharaoh, and Egypt, with their gods, and their **kings;** even Pharaoh, and all them that trust in him:

II Kings 7:6 For the Lord had made the host of the Syrians to hear a noise of chariots, and a noise of horses, even the noise of a great host: and they said one to another, Lo, the king of Israel hath hired against us the kings of the Hittites, and the **kings** (plural) of the Egyptians, to come upon us.

Psalms 105:30 Their land brought forth frogs in abundance, in the chambers of their **kings**. (kings plural of Egypt)

SUMMARY OF BIBLICAL LINKS TO ENABLE CHRONOLOGY FROM ADAM TO THE BIRTH OF CHRIST

The time of man on earth from Adam to Christ Jesus was a period of 4000 years. (Idealised)

From Adam to Abraham's 99th year   = 2107 +

ADAM - Noah and the Flood 1656 years +
451 years (?) =2107

Abraham's 99th year to the Exodus 430 years
**   = 2537 +**

Exodus 12:40 Now the sojourning of the children of Israel, who dwelt in Egypt, was four hundred and thirty years. 41 And it came to pass at the end of the four hundred and thirty years, even the selfsame day it came to pass, that

all the hosts of the Lord went out from the land of Egypt.

Period of Judges 480 years Joshua – King Saul
**   = 3017**

1 Kings 6:1 And it came to pass in the four hundred and eightieth year after the children of Israel were come out of the land of Egypt, in the fourth year of Solomon's reign over Israel, in the month Zif, which is the second month, that he began to build the house of the Lord.

4th year of Solomon to end of reign 36 years
**   = 3053 +**

1 Kings 11:42 And the time that Solomon reigned in Jerusalem over all Israel was forty years. (4th year to end of reign = 36 years)

Kings of Israel Rehoboam – Zedekiah 393 years
**   = 3446 +**

The list of Kings and length of reign is identical in both Kings and Chronicles

End of 70 years Captivity 1st of Cyrus   = 3476 +

Jeremiah 25:11 And this whole land shall be a desolation, and an astonishment; and these nations shall serve the king of Babylon seventy years.

1st Year of Cyrus to birth of Christ + 483 years

= 3999

Daniel 9:25 Know therefore and understand, that from the going forth of the commandment to restore and to build Jerusalem unto the Messiah the Prince shall be seven weeks, and threescore and two weeks: (7x7=49 + 62x7= 434 = 483) the street shall be built again...

5th 2 B.C. - 96 A.D.

Then Christ was born, brought the New Law of Love, and died in or around 30 A.D. Progressive revelation continued up until the revelation of the mystery in 63 A.D., ending with the book of Revelation in 96 A.D. So from 33 A.D., to the end of the 1st Century A.D., there are 40 years of only very hazy information.

6th 96 A.D. - 2nd Advent - Millennium

The time of man on earth from Christ Jesus to the Second Advent appears to be a period of 2000 years. (Idealised)

The number of man is six, and the Bible seems to indicate that man's time on earth will be 6000 years, followed by God's number of seven, the beginning of the Kingdom of God, and the Millennium of 1000 years making 7000 years.

-2/3 B.C. - 33 A.D.

Christ's birth, His life, ministry, death and resurrection.
33 A.D. - 96 A.D.

The development of Christianity, the revelation of the mystery, and the canonisation of the New Testament. Perversion of pure Christianity begins.

96 A.D. - Second Advent A.D.

A period of 1900 years of the perversion of the Gospel of Jesus Christ being mingled and taken over with the absorption of pagan and idolatrous practices by false prophets and ministers.

7th Post Second Advent – the Millennium - Eternity

At the time of the Second Advent, Christ's rule will begin on Earth.

Revelation 11:15 And the seventh angel sounded; and there were great voices in heaven, saying, The kingdoms of this world are become the kingdoms of our Lord, and of his Christ; and he shall reign for ever and ever.

After the Millennium, there will be a period that appears to be around a hundred years. Then God makes a new Earth, and prepares it to be His Centre of Activity for Eternity.

Revelation 21:1 And I saw a new heaven and a new earth: for the first heaven and the first earth were passed away; and there was no more sea. 2 And I John saw the holy city, new Jerusalem, coming down from God out of heaven, prepared as a bride adorned for her husband. 3 And I heard a great voice out of heaven saying, Behold, the tabernacle of God is with men, and he will dwell with them, and they shall be his people, and God himself shall be with them, and be their God.

God will begin to extend his Government forever.

Isaiah 9:7 Of the increase of his government and peace there shall be no end, upon the throne of David, and upon his kingdom, to order it, and to establish it with judgment and with justice from henceforth even for ever. The zeal of the Lord of hosts will perform this.

The next chapter will address the need to appreciate 'systematic' and 'dogmatic' theology.

CHAPTER 7
SYSTEMATIC & DOGMATIC THEOLOGY

According to a survey made in 1980, there are over 20,800 different Christian denominations all over the world. This is a puzzle to those who wonder how it is that there is one God, one Holy Bible, yet there are all these people with such very different ideas as to what exactly Christianity is.

Why, many ask, can all these people not agree upon what appears to be a simple issue. To the non-religious person, Christianity should be simply a matter of reading the Book and going along with what it teaches. Or more particularly, reading the teachings of Christ Jesus, and simply doing what He told us to do. Sadly such is not the case.

Any study of the Bible involves 'theology'. This word is made up of two Greek words, 'theos' meaning God, and 'logos' which means word; so we are studying the Word of God as Christ commanded us to do.

Matthew 4:4 But he answered and said, It is written, Man shall not live by bread alone, but by every word that proceedeth out of the mouth of God.

Sincere students of the Bible when led by Christ and the Holy Spirit are only interested in the truth it contains, and this 'truth' has to be carefully studied; while at the same time disregarding the thousands of misinterpretations that abound in the Christian world.

It is essential to study carefully to determine what applies to us today as Christians, and what does not.

So what is wrong? Why is there is so much dissension among Christians as to what constitutes the Christian faith? Peter, chief of the Apostles was inspired to write:

2 Peter 1:16 For we have not followed cunningly devised fables, when we made known unto you the power and

coming of our Lord Jesus Christ, but were eyewitnesses of his majesty.

Paul mentions the same theme.

2 Corinthians 11:3 But I fear, lest by any means, as the serpent beguiled Eve through his subtilty, so your minds should be corrupted from the simplicity that is in Christ.

Regrettably millions, if not billions of sincere people have been ensnared by 'cunningly devised fables'. Also by the deceptive devices of the god of this world without realising how far they have been drawn away from the simplicity which is in Christ Jesus.

It is essential for Christians to believe absolutely in the veracity and accuracy of the original inspired texts of the Bible. Christ Jesus said the scriptures cannot be broken or proved incorrect.

John 10:34 Jesus answered them, Is it not written in your law, I said, Ye are gods? 35 If he called them gods, unto whom the word of God came, and *the scripture cannot be broken;* 36 Say ye of him, whom the Father hath sanctified, and sent into the world, Thou blasphemest; because I said, I am the Son of God?

Rightly dividing the Word of Truth

We are exhorted to grow in Grace and Knowledge of God's Word.

2 Peter 3:18 But grow in grace, and in the knowledge of our Lord and Saviour Jesus Christ. To him be glory both now and for ever. Amen.

The way to growth in Grace and Knowledge is to draw close to God.

James 4:8 Draw nigh to God, and he will draw nigh to you. Cleanse your hands, ye sinners; and purify your hearts, ye double minded.

If we ask for them, we can receive the gifts of repentance, the Holy Spirit, and an open mind and heart to study His Word.

2 Timothy 2:15 Study to shew thyself approved unto God, a workman that needeth not to be ashamed, rightly dividing (partitioning) the word of truth.

So for the earnest seeker after Truth, there is clearly a need to establish both a **systematic** and **dogmatic** approach to the study of the Bible. These are not fancy academic or complex terms.

A 'SYSTEMATIC' approach to Theology

The definition of 'systematic' is: doing or acting according to a fixed plan or system; methodical.

The synonyms are: structured, methodical, organised, orderly, well ordered, planned, systematised, regular, routine, standardised, standard, normal, logical, coherent, consistent, efficient, businesslike, practical, careful, fastidious, meticulous;the new

A '**systematic**' approach would mean that scholars of the subject would approach the study of the Bible much the same as one might approach a textbook on geography or mathematics. We would need to take each section, and progress through the facts of the geography of this world, or the principles of mathematics, in a systematic manner, step by step. This could be relevant in the study of geography or mathematics, but to attempt to use this approach with the Bible is to misapply the 'systematic' principle.

The reason that a purely 'systematic' approach is not appropriate in relation to Bible study is because of the way Christ has structured His Word. It is not written in such a way that it can truly be 'systematised' from start to finish in order to define Christianity. This is why so many earnest scholars with all their knowledge fail to get the whole 'picture' when they attempt to 'systematise' the Bible.

A study of mathematics or geography or any other science can be 'systematised' to a degree because study reveals rules and principles that do not change. Whereas in the field of Theology, due to the development of God's Plan through six thousand years of human history, and His principle of 'Progressive Revelation', any attempt to systematise the Scriptures leads to confusion.

The Bible is made up of thousands of stories about events, about people, and other aspects of life on earth. There are 'cameos', 'snapshots', and glimpses of moments in history. Rarely is the whole story about any matter in one place. Information about any subject is scattered through the Bible, and all need to be considered carefully in order to arrive at a true understanding of the topic.

So each topic has to be explored in its context, and in relation to other scriptures that are related to that topic. In a way, it could be said that the Bible contains many 'jigsaw puzzles', in the sense that we need to study carefully to find as many of the pieces of each puzzle in order to get the whole 'picture' that we need for proper understanding of that subject.

Isaiah 28:10 For precept must be upon precept, precept upon precept; line upon line, line upon line; here a little, and there a little:

Whenever a concept is repeated in the Bible, as for instance the two verses quoted here, it is for emphasis, and to indicate its importance.

Isaiah 28:13 But the word of the Lord was unto them precept upon precept, precept upon precept; line upon line, line upon line; here a little, and there a little; that they might go, and fall backward, and be broken, and snared, and taken.

God has written the Bible in this way so that the 'scholar', the 'false' prophet, or the carnal minded person who uses the Bible for their own ends and their own purposes will 'fall backward, be broken, snared, and taken'.

Many 'theologians' can get into total confusion if they base a belief or doctrine on just one text, without ever looking carefully to see if what that text says is modified or clarified by other passages in the Bible.

However, it does help to be somewhat 'systematic' in our study of any particular subject. Our time in study would be best spent in a 'structured, methodical, organised, orderly, and well ordered' approach to our work.

For instance, we could find the first place in the Bible that any matter is mentioned, and then proceed through different parts of the Bible to see how it deals with that subject, and to get a balanced view of the subject.

What simply does not work is to attempt to 'systematise' the whole Bible into a single thread to define Christianity, or base beliefs or doctrines on one or two texts. To do so leads to real confusion and has resulted in the development of the now reportedly between 20,000 and 33,000 different denominations. A careful study will reveal that none of those denominations is completely free from the influence, or the inclusion in their body of beliefs, of 'doctrines and commandments of men', and pagan idolatrous notions.

Romans !:21 Because knowing God, they didn't glorify him as God, and didn't give thanks, but became vain in their reasoning, and their senseless heart was darkened. 22 Professing themselves to be wise, they became fools, 23 and traded the glory of the incorruptible God for the likeness of an image of corruptible man, and of birds, four-footed animals, and creeping things. 24 Therefore God also gave them up in the lusts of their hearts to uncleanness, that their bodies should be dishonored among themselves; 25 who exchanged the truth of God for a lie, and worshiped and served the creature rather than the Creator, who is blessed forever. Amen.

A 'DOGMATIC' approach to Theology

Definition of the word 'dogmatic': Inclined to lay down principles as undeniably true. Expressing personal opinions or beliefs as if they are certainly correct and cannot be doubted.

Each of the thousands of denominations, at some level, tend dogmatically to assert that they are 'right', even if they do not say others are 'wrong'.

Notice the authoritative nature of synonyms of the word 'dogmatic':

opinionated, imperative, assertive, insistent, emphatic, adamant, doctrinaire, authoritarian, authoritative, domineering, imperious, high-handed, pontifical, arrogant, overbearing, dictatorial, uncompromising, unyielding, unbending, inflexible, rigid, entrenched, unquestionable, unchallengeable; intolerant, narrow-minded, small minded.

Most people, especially Christians, would not prefer to be thought of or seen as being this insistent or arrogant about their being 'right'!

Say a person were to take a **dogmatic** stand about the physical characteristics of water for instance. One person might assert dogmatically that the freezing point of water is 0°C, and the boiling point of water is 100°C. While this is true under certain conditions, both the freezing point and the boiling point of water actually depend upon a number of factors.

These figures of 0°C and 100°C are generally considered correct if the measurements are being made at sea level where, and if, the atmospheric pressure is 29.92 in. Hg (inches of mercury) or 14.696 psi. However, people climbing mountains can notice that the water boils at a lower temperature because of the reduction of atmospheric pressure at high altitudes. At approximately 1 mile above sea level, atmospheric pressure drops to approximately 12.2 PSI and water boils at 92°C or 198°F.

Another factor that would determine freezing and boiling points of water could be the purity and mineral content of the water itself. So to be dogmatic about these natural laws concerning water is not wise unless we take into account the factors that can make a difference to any of the laws of physics. It might be a good idea to avoid being dogmatic, and to state our opinion about the freezing and boiling points of water in a rather more broad way which allows for there to be several answers to the question.

'If water is exposed to low enough temperatures it will freeze solid, and if water gets hot enough, it will boil.' Thus this law of physics could be stated in a down to earth way, in a firm accurate manner, without being unduly dogmatic.

The same thing applies to God's Laws. While God's Laws may be defined in a certain way at one time, to a certain people; they may be redefined to another people at a different time. In fact we see that this is actually the case as we consider 'Progressive Revelation'. It is unwise to express our beliefs to others in any manner that might give offence, or appear in any way to give an impression that we are assuming the attitude of any of those unfortunate synonyms of the word 'dogmatic'.

However, it is necessary to be 'dogmatic' when laying down the foundation of those things that are given to us by Christ, and are fundamental to the basis of Christianity.

For instance, I could state categorically, dogmatically that 'The Holy Bible is the Word of God'. I can know this personally from my studies, and only because God has given me the gift of that knowledge. For me to state the same fact dogmatically to others who have not arrived at the absolute conviction for themselves, may only tend to alienate them.

Jesus Christ warns us as Christians that we have a very serious responsibility to be careful not to offend others, especially those who are 'young' in the belief and faith in Jesus Christ.

Matthew 18:6 But whoso shall offend one of these little ones which believe in me, it were better for him that a millstone were hanged about his neck, and that he were drowned in the depth of the sea.

These strong words of warning from our Master should cause us to be very cautious about how we speak to others, especially those new to the faith.

It could be stated 'dogmatically' that every human who has lived, is living now, or will ever live, will die. This is a fact that is unarguable and not open to discussion. However, that fact is still better stated without the additional emphasis of dogmatic fervour. The verses about human mortality in the Bible are dogmatic enough. In this case, a clear picture of this truth can be established with just two or three verses, although there are many more that support the same fact.

Romans 5:12 Wherefore, as by one man sin entered into the world, and death by sin; and so death passed upon all men (human beings), for that all have sinned:

Ezekiel 18:4 Behold, all souls are mine; as the soul of the father, so also the soul of the son is mine: the soul that sinneth, it shall die.

Hebrews 9:27 And as it is appointed unto men (and women) once to die, but after this the judgment.

Paul, in 1 Corinthians 10 goes into some detail about the need for a Christian to avoid giving offence to others in the manner in which we conduct ourselves. Paul is talking about and advising us on our conduct at a dinner party.

1 Corinthians 10:24 Let no man seek his own, but every man another's wealth (welfare). 25 Whatsoever is sold in the shambles, that eat, asking no question for conscience

sake: 26 For the earth is the Lord's, and the fulness thereof. 27 If any of them that believe not bid you to a feast, and ye be disposed to go; whatsoever is set before you, eat, asking no question for conscience sake.

Meat that was sold in the 'shambles' in Corinth, the meat market, had in all probability been offered to idols at some stage in its preparation. Paul is saying, this is no big deal! Do not upset your host by questioning him about it. Just eat it, it won't hurt you, or offend God if you do!

But on the other hand, if your host or anyone makes an issue of it, and challenges you to eat something he tells you has been offered to an idol, then that is the time to take a stand, and refuse politely.

1 Corinthians 10:28 But if any man say unto you, this is offered in sacrifice unto idols, eat not for his sake that shewed it, and for conscience sake: for the earth is the Lord's, and the fulness thereof. 29 Conscience, I say, not thine own, but of the other: for why is my liberty judged of another man's conscience? 30 For if I by grace be a partaker, why am I evil spoken of for that for which I give thanks? 31 Whether therefore ye eat, or drink, or whatsoever ye do, do all to the glory of God.

Eat what is set before you, but not in a self-righteous manner which might give offence to others. The theme of this chapter is not to give offence to others by making a dogmatic issue of our beliefs if it is not necessary.

1 Corinthians 10:32 Give none offence, neither to the Jews, nor to the Gentiles, nor to the ~~church~~ ekklesia ~~of~~ God: 33 Even as I please all men in all things, not seeking mine own profit, but the profit of many, that they may be saved.

In our life as Christians, to take a 'dogmatic' approach means that we need to study very carefully to determine which are those doctrines or 'dogmas' which are eternal and unchanging and unchangeable. Also consider as well as those which have altered in substance and application over time; and understand how both of these categories apply to us in the conduct of our Christian life today.

Examples of 'dogma' or doctrines that will never change are faith, hope, and love. These are universal and timeless values. Without faith in God, understanding is impossible.

Without hope, we have nothing. Love is the prime dogma that should govern every aspect of the Christian life.

1 John 4:8 He that loveth not knoweth not God; for God is Love.

1 Corinthians 13:13 And now abideth faith, hope, charity, these three; but the greatest of these is charity. (Charity is the old 1611 English word for love.)

Well known examples of dogma, laws and values that have changed are the laws concerning circumcision, and the practice of the sacrificial system. There are very few in the Christian realm who would have any problem with these doctrines being no longer relevant to Christians today.

Firstly then, it is not possible to **'systematise'** the doctrines of the whole Bible into one thread called Christianity, because the teachings in its different books and sections record changes of emphasis over time to different peoples, in different places and eras. This is true because the teachings of the Bible do reveal the fact of "Progressive Revelation".

Very few of even the top scholars and evangelists of the various denominations seem to be aware of, understand, or teach this vital aspect of the Biblical revelation.

"Progressive Revelation" Not all teaching is relevant for all time.

"Progressive Revelation" means that God revealed some basic information to Adam, gave more information to the

Patriarchs, first Noah, then successively to Abraham, Isaac and Jacob, and the Prophets.

When Christ came, he taught his disciples some more advanced truths. Later He gave Paul inspired revelations concerning the 'mystery', and finally He gave the book of Revelation to John.

The Ten Commandments were written by the finger of God **on stone**, but they were not **'set in stone',** as in 'absolute' or 'unchangeable', but the Ten Commandments have been subject to change under different circumstances and periods of time for different peoples.

A close examination of many of the laws in the five books of Moses reveals changes. The Laws of Exodus were given against the backdrop of itinerant wandering in the Desert. Many of those laws were given different emphasis in Deuteronomy when the children of Israel were to be located in one place, in towns and cities.

Here an example of the changing of a law concerns the Mosaic Law of punishment for idolatry, a sin that God hates above most sins which states:

Deuteronomy 5:9 Thou shalt not bow down thyself unto them, nor serve them: for I the Lord thy God am a jealous God, visiting the iniquity of the fathers upon the children unto the third and fourth generation of them that hate me, (Or love God less, or fail to worship Him above all else.)

This aspect of the law of God punishing the children for the sins of their fathers was abrogated later in the inspired writings of Ezekiel.

Ezekiel 18:19 Yet say ye, Why? doth not the son bear the iniquity of the father? When the son hath done that which is lawful and right, and hath kept all my statutes, and hath done them, he shall surely live. 20 The soul that sinneth, it shall die. The son shall not bear the iniquity of the father, neither shall the father bear the iniquity of the son: the righteousness of the righteous shall be upon him, and the wickedness of the wicked shall be upon him.

So God, through Christ changes aspects of His Law whenever He chooses to do so, as of course it is his total prerogative.

Christ came to change the Law

Two and a half thousand years later, Christ Jesus gave more advanced information to His disciples, but even then He did not give them the whole final version of the story of the Gospel of God's Plan.

Isaiah 42:21 The Lord is well pleased for his righteousness' sake; He (Christ) will magnify the law, and make it honourable.

Religious people often quote a part of Christ's teaching:

Matthew 5:17 Think not that I am come to destroy the law, or the prophets: I am not come to destroy, but to fulfil.

Christ came to **complete** and *fulfil* the old law, and prepare the way for the new era of **the law of love.** Christ inspired Paul to define the meaning of the word 'fulfilled'.

Galatians 5:14 For all the law is **fulfilled** in one word, even in this; Thou shalt love thy neighbour as thyself.

Many ministers use this verse to say that Christ has done away with the Law, and in 'fulfilling' it that the commandments are abolished. How can they think and teach that when Christ clearly says: *Think **not** that I am come to destroy the law*. That does not make any sense at all. Nothing could be further from the truth. Why call yourself a Christian, and contradict Christ's teachings?

Luke 6:46 And why call ye me, Lord, Lord, and do not the things which I say?

Other religious leaders may take the opposite view and want to show that the Law of Moses still stands exactly as it was in Moses' time, and insist on binding obedience to its commands on their followers. They preach that: 'If there is a command in the Scripture, it must be kept.' They teach that the Ten Commandments were written in stone, and therefore are 'set *in stone*', and they apply for all time. They teach dogmatically that they apply today as much as when they were given to Moses and Israel on the Mount Sinai.

They quote Revelation to show that the 'commandments' will be law in the Kingdom of God, and those who do not keep them will not be in the Kingdom of God.

Revelation 12:7 And the dragon was wroth with the woman, and went to make war with the remnant of her seed, which keep the **commandments of God**, and have the testimony of Jesus Christ.

Revelation 14:12 Here is the patience of the saints: here are they that keep the **commandments of God**, and the faith of Jesus.

Are the 'commandments of God' referred to in Revelation the ten commandments of Sinai? In a sense, yes, however Jesus said:

John 14:15 If ye love me, keep **my** commandments.

John 14:21 He that hath **my** commandments, and keepeth them, he it is that loveth me: and he that loveth me shall be loved of my Father, and I will love him, and will manifest myself to him.

John 15:10 If ye keep **my** commandments, ye shall abide in my love; even as I have kept my Father's commandments, and abide in his love.

Notice carefully that Christ said **'my'** commandments, not **'the'** commandments. The Commandments given to Moses on Sinai were specifically intended for those people to whom they were given at the time they were given. They were laws emphasising the physical, because the Children of Israel did not have access to God's Power of the Holy Spirit.

The Commandments given on Sinai were not intended to be totally unchangeable absolutes; the principles were, yes, but the letter no! Paul makes that really clear.

2 Corinthians 3:6 Who also hath made us able ministers of the **new testament** or commandment; **not of the letter**, but of the spirit: for the letter killeth, but the spirit giveth life.

Paul warned of this form of religious slavery, and the tendency of religious people to want to stay in the Primary School of the Law when they should be graduating away from the need for physical laws and a physical 'schoolmaster'. Christians need to 'graduate' to being directly under our spiritual leader, Christ Jesus.

Galatians 3:23 But before faith came, we were kept under the law, shut up unto the faith which should afterwards be revealed. 24 Wherefore the law was our schoolmaster to bring us unto Christ, that we might be justified by faith. 25 But after that faith is come, we are no longer under a schoolmaster. 26 For ye are all the children of God by faith in Christ Jesus.

Paul's statement in very plain language that we are no longer under the 'schoolmaster' is frequently twisted by those who wrest the scriptures to fit their own notions.

Many 'theologians' also teach that whenever the word 'commandments' is mentioned in the New Testament it is referring to the commandments of the Old Testament, and that they are 'eternal'. This makes a nonsense of Christ's teachings, who came to 'magnify the law', make significant changes, and to lead His flock, His group, His ecclesia, into a new and greater understanding of the Spiritual Law of Love.

This is one way in which 'Christians' deny the Lord that bought them, and His message, and embrace and adhere to 'another Gospel'.

The earnest Bible student, under the guidance of the Holy Spirit will come to realise that there are 'dispensations'. The Old Testament Law was a dispensation to a physical people. The New Testament Law is a Spiritual dispensation to a spiritual people.

1 Corinthians 9:17 For if I do this thing willingly, I have a reward: but if against my will, a dispensation of the gospel is committed unto me.

Ephesians 3:2 If ye have heard of the dispensation of the grace of God which is given me to you-ward:

The New Testament Law of love is a dispensation from Christ given to Paul. It is a Gospel of total forgiveness, the unmerited pardon of Grace given to a Spiritual nation. Grace leads to Eternal Life, when given to humans who are in the process of becoming a fully born child of God as a Spirit Being. This was all totally new information.

Such religious leaders who want to keep people under the old Law do not understand what Christ meant when he said 'to fulfil'. Christ did not come to destroy the Law but to magnify it, to make huge changes to make it larger and more encompassing.

Isaiah 42:21 The Lord is well pleased for his righteousness' sake; he will magnify the law, and make it honourable.

There was nothing dishonourable about the Mosaic Law, but Christ came to fulfil it, or expand it, lift it to a spiritual level rather than just a physical law for a physical people, and actually make it even more difficult (actually impossible) for a human to obey and keep.

Christ came to change the Law – Examples in The Sermon on the Mount.

In the very important Sermon on the Mount, Christ announces some of His changes to the Law, and how He wants them to be understood and practised from now on. Several times in Matthew the 5th chapter, Christ says to

His disciples: *'Ye have heard that it was said of them of old time'*. Christ is saying, 'this is how it has always been understood'.

Matthew 5:21 Ye have heard that it was said of them of old time, Thou shalt not kill; and whosoever shall kill shall be in danger of the judgement:

Then Christ uses the very important word **BUT.** The word **'But'** is the great negator, and sweeps away what has gone before in any sentence. The word **'but'** introduces a completely new way of approaching the subject.

Matthew 5:22 **But** I say unto you, That whosoever is angry with his brother without a cause shall be in danger of the judgment: and whosoever shall say to his brother, Raca, shall be in danger of the council: but whosoever shall say, Thou fool, shall be in danger of hell fire.

So Christ clearly has 'upgraded' the nature of the law against 'killing' a person. He is now saying in effect, 'Never mind not killing anyone, it is also against the New Law I am giving you even to be angry without due cause, or to say to a 'brother' RACA'.

What did Christ mean by RACA? It means vain, empty, worthless. The Jews used it as a word of contempt. It is derived from a root meaning "to spit." So Christ is saying that that level of criticism of anyone is against the New Law He is now explaining. That places a very different emphasis on the law not to kill. As spiritual Christians, we are not even to express hateful or condemnatory thoughts to others.

Christ continues in the Sermon on the Mount to modify and upgrade more of the Ten Commandments. All the modifications Christ made to the Ten Commandments present an enormous challenge to any human being. They are huge changes in what is required as a standard of Christian behaviour.

Obeying Christ in regard to these changes can and must be attempted with all our heart and mind, but inevitably we will slip, sin, or 'chattah'- fall short, or miss the mark as when an arrow misses the target.

This is why we have to be in a constant close spiritual relationship with Christ, believing in, and having faith and confidence in His sacrifice, His Grace, His forgiveness, and His willingness to regard us as His brothers and sisters in His Family.

Adultery

Matthew 5:27 Ye have heard that it was said by them of old time, Thou shalt not commit adultery: 28 **But** I say unto you, That whosoever looketh on a woman to lust after her hath committed adultery with her already in his heart.

It is one thing to be able to resist physically getting into bed with someone, but to control the lustful aspects of the human mind is very much more difficult.

Divorce

Matthew 5:31 It hath been said, Whosoever shall put away his wife, let him give her a writing of divorcement: 32 **But** I say unto you, That whosoever shall put away his wife, saving for the cause of fornication, causeth her to commit adultery: and whosoever shall marry her that is divorced committeth adultery.

The law of divorce takes on different aspects, often connected with the laws of a country at a given time. David and Solomon had plural wives and concubines. There is nothing to indicate that they were adulterous. Christ divorced Israel because of their persistent disobedience and idolatry.

Laws of divorce have become watered down over time, and now even 'quickies' are permitted for trivial and superficial reasons to our shame.

Matthew 19:8 He saith unto them, Moses because of the hardness of your hearts suffered you to put away your wives: but from the beginning this was not so. It was God's intention from the outset that the human marriage relationship should be a loving one. Hardness of heart is not a Christian trait.

Swearing

Matthew 5:33 Again, ye have heard that it hath been said by them of old time, Thou shalt not forswear thyself, but shalt perform unto the Lord thine oaths: 34 **But** I say unto you, Swear not at all; neither by heaven; for it is God's throne: 35 Nor by the earth; for it is his footstool: neither by Jerusalem; for it is the city of the great King. 36 Neither shalt thou swear by thy head, because thou canst not make one hair white or black. 37 But let your communication be, Yea, yea; Nay, nay: for whatsoever is more than these cometh of evil.

Swearing, the use of foul words, and blasphemy has become a national curse to the nations of America, Britain, Australia, and the Commonwealth of Nations and those they influence. Every conversation is peppered with blasphemy, OMG, "Christ", "God knows", "Jesus" with words so awful that they will not be recorded here.

Controlling the tongue is a most difficult challenge also. Over the last few decades, swearing has changed from being socially and morally unacceptable, to those words being used and broadcast by the media without let or hindrance. Foul language now permeates almost every television program or film in our era.

Proverbs 18:21 Death and life are in the power of the tongue: and they that love it shall eat the fruit thereof.

James compares the tongue to the rudder of a great ship. Just one tiny movement, and the course of the whole journey of the ship is changed.

James 3:4 Behold also the ships, which though they be so great, and are driven of fierce winds, yet are they turned about with a very small helm, whithersoever the governor listeth. 5 Even so the tongue is a little member, and boasteth great things. Behold, how great a matter a little fire kindleth 6 And the tongue is a fire, a world of iniquity: so is the tongue among our members, that it defileth the whole body, and setteth on fire the course of nature; and it is set on fire of hell. 7 For every kind of beasts, and of birds, and of serpents, and of things in the sea, is tamed, and hath been tamed of mankind: 8 But the tongue can no man tame; it is an unruly evil, full of deadly poison. 9 Therewith bless we God, even the Father; and therewith curse we men, which are made after the similitude of God. 10 Out of the same mouth proceedeth blessing and cursing. My brethren, these things ought not so to be.

Christ also told the Pharisees that it is the heart that speaks through the tongue, and our speech reveals what our hearts and minds are thinking.

Matthew 12:34 O generation of vipers, how can ye, being evil, speak good things? for out of the abundance of the heart the mouth speaketh.

It is a good Christian habit to listen to what comes out of our own mouths, and also out of the mouths of others, and check whether how we speak measures up to the Law of Love that Christ brought or not.

Revenge

Matthew 5:38 Ye have heard that it hath been said, An eye for an eye, and a tooth for a tooth: 39 **But** I say unto you, That ye resist not evil: but whosoever shall smite thee on thy right cheek, turn to him the other also. 40 And if any man will sue thee at the law, and take away thy coat, let him have thy cloak also.

To attempt to take revenge upon someone is not the act of a Christian.

Obey the law of the land willingly

Matthew 5:41 And whosoever shall compel thee to go a mile, go with him twain.

Under the laws of the Roman occupation, and Roman could make a citizen of Israel carry his burden for one mile. Christ said, go above and beyond in being helpful. We need to apply this principle, and give respect and compliance to those who have the rule over us.

Be a giver

Matthew 5:42 Give to him that asketh thee, and from him that would borrow of thee turn not thou away.

Be a giver, and take care of your resources and protect them from those who would take advantage of your generosity, and squander or misuse anything they can get or take from any person who has a giving attitude.

Matthew 10:16 Behold, I send you forth as sheep in the midst of wolves: be ye therefore wise as serpents, and harmless as doves.

Love your enemies

Matthew 5:43 Ye have heard that it hath been said, Thou shalt love thy neighbour, and hate thine enemy. 44 *But* I say unto you, Love your enemies, bless them that curse you, do good to them that hate you, and pray for them which despitefully use you, and persecute you; 45 That ye may be the children of your Father which is in heaven: for he maketh his sun to rise on the evil and on the good, and sendeth rain on the just and on the unjust. 46 For if ye love them which love you, what reward have ye? do not even the publicans the same? 47 And if ye salute your brethren only, what do ye more than others? do not even the publicans so?

Again, this is not an easy directive to comply with! It is possibly one of the hardest laws to live with. It takes a lot of God's Spirit working in us to enable us even to begin to comply with this law.

At the end of Matthew 5, Christ says in verse 48: Be ye therefore perfect, even as your Father which is in heaven is perfect.

But this is humanly impossible, we can only be 'perfect' if Christ lives in us and we in him, and we are in a constant attitude of repentance and trust in His constant ongoing forgiveness and His love towards us, even with and despite all our faults and failings.

The Sermon on the Mount continues in Matthew chapter 6:

Giving money to others or to charities

Matthew 6:1 Take heed that ye do not your alms before men, to be seen of them: otherwise ye have no reward of your Father which is in heaven. 2 Therefore when thou doest thine alms, do not sound a trumpet before thee, as the hypocrites do in the synagogues and in the streets, that they may have glory of men. Verily I say unto you, They have their reward. 3 **But** when thou doest alms, let not thy left hand know what thy right hand doeth: 4 That thine alms may be in secret: and thy Father which seeth in secret himself shall reward thee openly.

It is one thing to give to those one knows are in special need, and the principle is to 'prime the pump' to help anyone on their way. However, if any money given is used for purposes other than was intended, then the situation needs to be looked at again. When the same individuals ask for more, then again, that is another matter.

Giving to charities in this era is fraught with difficulty, as it is almost impossible to know just how much of a donation actually reaches those for whom the charity is claiming to help.

Much donated money is used up in 'expenses', 'salaries', 'administration' to the point where a very small proportion any money given actually reaches those needing help.

This is mentioned simply to suggest that one takes care in giving. Be 'wise as serpents...'

Praying in public and in private

Matthew 6:5 And when thou prayest, thou shalt not be as the hypocrites are: for they love to pray standing in the synagogues and in the corners of the streets, that they may be seen of men. Verily I say unto you, They have their reward. 6 **But** thou, when thou prayest, enter into thy closet, and when thou hast shut thy door, pray to thy Father which is in secret; and thy Father which seeth in secret shall reward thee openly.

Simple enough, prayer is a private matter between ourselves and God. On occasions it might be that a public prayer where someone leads it for a group, might be something to participate in, or not, depending upon circumstances.

People are led to pray in churches in a manner that might be considered to be vain and is frequently highly repetitious. Only those attending can decide whether they are or not.

Matthew 6:7 But when ye pray, use not vain repetitions, as the heathen do: for they think that they shall be heard for their much speaking.

In some countries, adherents to some religions use mechanical devices like prayer wheels to send thousands of 'prayers' with a twist of the wrist. Most of the prayers in churches are very repetitive also. The worshipper's concept of the nature of God in these instances is hardly consistent with the God of the Bible.

God is our Heavenly Father, and when we talk to Him, we are invited to talk to Him as we would our Earthly father, but in an attitude somewhat different towards our Creator. We need to hallow, to respect greatly His name, and honour

Him with the most profound veneration as we are talking to the King of Kings.

The 'Lord's Prayer is only a format, or a guide. Mumbling it repetitiously by heart is not the manner of prayer that should be used by a Christian.

Matthew 6:8 Be not ye therefore like unto them: for your Father knoweth what things ye have need of, before ye ask him. 9 After this manner therefore pray ye: Our Father which art in heaven, Hallowed be thy name. 10 Thy kingdom come, Thy will be done in earth, as it is in heaven. 11 Give us this day our daily bread. 12 And forgive us our debts, as we forgive our debtors. 13 And lead us not into temptation, but deliver us from evil: For thine is the kingdom, and the power, and the glory, for ever. Amen.

This is a simple framework, not something to be used repetitiously.

Forgiveness, unmerited pardon is by Grace, and is conditional

Matthew 6:14 For **if** ye forgive men their trespasses, your heavenly Father will also forgive you: 15 **But if** ye forgive not men their trespasses, neither will your Father forgive your trespasses.

To receive forgiveness, we are required to have an attitude of willing forgiveness towards our fellow human beings.

Many espouse the righteous sounding concept of 'unconditional love', but this concept is not supported in God's Word.

Fast in private

Matthew 6:16 Moreover when ye fast, be not, as the hypocrites, of a sad countenance: for they disfigure their faces, that they may appear unto men to fast. Verily I say unto you, They have their reward. 17 **But** thou, when thou fastest, anoint thine head, and wash thy face; 18 That thou appear not unto men to fast, but unto thy Father which is in secret: and thy Father, which seeth in secret, shall reward thee openly.

We cannot serve God *and* money or earthly 'treasures'

Matthew 6:19 Lay not up for yourselves treasures upon earth, where moth and rust doth corrupt, and where thieves break through and steal: 20 **But** lay up for yourselves treasures in heaven, where neither moth nor rust doth corrupt, and where thieves do not break through nor steal: 21 For where your treasure is, there will your heart be also. 22 The light of the body is the eye: if therefore thine eye be single, thy whole body shall be full of light. 23 **But** if thine eye be evil, thy whole body shall be full of darkness. If therefore the light that is in thee be darkness, how great is that darkness! 24 No man can serve two masters: for either he will hate the one, and love the other; or else he will hold to the one, and despise the other. <u>**Ye cannot serve God and mammon (worldly things and money).**</u>

It is all too easy to be caught up in chasing 'success'. The pursuit of money is like a drug, before you know where you are, it is dominating your time, your thoughts, your emotions. Pursuit of money is 'mammon' or 'worldliness'. There is absolutely nothing wrong with prosperity or doing well in life, but when it becomes our all-consuming dominant activity we enter dangerous waters.

Take no <u>anxious</u> thought in daily life, trust that God knows what we need.

Matthew 6:25 Therefore I say unto you, Take no (anxious) thought for your life, what ye shall eat, or what ye shall drink; nor yet for your body, what ye shall put on. Is not the life more than meat, and the body than raiment? 26 Behold the fowls of the air: for they sow not, neither do they reap, nor gather into barns; yet your heavenly Father feedeth them. Are ye not much better than they?

Matthew 6:31 Therefore take no thought, saying, What shall we eat? or, What shall we drink? or, Wherewithal shall we be clothed? 32 (For after all these things do the Gentiles

seek:) for your heavenly Father knoweth that ye have need of all these things. 33 **But** seek ye first the kingdom of God, and his righteousness; and all these things shall be added unto you. 34 Take therefore no (anxious) thought for the morrow: for the morrow shall take thought for the things of itself. Sufficient unto the day is the evil thereof.

God the Father and His Son do not want Their flock to live in a perpetual state of anxiousness as so many do. We can conduct our lives in the knowledge that God is taking care of our every need. Yes, life as a Christian will certainly not be easy, it takes hard work and earnest attention to everything we do to make the best of the gifts God has entrusted to each of us in measure. Even when things go wrong as we see it, remember that "all things (ultimately) work together for good to those who love God" even if it may not seem so at the time.

What are 'all *these things'?* They are the necessities in life, food and drink, clothing, and shelter. Does this mean we will never be without these things as Christians? There may be times when God allows us to suffer somewhat, but if we are constantly seeking the Kingdom and obedience to His Law, we need to ask for the Faith to know that He knows our state and what we need, even if and when things get difficult in our lives.

Do not judge or be critical of others

Matthew 7:1 Judge not, that ye be not judged. 2 For with what judgment ye judge, ye shall be judged: and with what measure ye mete, it shall be measured to you again. 3 And why beholdest thou the mote that is in thy brother's eye, **but** considerest not the beam that is in thine own eye? 4 Or how wilt thou say to thy brother, Let me pull out the mote out of thine eye; and, behold, a beam is in thine own eye? 5 Thou hypocrite, first cast out the beam out of thine own eye; and then shalt thou see clearly to cast out the mote out of thy brother's eye.

When anyone points the finger at another, three fingers of their hand point back at them. When anyone indulges in criticising others, it is well to remember that we are all guilty of exactly the same thing. If we can see it in others, then it is because we know that it is within ourselves.

Romans 2:1 Therefore thou art inexcusable, O man, whosoever thou art that judgest: for wherein thou judgest another, thou condemnest thyself; for thou that judgest doest the same things.

It is so very easy to see the speck in someone else's eye, without realising we have a plank in our own.

Treasure the pearls of wisdom God has given us

Matthew 7:6 Give not that which is holy unto the dogs, neither cast ye your pearls before swine, lest they trample them under their feet, and turn again and rend you.

The word 'dogs' in the Bible can refer to ministers of religion, and those who are godless, and openly practice things against God's Law. If we attempt to share truly spiritual truths with the 'heathen' or those of other faiths, we risk rebuttal and rejection at the very least. In some countries we may even risk imprisonment or death.

1 Peter 3:15 But sanctify the Lord God in your hearts: and be ready always to give an answer to every man that asketh you a reason of the hope that is in you with meekness and fear:

Christians are authorised to share with great care what knowledge we have been given, but only to those who sincerely ask. This can be a trap when the one asking may pounce on the unsuspecting Christian and reveal that they did not want to learn anything, but just wanted to start an argument.

Ask God for our spiritual needs and Christians will receive

Matthew 7:7 Ask, and it shall be given you; seek, and ye shall find; knock, and it shall be opened unto you: 8 For every one that asketh receiveth; and he that seeketh findeth; and to him that knocketh it shall be opened.

God does bless with physical things, but that is not where our hearts should be. We should be seeking spiritual gifts, belief, faith, repentance, trust, and a closer walk with Christ and our Father. Our spiritual 'treasures' are stored up for us in Heaven.

Treat others as you would like to be treated

Matthew 7:12 Therefore all things whatsoever ye would that men should do to you, do ye even so to them: for this is the law and the prophets.

Sometimes the way we like to be treated is not always shared by others. Some people like to take risks, are not afraid of heights, and so on. Others do not like taking risks and are terrified of heights. So we need to be sensitive to the feelings of others and how they would like to be treated in ways that might differ from what we might like or enjoy.

The Christian life is not the easy path, *very* few find the true way

Matthew 7:13 Enter ye in at the strait gate: for wide is the gate, and broad is the way, that leadeth to destruction, and many there be which go in thereat: 14 Because strait is the gate, and narrow is the way, which leadeth unto life, and *few* there be that find it.

Clearly, God is not opening the eyes, ears, and minds of the majority of the billions on the planet earth at this time.

Christ warns often of false prophets – are we listening?

Matthew 7:15 Beware of false prophets, which come to you in sheep's clothing, but inwardly they are ravening wolves.

How can you tell if someone is a false prophet or one who is not motivated by God's Spirit? The Bible and Christ in His ministry tells us so many times not to be taken in by anyone.

There is only ONE Mediator between God and man, Christ. Any person, especially 'minsters' of any type who assume the role of mediating is putting him or herself between people and God, which is clearly forbidden.

Matthew 23:7 And greetings in the markets, and to be called of men, Rabbi, Rabbi. **But** be not ye called Rabbi: for one is your Master, even Christ; and all ye are brethren.

The leaders of the Jewish faith to this day call themselves and are called, 'Rabbi'. Christ said do not allow anyone to call you Rabbi, which means master, for One is your Master, even Christ, and you are all brothers, that is with the same rank. No human is 'over' us in authority, only Christ is our Elder Brother, and our Mediator.

Matthew 23:9 And call no man your 'father' upon the earth: for one is your Father, which is in heaven.

Of course, Christ was not talking here about calling your human Dad 'father'. The priests and ministers of the world's largest Christian denomination are called 'Father', which Christ said is not to be done in any religious or theological context.

The 'Fathers' of the Church, mere men, hear confession, and hand out punishments of various kinds, and grant 'forgiveness' of sins to those who go to 'confession'. There is only one who can and does forgive sin, and that is Christ.

Matthew 23:10 Neither be ye called masters: for one is your Master, even Christ. 11 But he that is greatest among you shall be your servant.

The religions of the world are run by people who want to control others, to control how they worship God, to control what they believe and think, and even control aspects of their private lives. God, No human is qualified to do that.

Part of a Christian's work is to use all our might to control ourselves, and to avoid any attempt to control others. We need to practice relinquishing the desire to control others. It is not an easy challenge, as almost everyone does it in everyday conversation.

Avoid any attempt to control others

We all need to be aware of any attempt to control others. There is a strong part of human nature that has a desire to control others. We have all seen when some people are given even a modest amount of authority over others, immediately begin to use it unwisely and become petty tyrants.

Children at play are an absolute prime example. "Now you do this and I'll do that." If you don't do this, I won't let you play with me. " Controlling, or attempting to control others starts young, and is part of everyday adult life.

Most of the English speaking world is largely unconscious and unaware of the words they use constantly which amount to an attempt to control or criticise others.

"YOU" is possibly the most used word in attempts to control others. When the word "YOU" is followed by any of the following: you are, you could, you might have, you should, you should not, you ought to, you ought not to, you must or you must not, they all imply a measure of control. Also "You always' and "You never" are best avoided, as they are rarely fair comment or true.

"WHY?..." Nobody likes being called into question, or to account for their actions. From our earliest childhood, we were asked "Why did you do this or that?" It is invariably linked to a critical frown. Or worse still, some form of punishment. We grow up learning that every time we hear the word "WHY? to have a very negative feeling about the word "WHY".

"TRY to..." the word "TRY" is actually interpreted by the brain as confusion. "TRY" means to make an attempt to do something but falls short of achieving a result. As long as anyone is 'trying' to do something they are not succeeding. Repeating the instruction to "TRY" usually results in frustration. Christ does not tell us to 'try', He tells us to "do".

"SURELY": This word has negative connotations with superior and patronising overtones. It implies that you don't know what you are talking about, or that you have got it wrong." Surely you don't mean...?" "Surely you ought to..." "Surely you should …".

"BUT" – this word is the great negator. If you tell someone what a great job they have done, and that you are pleased with them, **but...** The word **'but'** sweeps away all the nice compliments. All the person hears and feels are the words after the word 'but', and they feel they are critical, judgemental, and not accepting of them. "Yes, BUT...", actually means 'No! I do not agree with you at all!' It is wise to avoid the use of "BUT" at all in these circumstances.

Many people do not believe that the Bible is God's Word. However, if anyone asks for the help of the Holy Spirit and devotes time in careful **study** rather than just reading it casually, their greater Knowledge Understanding and Wisdom will be the result.

"ASSUME": "I assume you mean...", "I assume you think...", When people 'assume' they are often acting in a pretentious, superior or presumptuous manner, and this is not wise. It is always much better to ask a person what they mean by what they said. Making assumptions about what others mean or think is dangerous ground indeed.

"I was only JOKING!" People frequently, laughingly, make all kinds of unkind, cruel, or thoughtless personal comments, and as soon as they see the effect on the recipient, they immediately say, ***"I was only joking!"*** Actually, they meant every word of it. Christ says: "Out of the abundance of the heart, the mouth speaks." Without realising it, what a person says is almost always based on what they truly feel in their hearts.

There is another old proverb which states: "As an arrow loosed from the bow, so a word once uttered cannot be recalled." Once something is said, it has an effect on the hearer. So we do well to think before we speak.

As Christians we will want to avoid using controlling words, or even attempt to control others, and instead, think how we can speak kindly and respectfully, and build each other up.

1 Thessalonians 5:9 For God hath not appointed us to wrath, but to obtain salvation by our Lord Jesus Christ, 10 Who died for us, that, whether we wake or sleep, we should live together with him. 11 Wherefore comfort yourselves together, and edify one another, even as also ye do.

Romans 12:10 Be kindly affectioned one to another with brotherly love; in honour preferring one another;

Ephesians 4:32 And be ye kind one to another, tenderhearted, forgiving one another, even as God for Christ's sake hath forgiven you.

Christ, tells us how He wants His called out ones to live this life today, and attempting to control others is not part of the Christian way.

Yes, Christ warns often of false prophets

So how are we to know if someone is a false prophet or whether anyone who purports to represent Christ is a false minister? Again Christ warns:

Matthew 7:15 Beware of false prophets, which come to you in sheep's clothing, but inwardly they are ravening wolves. 16 Ye shall know them by their fruits. Do men gather grapes of thorns, or figs of thistles? 17 Even so every good tree bringeth forth good fruit; but a corrupt tree bringeth forth evil fruit. 18 A good tree cannot bring forth evil fruit, neither can a corrupt tree bring forth good fruit. 19 Every tree that bringeth not forth good fruit is hewn down, and cast into the fire. 20 Wherefore by their fruits ye shall know them.

In the 21st century, there have been countless appalling accounts of the degree to which religious and other leaders of schools and groups have been involved in preying sexually on children, men and women. These many reports are only those which have come to light, sometimes several decades after the offences took place. Nobody knows the extent to which these perversions are happening today behind the scenes of organisations in which people are still entrusted with the care of others.

These activities are part of the fruits of the flesh, and parents and families need to be aware of the possibility of it happening in their area. Especially 'Online'! We can indeed know them by their fruits, and it would be wise not to be gullible in our trust of others. They may be indulging in the 'fruits' of going against the very instructions of Christ who they claim to represent.

Just because anyone knows how to quote the Bible, or mentions the name of "Jesus" or "God", or wear certain clothes, does not mean that they are genuine God-fearing people. **Especially be careful "ONLINE" where evil**

people masquerade as tantalizingly interesting and helpful, whereas they are masters of deception.

Matthew 7:21 Not every one that saith unto me, Lord, Lord, shall enter into the kingdom of heaven; but he that doeth the will of my Father which is in heaven.

'Dogmatic' – Certain teachings that cannot and will never change.

Here are some examples of teachings, concepts, and principles that will never change: Love, Faith, Hope, which are universal, permanent in value and importance dogmatically. No discussion. They are imparted to God's children by way of God's Power, the Holy Spirit.

In John chapters 13-17, Christ is teaching His disciples just before His crucifixion, and many of His statements supersede earlier definitions.

When the serpent told Eve that God was lying when He said they would die if they ate of the Tree of the Knowledge of Good and Evil, this was the beginning of the doctrine of the 'Immortality of the Soul' which coupled with belief in 'Reincarnation' is so widely believed in the world today.

If the doctrine of the 'Immortality of the Soul' is true, then Christ did not die on the tree of crucifixion, he was not dead in the tomb, but alive somewhere else (some say visiting the spirits in prison!), then we cannot be saved, and we are still in our sins. The penalty of sin is **death,** the complete cessation of life, and Christ had to **die** for our sins for them to be removed so that we could have eternal life.

John 3:16 For God so loved the world, that he gave his only begotten Son, that whosoever believeth in him should not perish, but have everlasting life.

Some Christians seem to want it both ways, they want to believe in the 'Immortality of the Soul', and to be saved by the death of Christ. Both cannot be true. If Christ did not die, then nobody is saved.

Ezekiel 18:4 Behold, all souls are mine; as the soul of the father, so also the soul of the son is mine: the soul that sinneth, it shall die.

Hebrews 19:27 And as it is appointed unto men once to die, but after this the judgement:

Ecclesiastes 9:10 Whatsoever thy hand findeth to do, do it with thy might; for there is no work, nor device, nor knowledge, nor wisdom, in the grave, whither thou goest.

Christ says: When we die, we die, we cease to exist completely.

Ten Commandment variations

Interpretation of Scripture is of vital importance, and has to be tempered with great care. Dispensations, circumstances, exceptions, chronology, ethnicity, all have to be taken into account in the understanding and application of law. Only by earnest study can we be sure what applies to us in this age and what does not.

Graven Images

Exodus 20:4 Thou shalt not make unto thee any graven image, or any likeness of any thing that is in heaven above, or that is in the earth beneath, or that is in the water under the earth.

This commandment is very clear, that no type of graven image or any likeness of anything is to be made and used in connection with worship.

Genesis 3:24 So he drove out the man; and he placed at the east of the garden of Eden

Cherubims, and a flaming sword which turned every way, to keep the way of the tree of life.

Cherubims were spirit beings placed in the garden of Eden to prevent Adam or anyone else from going near the Tree of Life.

So despite the clear law about making any graven image, there is an exception in the case of Cherubim. God tells Moses to make two of them and place them in the Tabernacle, and later they were placed in the Temple when it was built.

Exodus 25:18 And thou shalt make two cherubims of gold, of beaten work shalt thou make them, in the two ends of the mercy seat. 19 And make one cherub on the one end, and the other cherub on the other end: even of the mercy seat shall ye make the cherubims on the two ends thereof. 20 And the cherubims shall stretch forth their wings on high, covering the mercy seat with their wings, and their faces shall look one to another; toward the mercy seat shall the faces of the cherubims be.

But while Moses was still upon the mountain receiving the commandments from God, Aaron, a priest of the Most High God gave in to the demands of the Israelites and made them a golden image of a calf to worship.

Exodus 32:3 And all the people brake off the golden earrings which were in their ears, and brought them unto Aaron. 4 And he received them at their hand, and fashioned it with a graving tool, after he had made it a molten calf: and they said, These be thy gods, O Israel, which brought thee up out of the land of Egypt.

Aaron was a priest of the Most High God. He not only made a molten calf, but told the Israelites that this was the god that brought them out of Egypt; he told the Israelites to be naked, no doubt to prepare for sex worship; then lied by making the ridiculous excuse that the calf made itself!

Exodus 32:24 And I said unto them, Whosoever hath any gold, let them break it off. So they gave it me: then I cast it into the fire, and there came out this calf. 25 And when Moses saw that the people were naked; (for Aaron had made them naked unto their shame among their enemies:)

God's immediate reaction was to want to destroy them all. Moses pleaded for their lives, and God relented, but three thousand people died for this transgression of the second commandment, and God continued to plague the Children of Israel for this vile act.

It is interesting to note that the idolatry of the Golden Calf involved nudity and no doubt sinful and unlawful sexual activity. This was also true of those who indulged in the worship of false gods throughout history.

Exodus 32:28 And the children of Levi did according to the word of Moses: and there fell of the people that day about three thousand men. 33 And the Lord said unto Moses, Whosoever hath sinned against me, him will I blot out of my book   34 Therefore now go,

lead the people unto the place of which I have spoken unto thee: behold, mine Angel shall go before thee: nevertheless in the day when I visit I will visit their sin upon them. 35 And the Lord plagued the people, because they made the calf, which Aaron made.

Taking God's Name in vain

It is not intended to enter into any discussion here about the names of God. What is clear from the context of the commandment is that to use any word that we or others associate with God in a disrespectful or blasphemous manner is against spiritual law.

When the King James Bible was first translated and printed in 1611, there was no such letter in the English alphabet as J. It was only over a century later that a J was included in the alphabet. Prior to that time, there were of course many names of God, most of which we have no way of knowing how to pronounce the original Hebrew words. The Hebrew language does not put the vowels into written words, so to any attempts to pronounce accurately the Tetragrammaton YHWH are futile.

Some people pronounce YHWH as 'Jehovah'. Others use the pronunciation 'Yahweh'. Others might use 'Yaheshua' which would mean 'God is deliverer'. Some use the word 'Yashua' which would literally mean 'God is crying out for help' which would be totally inappropriate.

Regrettably, out of total ignorance the masses use the words "God", "Jesus", "Christ", and "Jesus Christ" together with unprintable other words, in a manner of blasphemous epithets in everyday language. This is one reason why the word "Jesus" has been eliminated from this book except where it is quoting the Bible directly. They have even created 'shorthand' for blasphemy, such as "OMG", which is used in every other sentence by many, especially young people. That is certainly very sad, and to be avoided by Christians.

Christians will use the third commandment as a guide to be very careful only to use words to refer to God in a manner of absolute reverence, respect and honour.

Law on killing and murder

Exodus 20:13 Thou shalt not kill.

The Mosaic Law details a large number of crimes for which capital punishment was the automatic penalty.

The Old Testament is full of accounts where God commanded the killing, and even the apparent mass 'ethnic cleansing' of peoples who had descended into depravity and Godlessness. Also clearly this does not apply to the killing of animals under certain circumstances, as in sacrificing the ram for Isaac, and the thousands of animal and bird sacrifices involved with worshipping God in the Temple sacrificial system.

So again, the caveats of 'Dispensations, circumstances, exceptions, chronology, ethnicity', all have to be taken into account in our understanding and application of law.

Adultery

Exodus 20:14 Thou shalt not commit adultery.

Under Mosaic Law, adultery was punished with the death penalty.

Yet, the Patriarchs with whom God was dealing on a personal level often had more than one wife, and they also had concubines.

Genesis 25:1 Then again Abraham took a wife, and her name was Keturah. 6 But unto

the sons of the concubines, which Abraham had, Abraham gave gifts, and sent them away from Isaac his son, while he yet lived, eastward, unto the east country.

David committed adultery in a particularly horrific manner and also married many wives, and took concubines, yet he above so many men, was a 'man after God's own heart'.

2 Samuel 5:13 And David took him more concubines and wives out of Jerusalem, after he was come from Hebron: and there were yet sons and daughters born to David.

Solomon, who was used by God to build his Temple, had hundreds of wives and concubines and was not accused of adultery. But he had transgressed God's commands regarding women of other races.

1 Kings 11:1 But king Solomon loved many strange women, together with the daughter of Pharaoh, women of the Moabites, Ammonites, Edomites, Zidonians, and Hittites: 2 Of the nations concerning which the Lord said unto the children of Israel, Ye shall not go in to them, neither shall they come in unto you: for surely they will turn away your heart after their gods: Solomon clave unto these in love. 3 And he had seven hundred wives, princesses, and three hundred concubines: and his wives turned away his heart.

In our society in this era, we are required as Christians to obey the laws of the land. Adultery is against common law, but those who commit it are not required to submit to the death penalty. Bigamy, marrying more than one wife at a time is also against the law, but the sentence of capital punishment is not handed down.

Paul says that in his era a minister and deacons should be the husband of one wife, but he does not exclude the practice of anyone having more than one wife in the society in which he lived at the time.

1 Timothy 3: 2 A bishop then must be blameless, the husband of one wife, vigilant, sober, of good behaviour, given to hospitality, apt to teach;...12 Let the deacons be the husbands of one wife, ruling their children and their own houses well.

Yes Exodus 20:14 Thou shalt not commit adultery was true in former times, but the law against adultery is now not only against the physical act, but also to do with the thoughts of the heart.

Again the law of adultery has been interpreted differently according to circumstance, times, and different peoples positions.

The Sabbath

Christ came to fulfil the law, and He did it perfectly, which meant that He observed the keeping of the Sabbath correctly in every detail. Ministers and pastors of many denominations use the fact that Christ kept the Sabbath during his ministry, to insist therefore that it is binding on Christians to keep it today.

Firstly, it is virtually impossible to observe all the constraints and aspects of the Law of Sabbath keeping in our era. Some sincere religious but self-righteous people are content to keep some parts of the Law of the Sabbath, feel good about that, but conveniently ignore others, and in so doing are not actually keeping the Sabbath at all. If we offend in one point, we offend in all.

Isaiah 64:6 But we are all as an unclean thing, and all our righteousnesses are as filthy rags; and we all do fade as a leaf; and our iniquities, like the wind, have taken us away.

The Sabbath was a command to be observed 'forever'. The Hebrew word Olam means age lasting, and olam is not forever, but for as long as the 'olam' lasted. God does not keep the Sabbath. Actually Christ did work on the Sabbath during His ministry, and when challenged by the religious people, He replied, "My Father works, and I work". He plucked grain with his disciples to eat which was against the Pharisaical interpretation of the law. He also healed on the Sabbath against the 'law' of the religious leaders.

Christ is the Lord of the Sabbath. The Sabbath was made for man not the other way around. Christians in Christ are now under the dispensation of a different 'Sabbath' rest. Hebrews 4 explains that Christians are now in the period of the Sabbath spiritual 'rest' of Jesus Christ.

Stealing

In Numbers 31 God told the Israelites to 'spoil' the Midianites. Even 'stealing' had variations and different dispensations in the law. Theft is still wrong, and always will be as it is one of those permanent dogmatic teachings that will never change, yet even that law can be modified by Divine Fiat. Now in this era we have 'identity' theft, and 'intellectual property' theft, stealing a person's identity and their ideas is still against the law.

Be very careful 'online' and even on your phone, SCAMS are rife. Look into how they are done so as to avoid them, and not be ensnared.

Coveting

'Coveting' which is an illicit desire, wanting for yourself that which belongs to another. It is destructive to Godly character, and our Lawgiver wants us to respect our neighbours and the Laws that govern our thoughts regarding them.

Exodus 20:17 Thou shalt not covet thy neighbour's house, thou shalt not covet thy neighbour's wife, nor his manservant, nor his maidservant, nor his ox, nor his ass, nor any thing that is thy neighbour's.

The origin of this law in Exodus 20 refers to your neighbour's house, wife, servant, ox, ass, etc. The intent at that time was not to covet your *Israelite* neighbour's things. But God did decide that the Israelites were entitled to 'spoil' the Midianites, and kill the Canaanites, and in other ways, contravene the letter of the commandment laws.

Covetousness also breaks the law of idolatry, putting illegal desire for other things before our love for God.

Colossians 3:5 Mortify therefore your members which are upon the earth; fornication, uncleanness, inordinate affection, evil concupiscence, and covetousness, which is idolatry:

We do not have any instructions in this day and age from God that it is alright for us to break these physical laws, but rather take to them to a heart and spiritual level.

More "Progressive Revelation" - The 'Mystery' hidden since before the world began.

Christ Jesus came to introduce the beginning of the next stage of the Divine Plan relationship between God and humankind. Christ transformed the law by His life, by bearing the entire sins of human beings, by His death to pay the penalty for everyone, His resurrection, His being judged by the Father as perfect, and His sacrifice enabled Him to present all human beings to the Father without spot, wrinkle or any type of sin, so they could ultimately enter into eternal life with God and Christ Jesus.

John 3:14 And as Moses lifted up the serpent in the wilderness, even so must the Son of man be lifted up:

15 That whosoever believeth in him should not perish, but have eternal life 16 For God so loved the world, that he gave his only begotten Son, that whosoever believeth in him should not perish, but have everlasting life. 17For God sent not his Son into the world to condemn the world; but that the world through him might be saved.

So then when the Holy Spirit was given at Pentecost 31 A.D., we were already released from the bondage of the Law, and from the penalty of our sin, and sealed with that promise of salvation which we had been accorded since before the world began.

Paul, (Saul) a Benjamite Pharisee who had been causing Christians to be killed, who was present at the stoning of Steven the first martyr, was blinded on the road to Damascus.

From then on, Christ appeared to him in vision, and began and continued to work with his mind, and give him more "Progressive Revelation".

Acts 9:9 And Saul, yet breathing out threatenings and slaughter against the disciples of the Lord, went unto the high priest, 2 And desired of him letters to Damascus to the synagogues, that if he found any of this way, whether they were men or women, he might bring them bound unto Jerusalem. 3 And as he journeyed, he came near Damascus: and suddenly there shined round about him a light from heaven: 4 And he fell to the earth, and heard a voice saying unto him, Saul, Saul, why persecutest thou me? 5 And he said, Who art thou, Lord? And the Lord said, I am Jesus whom thou persecutest: it is hard for thee to kick against the pricks.

Christ was dealing directly with Paul, and gave him the title and authority of an Apostle, because Christ had a special work for him to do.

Acts 9:10,15 And he trembling and astonished said, Lord, what wilt thou have me to do? And the Lord said unto him

(Ananias), Arise, and go into the city, and it shall be told thee what thou must do... verse 15 But the Lord said unto him, Go thy way: for he is a chosen

vessel unto me, to bear my name before the Gentiles, and kings, and the children of Israel:... Read the chapter.

Romans 1:1 Paul, a servant of Jesus Christ, called to be an apostle, separated unto the gospel of God,

In Romans the eighth chapter, often called the Holy Spirit chapter, Paul reveals more detail about the relationship of God to human beings than had been known previously.

Romans 8:1 There is therefore now no condemnation to them which are in Christ Jesus, who walk not after the flesh, but after the Spirit.

Christ paid the penalty for all sin, so nobody is under condemnation (of death), but will inherit life. Whatever was necessary for a human being to become a fully fledged child of God was done for us by Christ Jesus who knew each of us before He created the world and the Universe.

Romans 8:2 For the law of the Spirit of life in Christ Jesus hath made me free from the law of sin and death. 3 For what the law could not do, in that it was weak through the flesh, God sending his own Son in the likeness of sinful flesh, and for sin, condemned sin in the flesh: 4 That the righteousness of the law might be fulfilled in us, who walk not after the flesh, but after the Spirit. 5 For they that are after the flesh do mind the things of the flesh; but they that are after the Spirit the things of the Spirit.

Even the most sincerely religious people have a carnal mind and a heart that is at enmity to God, unless He has called them and given them His Holy Spirit. This accounts for the evil behaviour that runs rampant in many so-called Christian organisations.

Romans 8:6 For to be carnally minded is death; but to be spiritually minded is life and peace. 7 Because the carnal mind is enmity against God: for it is not subject to the law of God, neither indeed can be. 8 So then they that are in the flesh cannot please God. 9 But ye are not in the flesh, but in the Spirit, **if** so be that the Spirit of God dwell in you. Now **if** any man have not the Spirit of Christ, he is none of his. 10 And if Christ be in you, the body is dead because of sin; but the Spirit is life because of righteousness. 11 **But if** the Spirit of him that raised up Jesus from the dead dwell in you, he that raised up Christ from the dead shall also quicken your mortal bodies by his Spirit that dwelleth in you. 12 Therefore, brethren, we are debtors, not to the flesh, to live after the flesh. 13 For *if* ye live after the flesh, ye shall die: **but if** ye through the Spirit do mortify the deeds of the body, ye shall live.

Notice all the conditionall 'ifs'! Once we have been sealed with the gift of the Holy Spirit we become potential Spirit children of the Most High God, and are allowed to call Him Father, or 'Abba' or Dad.

Romans 8:14 For as many as are led by the Spirit of God, they are the sons of God. 15 For ye have not received the spirit of bondage again to fear; but ye have received the Spirit of adoption, whereby we cry, Abba, Father.

We can call the Father, Dad! God the Father has adopted all human beings into His family. Amazing Grace!

Romans 8:16 The Spirit itself beareth witness with our spirit, that we are the children of God: 17 **And if children, then heirs; heirs of God, and joint-heirs with Christ; if so be that we suffer with him, that we may be also glorified together.**

The enormity of the implication of that last sentence is so awesome, yet is glossed over by so many people. This can only be regarded with a 'ho-hum' attitude if that person has not been given the spiritual enlightenment to be able to appreciate the majesty of our future as members of the Royal Household of God.

Christ then says through Paul that we may have to go through the 'slings and arrows of outrageous fortune' in this life, but when we look past our trials and tribulations of this life to our glorious future, they are nothing.

Romans 8:18 For I reckon that the sufferings of this present time are not worthy to be compared with the glory which shall be revealed in us. 19 For the earnest expectation of the creature (the whole creation) waiteth for the manifestation of the sons of God. 20 For the creature was made subject to vanity, not willingly, but by reason of him who hath subjected the same in hope, 21 Because the creature itself also shall be delivered from the bondage of corruption into the glorious liberty of the children of God. 22 For we know that the whole creation groaneth and travaileth in pain together until now.

Our Messiah, Christ Jesus, was appointed by the Father to be over all of creation.

Romans 8:23 And not only they, but ourselves also, which have the firstfruits of the Spirit, even we ourselves groan within ourselves, waiting for the adoption, to wit, the redemption of our body. 24 For we are saved by hope: but hope that is seen is not hope: for what a man seeth, why doth he yet hope for? 25 But if we hope for that we see not, then do we with patience wait for it.

We do not even know how to pray, or what we should pray for, but God even takes care of that for us.

Romans 8:26 Likewise the Spirit also helpeth our infirmities: for we know not what we should pray for as we ought: but the Spirit itself maketh intercession for us with groanings which cannot be uttered. 27 And he that searcheth the hearts knoweth what is the mind of the Spirit, because he maketh intercession for the saints according to the will of God. 28 And we know that all things work together for good to them that love God, to them who are the called according to his purpose.

So whatever trials we experience in this life, we can have the absolute assurance that everything will work together (ultimately) for good for those of Christ's ecclesia who are the called according to His purpose, because God knew each of us personally before the creation of the world.

Romans 8:29 For whom he did foreknow, he also did predestinate to be conformed to the image of his Son, that he might be the firstborn among many brethren. 30 Moreover whom he did predestinate, them he also called: and whom he called, them he also justified: and whom he justified, them he also glorified.

If people who consider themselves to be Christians actually really believed what verses 29 and 30 are saying, 'how can we (they) neglect (disregard or treat so lightly) so great salvation'; (Hebrews 3:) which at the first began to be spoken by our Lord Jesus Christ.

Romans 8:31 What shall we then say to these things? If God be for us, who can be against us? 32 He that spared not his own Son, but delivered him up for us all, how shall he not with him also freely give us all things? 33 Who shall lay any thing to the charge of God's elect? It is God that justifieth. 34 Who is he that condemneth? It is Christ that died, yea rather, that is risen again, who is even at the right hand of God, who also maketh intercession for us. 35 Who shall separate us from the love of Christ? shall tribulation, or distress, or persecution, or famine, or nakedness, or peril, or sword? 36 As it is written, For thy sake we are killed all the day long; we are accounted as sheep for the slaughter. 37 Nay, in all these things we are more than conquerors through him that loved us. 38 For I am persuaded, that neither death, nor life, nor angels, nor principalities, nor powers, nor things present, nor things to come, 39 Nor height, nor depth, nor any other creature, shall be able to separate us from the love of God, which is in Christ Jesus our Lord.

When Christ came to deliver us, the Mosaic Law had served its purpose, as a schoolmaster for kindergarten physical humans, and now Christ brought Faith and Grace, the physical Law would be superseded by the Spiritual Law of Love for those who are spiritually circumcised of the heart.

Galatians 3:21 Is the law then against the promises of God? God forbid: for if there had been a law given which could have given life, verily righteousness should have been by the law. 22 But the scripture hath concluded all under sin, that the promise by faith of Jesus Christ might be given to them that believe. 23 But before faith came, we were kept under the law, shut up unto the faith which should afterwards be revealed. 24 Wherefore the law was our schoolmaster to bring us unto Christ, that we might be justified by faith.

But then Christ brought Faith and Grace, unmerited pardon, and the promise of eternal life as a gift.

Galatians 3:25 But after that faith is come, we are no longer under a schoolmaster. 26 For ye are all the children of God by faith in Christ Jesus. 27 For as many of you as have been baptized into Christ have put on Christ.

The rite of physical baptism is no longer necessary, as when Christ was baptised, so in effect was every human being. When we are 'in Christ' we are also baptised into Christ.

Galatians 3:28 There is neither Jew nor Greek, there is neither bond nor free, there is neither male nor female: for ye are all one in Christ Jesus. 29 And if ye be Christ's, then are ye Abraham's seed, and heirs according to the promise.

This was more of the revelation that was staggering to those who first heard at the time that the uncircumcised 'heathen' Gentiles were also to inherit the Kingdom of God, and were to be given salvation.

Ephesians 1:3 Blessed be the God and Father of our Lord Jesus Christ, who hath blessed us with all spiritual blessings in heavenly places in Christ: 4 According as he hath chosen us in him before the foundation of the world, that we should be holy and without blame before him in love:

Every human being was chosen to inherit eternal life long before the world was created by Christ under the direction of the Father. Everyone was potentially 'saved' before the universe and the world were even created. We were known individually and personally to the Father and to Christ who were able to see the awesome nature of the future Plan they had devised to replicate themselves with an extended family.

Ephesians 1:5 Having predestinated us unto the adoption of children by Jesus Christ to himself, (and to the Father) according to the good pleasure of His will, 6 To the praise of the glory of his grace, wherein he hath made us accepted in the beloved. 7 In whom we have redemption through his blood, the forgiveness of sins, according to the riches of his grace; 8 Wherein he hath abounded toward us in all wisdom and prudence;

Philippians 3:20 For our conversation (citizenship) is in heaven; from whence also we look for the Saviour, the Lord Jesus Christ: 21 Who shall change our vile body, that it may be fashioned like unto his glorious body, according to the working whereby he is able even to subdue all things unto himself.

This verse in Philippians harks back to the first book of Corinthians the fifteenth chapter written around 52 A.D., known as the 'resurrection' chapter. Part of that chapter is included here because it gives such a clear account regarding the future resurrection from our human body to our new glorious body.

1 Corinthians 15:35 But some man will say, How are the dead raised up? and with what body do they come? 36 Thou fool, that which thou sowest is not quickened, except it die: 37 And that which thou sowest, thou sowest not that body that shall be, but bare grain, it may chance of wheat, or of some other grain: 38 But God giveth it a body as it hath pleased him, and to every seed his own body. 39 All flesh is not the same flesh: but there is one kind of flesh of men, another flesh of beasts, another of fishes, and another of birds. 40 There are also celestial bodies, and bodies terrestrial: but the glory of the celestial is one, and the glory of the terrestrial is another. 41 There is one glory of the sun, and another glory of the moon, and another glory of the stars: for one star differeth from another star in glory. 42 So also is the resurrection of the dead. It is sown in corruption; it is raised in incorruption: 43 It is sown in dishonour; it is raised in glory: it is sown in weakness; it is raised in power: 44 It is sown a natural body; it is raised a spiritual body.

There is a natural body, and there is a spiritual body. 45 And so it is written, The first man Adam was made a living soul; the last Adam was made a quickening spirit. 46 Howbeit that was not first which is spiritual, but that which is natural; and afterward that which is spiritual. 47 The first man is of the earth, earthy; the second man is the Lord from heaven. 48 As is the earthy, such are they also that are earthy: and as is the heavenly, such are they also that are heavenly. 49 And as we have borne the image of the earthy, we shall also bear the image of the heavenly. 50 Now this I say, brethren, that flesh and blood cannot inherit the kingdom of God; neither doth corruption inherit incorruption. 51 Behold, I shew you a mystery; We shall not all sleep, but we shall all be changed, 52 In a moment, in the twinkling of an eye, at the last trump: for the trumpet shall sound, and the dead shall be raised incorruptible, and we shall be changed. *(Revelation 11:15 And the seventh angel sounded; and there were great voices in heaven, saying, The kingdoms of this world are become the kingdoms of our Lord, and of his Christ; and he shall reign for ever and ever. Revelation 20:6 Blessed and holy is he that hath part in the first resurrection: on such the second death hath no power, but they shall be priests of God and of Christ, and shall reign with him a thousand years.)* 53 For this corruptible must put on incorruption, and this mortal must put on immortality. 54 So when this corruptible shall have put on incorruption, and this mortal shall have put on immortality, then shall be brought to pass the saying that is written, Death is swallowed up in victory.

So although the resurrection of the body had been preached by Paul earlier in his ministry, the fact that both Jew and Gentile were to be co-heirs with Christ, the understanding of the 'mystery' was completely new information.

Colossians 3:10 And have put on the new man, which is renewed in knowledge after the image of him that created him: 11 Where there is neither Greek nor Jew, circumcision nor uncircumcision, Barbarian, Scythian, bond nor free: but Christ is all, and in all.

Ephesians 1:9 Having made known unto us the mystery of his will, according to his good pleasure which he hath purposed in himself:

10 That in the dispensation of the fulness of times he might gather together in one all things in Christ, both which are in heaven, and which are on earth; even in him:

People talk blithely about 'going to heaven when you die' with about the same tone of voice as they might say 'we go down to the coast to be by the seaside'! Our inheritance deserves more attention than that!

Ephesians 1:11 In whom also we have obtained an inheritance, being predestinated according to the purpose of him who worketh all things after the counsel of his own will: 12 That we should be to the praise of his glory, who first trusted in Christ. 13 In whom ye also trusted, after that ye heard the word of truth, the gospel of your salvation: in whom also after that ye believed, ye were sealed with that holy Spirit of promise, 14 Which is the earnest of our inheritance until the redemption of the purchased possession, unto the praise of his glory.

In 63 A.D. after many years of his ministry, the Apostle Paul was to be given more personal teaching directly from the risen Christ Jesus about the 'mystery' of our ultimate future. This was completely new information, and another example of 'Progressive Revelation'. Paul was given more details regarding the full and complete understanding of the 'Mystery' that had been hidden from human beings since the beginning of time.

Ephesians 3:9 And to make all men see what is the fellowship of the mystery, which from the beginning of the world hath been hid in God, who created all things by Jesus Christ:

Colossians 1:25 Whereof I am made a minister, according to the dispensation of God which is given to me for you, to fulfil the word of God; 26 Even the mystery which hath been hid from ages and from generations, but now is made manifest to his saints: 27 To whom God would make known what is the riches of the glory of this mystery among the Gentiles; which is Christ in you, the hope of glory:

The matter of the Gentiles becoming heirs also must have been a difficult concept to accept for those steeped in the traditions of the Jews, so God repeats for emphasis:

Colossians 3:10 And have put on the new man, which is renewed in knowledge after the image of him that created him: 11 Where there is neither Greek nor Jew, circumcision nor uncircumcision, Barbarian, Scythian, bond nor free: but Christ is all, and in all.

Again, because God has seen fit to reveal His plan in stages, it is totally impractical and incorrect to take statements of doctrine and law given at one time, and to certain people for them to practice and obey, and then arbitrarily to apply them to people of different races, times and geographical locations throughout history without due regard for "Progressive Revelation".

Paul lived on for a few more years after 63 A.D., but died around 68 A.D.

The Bible does not tell us the exact time or manner of the apostle Paul's death, and secular history has yet to provide us with any definitive information. However, evidence highly suggests the apostle Paul's death occurred after his fifth missionary journey ended in 67 A.D. Paul was likely beheaded by the Romans, under Emperor Nero, sometime around May or June of 68 A.D. Nero himself died by suicide on June 9th of the same year.

After Paul's death, Christ gave final special inspired information in the Book of Revelation to the Apostle John, the forty-ninth book which put the capstone on the whole body of doctrine in 96 A.D., just before Christ through John Christ's brother canonised the Old and New Testament into the perfect arrangement of one Book made up of 49 books.

BEWARE DECEPTION

Religious people, ministers, and those in higher ranks of churches can appear totally sincere, and it is probable no doubt that some are sincere.

Both Dr. Martin, and the author who compiled this book were totally and utterly sincere for many years while associated with an organisation that claimed to be "the one and only church of God". We did not know we were being deceived until God opened our minds to see how false their teachings were, and how in fact they were actually not following the Bible at all, but were teaching, but we were following, the commandments of men.

Those who are deceived do not know that they are deceived, and it is only the flow of God's Holy Spirit in our hearts and minds that can give us the wisdom, and reveal to us the deceptiveness of words and behaviours.

Matthew 15:8 This people draweth nigh unto me with their mouth, and honoureth me with their lips; but their heart is far from me. 9 But in vain they do worship me, teaching for doctrines the commandments of men.

Utter sincerity is of no value if what you are sincere about is wrong!

James 4:7 Submit yourselves therefore to God. Resist the devil, and he will flee from you.

We can also pray: Matthew 6:13 And lead us not into temptation, but deliver us from evil: Or deliver us from the evil one.

We can thank God that the **KEY** to protection from deception is freely available to those that God, through Christ, is adding to His Ekklesia. **That KEY is to avoid the teachings of men, and rely completely on God's Word as we grow in Grace and knowledge.**

However, we know, and need to keep in mind, that God has built into the heart of man a deceitful nature. We need to keep our own deceitful nature well in check both towards ourselves and others, and that can only be done with God's help.

Jeremiah 17:9 The (human) heart is deceitful above all things, and desperately wicked: who can know it? We can, and we do!

Here once again for emphasis is the statement that is not only true, but disturbing:

Those who are deceived do not know that they are deceived.

If anyone knew that they were deceived, then they would not be deceived!

A disturbing thought, yes but only if we do not have the KEY to God's protection from being deceived.

Christ gave a clear warning about false ministers and those who would come using Christ's name and His Word the Bible as the authority for their teachings. Yes, they say that Jesus is the Christ, but they do not preach the true Gospel, but use the Bible to deceive.

Matthew 24:5 For **many** shall come in my name, saying, I am Christ; and shall deceive many.

Christ said, "many" shall come *in my name*. False teachers are good at using the name of Christ, and quoting the Bible to further their own ends. False ministers and false prophets do not go around wearing a sign which says 'False Prophet', of course not! It is up to each of us to use our knowledge of the Scriptures thoughtfully to make a careful and valid judgement of anyone who presents himself, or nowadays herself, as a minister of God. So religious organisations and their ministers may well have the appearance of piety or godliness, but Christ says inside they are dangerous ravening wolves.

Thinking about the fact that those who are deceived do not know they are is very disturbing, unless we have an assurance that we are not deceived. We can have that assurance.

So how can the ardent student of Theology, the study of God's Word know, and know that they know, that they are not deceived? We can have protection from deception.

The KEY: We have to protect our minds from, and ignore any and every doctrine, belief system, and dictates of the religious organisations of men or women.

There is an absolutely reliable KEY. **The KEY is only to believe and accept that there is only ONE Mediator between us and God, and that is the Man Jesus Christ, and His Word, the Holy Bible**. Our contact with Christ and with our Father can only be directly from that Source, never through other human beings.

How do we do that? It is important to maintain a close connection with our Father and Jesus Christ. In an attitude of humility, when we approach our studies, it is crucial to ask the tools we need for true understanding. What are these tools?

* Understand that there is only one standard of Truth, Christ, the Word of God, the Holy Scriptures, our Bibles are the only source of Truth we can trust implicitly.

* Ask God for a repentant attitude.

* Claim forgiveness through Christ.

* Ask for the guidance of God's Holy Spirit as we study.

John 16:13 Howbeit when he, the Spirit of truth, is come, he (it) will guide you into all truth: for he shall **not** speak of himself; but whatsoever he shall hear, that shall he speak: and he will shew you things to come.

How does the Spirit show us what God wants us to know? Not in words, or in an audible language, but God speaks to each of us by transmitting insights (like radio signals that cannot be heard without a radio which is our Godly Mind), thoughts, understandings, feelings, concepts, realisations, appreciations, joy and enlightenment to our minds as we study.

* Express gratitude. Be constantly grateful for our open minds and ears, very grateful indeed, for very few are being given these gifts in this era.

When in a right attitude, the Holy Spirit will guide us into all the Truth God wants us to have at that moment in time as we grow in Grace and Knowledge. We have seen that 'Progressive Revelation' has taken place over thousands of years as God reveals His plan. We will grow in knowledge 'progressively' as God reveals to each of us what He wants us to know and appreciate at any given time.

The chances are that every human being, regardless of denomination or ministerial rank that would have us follow his or her beliefs, ideas, doctrines are themselves deceived. To listen to, or follow their teachings would lead us to be deceived also.

BEWARE OF COUNTERFEITS

What is a counterfeit? To counterfeit means to imitate something. Counterfeit products are fake replicas of the real product that are virtually indistinguishable from the genuine article.

Indistinguishable that is, unless one has access to highly specialised knowledge concerning that article. We have that specialised knowledge. This whole book will certainly help the reader sort the wheat from the chaff.

If one has ever had the misfortune to be given a counterfeit bank note, they will know about the sinking feeling when they realise that the note is worthless. The art world has been plagued since time immemorial with fake pictures, spurious copies of masterpieces, especially when the original is worth millions. It takes a highly skilled specialist to determine whether a picture is genuine or a cleverly produced fake.

The world is full of many thousands of counterfeit 'Christian' religious organisations, each setting forth their beliefs as 'the Truth'.

How many 'Christian' denominations are there worldwide? World Christianity consists of 6 major groups divided into 300 major ecclesiastical traditions, composed at the last count of over 33,000 distinct denominations in 238 countries. The total number of 'Christians' is generally estimated to be in the region of two billion. How is it possible for so many people to be deceived? Satan is **the** master counterfeiter.

A denomination is defined as an organised Christian church or tradition or religious group or community of believers, whose congregations and members are called by the same denominational name in different areas. Each group regard themselves as one autonomous Christian church distinct from other denominations, churches and traditions by virtue of having similar ecclesiastical traditions and beliefs.

How is this possible? Satan is **the** master counterfeiter!

2 Corinthians 11:13 For such are false apostles, deceitful workers, transforming themselves into the apostles of Christ. 14 And no marvel; for Satan himself is transformed into an angel of light. 15 Therefore it is no great thing if his ministers also be transformed as the ministers of righteousness; whose end shall be according to their works.

Revelation 12:9 And the great dragon was cast out, that old serpent, called the Devil, and Satan, which deceiveth the whole world: he was cast out into the earth, and his angels were cast out with him.

Satan the Devil has indeed deceived the whole world in every aspect of life, and especially in the relationship of human beings to God.

The Devil does not appear with horns and a tail. Both he and his myriad of fallen angels can and do present themselves in many most attractive forms.

In the day that Satan was created his name was Lucifer, the 'lightbringer', the morning 'star'. He was a very beautiful being covered in sparkling jewels. In this passage in

Ezekiel his origins are given as if the 'King of Tyrus', but this description cannot apply to a mere man.

Ezekiel 28:11 Moreover the word of the Lord came unto me, saying, 12 Son of man, take up a lamentation upon the king of Tyrus, and say unto him, Thus saith the Lord God; Thou sealest up the sum, full of wisdom, and perfect in beauty. 13 Thou hast been in Eden the garden of God; every precious stone was thy covering, the sardius, topaz, and the diamond, the beryl, the onyx, and the jasper, the sapphire, the emerald, and the carbuncle, and gold: the workmanship of thy tabrets and of thy pipes was prepared in thee in the day that thou wast created. 14 Thou art the anointed cherub that covereth; and I have set thee so: thou wast upon the holy mountain of God; thou hast walked up and down in the midst of the stones of fire. 15 Thou wast perfect in thy ways from the day that thou wast created, till iniquity was found in thee. 16 By the multitude of thy merchandise they have filled the midst of thee with violence, and thou hast sinned: therefore I will cast thee as profane out of the mountain of God: and I will destroy thee, O covering cherub, from the midst of the stones of fire. 17 Thine heart was lifted up because of thy beauty, thou hast corrupted thy wisdom by reason of thy brightness: I will cast thee to the ground, I will lay thee before kings, that they may behold thee.

The Apostle Peter warns Christians to be wary and vigilant concerning Satan and his wiles.

1 Peter 5:8 Be sober, be vigilant; because your adversary the devil, as a roaring lion, walketh about, seeking whom he may devour:

If anyone saw a lion running towards them, they would run from the terrifying sight, and from the possibility of being torn to shreds. That is not how Satan the Devil appears to humans. He appears as an angel of light.

In Isaiah 14, we get a glimpse of what turned Lucifer into Satan the Adversary of all who would follow Christ in honesty and truth. God created Lucifer with enormous power and capacity, but this led to pride, and to think that he was greater than God Himself, so he tried to attack God.

Isaiah 14:12 How art thou fallen from heaven, O Lucifer, son of the morning! how art thou cut down to the ground, which didst weaken the nations! 13 For thou hast said in thine heart, I will ascend into heaven, I will exalt my throne above the stars of God: I will sit also upon the mount of the congregation, in the sides of the north: 14 I will ascend above the heights of the clouds; I will be like the most High. 15 Yet thou shalt be brought down to hell, to the sides of the pit.

God will cause Satan to come to an end of his power over humankind, but until that time, God is using him to forward and execute His Glorious Plan.

The Devil has very cleverly got the majority of people in the world believing that he does not exist, how clever is that? The Devil also has a high proportion of human beings believing that God does not exist either!

Jeremiah 14:14 Then the Lord said unto me, The prophets prophesy lies in my name: I sent them not, neither have I commanded them, neither spake unto them: they prophesy unto you a false vision and divination, and a thing of nought, and the deceit of their heart.

When God leads us in our study of the Scriptures, it becomes clear that billions of people who think they are Christians are to one degree or another, deceived. In a way this is horrifying, but it is important for the 'called', His ecclesia, to recognise that God actively allows this situation to exist.

We do not use the word 'church' in this book to refer to Christians, as the origin of the word is the name of 'Circe' who was a mythical, foul immoral pagan god, who claimed to turn men into animals. 'Circe' pronounced 'kirky' which also gives rise to the Scottish and Welsh word Kirk.

There is also such a thing as 'selective' deafness and blindness. Many religious denominations choose parts of the Bible to believe and to quote to others, while leaving well alone other verses or section which do not support their ideas or teachings.

The ministers of one church which insists on obedience to the Mosaic Laws by their adherents, were adept at avoiding the book of Galatians for instance, which talks about Christians being no longer under the schoolmaster of that Code.

That organisation, presided over by a wicked, avaricious, lying, immoral man, and other sects, also teach that their members must 'tithe' to the 'Work', or they would be guilty of robbing God. The truth of God's Word is that tithing was only to be handled by the Levitical Priesthood, and the tithes were devoted to the provisioning and maintenance of the running of the Temple for as long as the Temple existed. If there is no Temple and no Levites, then to tell people to tithe is to break the Law, and those who tithe to false ministers are also breaking the Law!

In the first chapter of the book of Job, it records conversations between God and Satan the Devil. It is worth taking the time to meditate on that first chapter of Job. From those inspired words in the Holy Bible we can learn a very important principle. God does allow Satan to deceive and afflict people, but strictly under His watchful eye and total control.

We also know from our studies of the Bible that God has 'blinded' and 'deafened' the vast majority of human beings on the planet, so that they cannot 'see' or 'hear' the truth unless God actively gives anyone that gift.

Matthew 15:12 Then came his disciples, and said unto him, Knowest thou that the Pharisees were offended, after they heard this saying? 13 But he answered and said, Every plant, which my heavenly Father hath not planted, shall be rooted up. 14 Let them alone: they be blind leaders of the blind. And if the blind lead the blind, both shall fall into the ditch.

This is unfortunately true of religious leaders of every persuasion in this day and age. Jesus warns in His Holy Bible many times not to be taken in by 'false prophets'.

Matthew 7:15 Beware of false prophets (or pastors or ministers etc.,), which come to you in sheep's clothing, but inwardly they are ravening wolves. 16 Ye shall know them by their fruits. Do men gather grapes of thorns, or figs of thistles?

Sheep look so harmless, do they not? We cannot really know what goes on any organisation in secret, hidden from the 'flock'. Floods of evidence of evildoing by churchmen and women have come to light in recent years. Sometimes their activities are known to their colleagues and superiors, yet nothing is done to restrain them, sometimes over decades of depraved behaviour. And when their 'fruits' do come to light, sadly they are soon forgotten in a constant stream of media reports of horrors in this world.

Surely one might think that cannot apply to this pastor, he is such a nice man. Well, he may look fine in his 'sheep's clothing' he may carry and quote from a Bible, but is he a true minister of God?

Dr. Martin always placed great emphasis on the fact that a Christian needs to study the Bible very carefully. We need to be mindful of the knowledge of 'Progressive Revelation' in order to systematise our minds to understand exactly what applies to us today in this era, and what does not. He reminds us of the scripture we all know by heart:

2 Timothy 2:15 Study to shew thyself approved unto God, a workman that needeth not to be ashamed, rightly dividing (partitioning) the word of truth.

The 'Truth' cannot be divided, certainly not into what is right and wrong, or truth from error as there is no error, since the Truth IS the Truth. So what is meant? The word 'divided' actually means 'partitioning' or 'cutting' the truth into its dispensations, in order to be clear to whom, when, where, what, why, and how, and indeed whether different scriptures apply to us in our era.

Many are deceived into thinking that ALL the Bible applies to EVERYONE, always and for all time. This is just not so as we have seen.

Some truths applied specifically to Adam and Eve, some to Noah, some to Abraham, to Moses, to the Prophets, to Israelites, and these truths which were always truths have expanded over time. Truths have periods of being more relevant to some people than to others. The different dispensations cannot be absolutely 'systematised', or harmonised, or arbitrarily 'dognatised', as circumstances altered cases, as does the 'Progression of Revelation'. It is essential to understand the timing of different revelations.

You cannot make truth into error, but it is possible to be in error if it is misapplied or put to work inappropriately. We can review past truths, and glean more information. We can examine prophecy, history written by Christ in advance, to have an idea what is coming. We can be carefully systematic in our studies. We can be really dogmatic about absolute truths like the fruits of the Spirit, and avoid giving offence by being dogmatic inappropriately.

Truths that were emphatically 'physical', still have a physical aspect to them, but are now also spiritual and even more difficult or even impossible for the Christian to observe unless we have the help of the Holy Spirit.

Only with the ongoing help of our Elder Brother, and continually having the flow of the Holy Spirit renewed in our minds as we study can we grow in Grace and knowledge. Selah.

The next chapter will deal somewhat with Old Testament history.

CHAPTER 8
ESSENTIALS OF OLD TESTAMENT HISTORY

A 'broad brush' study of history is needed properly to understand doctrine, and what the Word of God has to teach us in this era. The world's scholars think that they are the 'authorities' on historical events, and that the Bible is in error in many areas. The exact opposite is true.

The Bible, written by our Creator, Jesus Christ, is *THE* authority. The Bible contains the truth about the significant events of the world since Adam, and should be our guide.

Where conventional knowledge about history differs from the Biblical record, we should look to see where men's ideas are at fault, and not blame the Scriptures.

The Bible is **the** standard to enable a proper understanding of Old Testament History. The Holy Scriptures give information about Palestine, Egypt, and other areas prior to the 6th Century which is not available anywhere else because of the almost total destruction of all available historical records by Nebuchadnezzar when he came to power.

Historians find it very difficult to piece together details of the centuries between the flood and the 6th Century B.C. The Bible does not give many details of this period, but what it does say about people and events of history are extremely important keys to the proper understanding of secular history. Not the other way around.

Archaeologists can only properly interpret finds from digs correctly if they harmonise their findings with the Biblical record. Towns and cities over millennia were built, and went into decay. When rebuilding took place, the new towns and cities were built on top of the old, often stones and materials were used from the old ruins to build the new buildings. This sometimes means that when a tel or site is excavated, there could be multiple layers, each one of which would yield fragments of history of the time it was built.

There are over twenty-five thousand tels or mounds yet to be explored, where no doubt vast amounts of information exist, lie buried waiting to be discovered.

To have a mental overview, it is important to bear in mind the dates of the various significant 'benchmarks' of history, which if taken as indications, can help us form a picture.

Adam to the Flood was 1656 years, (or 2369 B.C.), the period from the 1st Adam to the 2nd Adam Jesus Christ was 4000 years, give or take. When we add the 2000 years or so A.D., we arrive at 6000 years, the accepted probable approximate length of humankind's period on earth.

This does not mean to suggest at all that the earth was created only 6000 years ago, as the Bible gives indications that it was in existence for an indeterminate period before it was created, It was then reformed by God in six days to provide a suitable environment for His children as is described in the early chapters of Genesis.

The Tower of Babel was being built around 2160 B.C., when the confusion of languages took place. God worked with Abraham, Isaac, and Jacob (whose name was changed to Israel) between 1900 and 1700 B.C.

Egypt was a very highly developed civilisation prior to the Exodus. The Israelites were in Egypt for 430 years, between approximately 1920 – 1490, prior to the Exodus.

Exodus 12:40 Now the sojourning of the children of Israel, who dwelt in Egypt, was four hundred and thirty years. 41 And it came to pass at the end of the four hundred and thirty years, even the selfsame day it came to pass, that all the hosts of the Lord went out from the land of Egypt.

When the Israelites departed in approximately 1490 B.C., the ten plagues left the country of Egypt in a deplorable state from which it never really recovered.

Then came the four hundred and eighty years of the Judges, Kings, David and Solomon who built the Temple around 1015 B.C.

1 Kings 6:1 And it came to pass in the four hundred and eightieth year after the children of Israel were come out of the land of Egypt, in the fourth year of Solomon's reign over Israel, in the month Zif, which is the second month, that he began to build the house of the Lord.

The ten tribes of Israel were carried captive by the Assyrians in 721 B.C., and from that time forward, when they were released from captivity were dispersed and became known as the 'Lost Tribes' of Israel as their migrations were so diverse over time.

Judah was taken and held captive to Babylon around 586 B.C. for seventy years, after which around fifty thousand people returned to Palestine when they were allowed to do so by Cyrus. However many who had developed businesses preferred to remain in the area of Babylon.

2 Chronicles 36:21 To fulfil the word of the Lord by the mouth of Jeremiah, until the land had enjoyed her sabbaths: for as long as she lay desolate she kept sabbath, to fulfil threescore and ten years.

Notice carefully that the Decree of Cyrus was at the end of the exactly seventy years prophesied by Christ through Jeremiah, so that period must be correct. However if one takes the various different dates offered by 'scholars' for the captivity, and the return, there is rarely a difference of exactly seventy years.

2 Chronicles 36:22 Now in the first year of Cyrus king of Persia, that the word of the Lord spoken by the mouth of Jeremiah might be accomplished, the Lord stirred up the

spirit of Cyrus king of Persia, that he made a proclamation throughout all his kingdom, and put it also in writing, saying 23 Thus saith Cyrus king of Persia, All the kingdoms of the earth hath the Lord God of heaven given me; and he hath charged me to build him an house in Jerusalem, which is in Judah. Who is there among you of all his people? The Lord his God be with him, and let him go up.

So Cyrus, no doubt under the influence of God, wanted to build a Temple in Jerusalem, and ordered the Jews, mostly those who were of a religious persuasion, to return to Israel and build it. It is recorded in the Minor Prophets, that the religious leaders of the Jews failed to carry this decree out for at least nineteen years during which time they built nice houses for themselves. God was not impressed.

Haggai 1:3 Then came the word of the Lord by Haggai the prophet, saying 4 Is it time for you, O ye, to dwell in your cieled houses, and this house (the new Temple) lie waste? 5 Now therefore thus saith the Lord of hosts; Consider your ways.

Ezra 1:2 Thus saith Cyrus king of Persia, The Lord God of heaven hath given me all the kingdoms of the earth; and he hath charged me to build him an house at Jerusalem, which is in Judah.

Note: Dr. Martin was a very highly respected historian in many quarters, and especially at the Hebrew University, but the Compiler of this book is definitely not a historian. Secular historians and religious 'authorities' are not always in agreement with all the commonly used benchmark dates. For the purpose of this study, this is not important, so long as their calculations are in line with the Biblical record. However, disentangling all the many apparently so-called 'conflicting' chronological indicators in the Bible is no simple task.

Here it is only intended to give a broad brush picture of historical dates.

The Bible is a book about God's plan of redemption for His human children, it is not a complete history, but what it does include gives us glimpses of the past which would be impossible otherwise to understand. What it does do is to give us God's story, 'HisStory' so to speak, His way of looking at things, written in His 'language' and style which obscures the meaning from humans unless they have help from the Holy Spirit .

The 6th Century B.C., is pivotal as it was the start of the Babylonish type of world government which will remain in power, although largely hidden in our era, until Christ's second coming, when global powers will be beaten into powder and blown away, and the Kingdom of God will be established.

Daniel 2:34 Thou sawest till that a stone was cut out without hands, which smote the image upon his feet that were of iron and clay, and brake them to pieces. 35 Then was the iron, the clay, the brass, the silver, and the gold, broken to pieces together, and became like the chaff of the summer threshingfloors; and the wind carried them away, that no place was found for them: and the stone that smote the image became a great mountain, and filled the whole earth.

Daniel 2:38 And **wheresoever the children of men dwell,** the beasts of the field and the fowls of the heaven hath he given into thine hand, and hath made thee ruler over them **all.** Thou art this head of gold.

Wheresoever men dwell, that implies world, global control, total government. The government of Babylon will be established and control the activities of the whole world overtly for a period of time, then it will be hidden for millennia and will operate behind the scenes until the second coming of Christ.

Daniel 2:39 And after thee shall arise another kingdom inferior to thee, and another third kingdom of brass, which shall bear rule over all the earth. 40 And the fourth kingdom shall be strong as iron: forasmuch as iron breaketh in pieces and subdueth all things: and as iron that breaketh all these, shall it break in pieces and bruise....44 And in the days of these kings shall the God of heaven set up a Kingdom, which shall never be destroyed: and the kingdom shall not be left to other people, but it shall break in pieces and consume all these kingdoms, and it shall stand for ever.

The Babylonish system certainly exists worldwide today, unrealized by most, behind public view, and is nowunder the control of unseen powers both human and spiritual.

Ephesians 6:12 For we wrestle not (only) against flesh and blood, but (also) against principalities, against powers, against the rulers of the darkness of this world, against spiritual wickedness in high places.

In the time of Solomon his fabulous riches, power and control were worldwide. He sent ships around the world on voyages lasting three years gathering gold, wealth, fauna and flora for his estates. The amount of gold in the Temple that Solomon built was beyond our imagination now.

Solomon wrote 5000 books, and many songs and poems. We only have one song in the Bible, the Song of Solomon. Only one book and some proverbs, and it is to be wondered what happened to the other 4999. In the book of Ecclesiastes Solomon wrote:

Ecclesiastes 12:12 And further, by these, my son, be admonished: of making many books there is no end; and much study is a weariness of the flesh.

Kings and Queens came from all over the world to see the seven wonders of the world in Solomon's kingdom.

2 Chronicles 9:1 And when the queen of Sheba heard of the fame of Solomon, she came to prove Solomon with hard questions at Jerusalem, with a very great company,

and camels that bare spices, and gold in abundance, and precious stones: and when she was come to Solomon, she communed with him of all that was in her heart. 2 And Solomon told her all her questions: and there was nothing hid from Solomon which he told her not. 3 And when the queen of Sheba had seen the wisdom of Solomon, and the house that he had built, 4 And the meat of his table, and the sitting of his servants, and the attendance of his ministers, and their apparel; his cupbearers also, and their apparel; and his ascent by which he went up into the house of the Lord; there was no more spirit in her. 5 And she said to the king, It was a true report which I heard in mine own land of thine acts, and of thy wisdom: 6 Howbeit I believed not their words, until I came, and mine eyes had seen it: and, behold, the one half of the greatness of thy wisdom was not told me: for thou exceedest the fame that I heard. 7 Happy are thy men, and happy are these thy servants, which stand continually before thee, and hear thy wisdom. 8 Blessed be the Lord thy God, which delighted in thee to set thee on his throne, to be king for the Lord thy God: because thy God loved Israel, to establish them for ever, therefore made he thee king over them, to do judgment and justice. 9 And she gave the king an hundred and twenty talents of gold, and of spices great abundance, and precious stones: neither was there any such spice as the queen of Sheba gave king Solomon. 10 And the servants also of Huram, and the servants of Solomon, which brought gold from Ophir, brought algum trees and precious stones.

The Queen of Sheba gave Solomon 120 talents of gold, or $72,000,000 worth of gold at

$400.00 per ounce, to add to his already massive wealth.

Psalm 72:10 The kings of Tarshish and of the isles shall bring presents: the kings of Sheba and Seba shall offer gifts. 11 Yea, all kings shall fall down before him: all nations shall serve him.

Solomon's power was worldwide. Yet, secular historians find it impossible to believe the extent of Solomon's wealth, and have great difficulty in finding any reference to his works in his time. For this reason many scholars even question whether Solomon ever existed. Why might there be no evidence of his glory? Such wealth would definitely be the prime target of those who came after his time.

The wonders of Solomon's kingdom were plundered to the point where no evidence of them exists in our era. Even Josephus, the renowned Jewish historian writing in the 1st Century B.C., could only find two brief references to Solomon in that he exchanged riddles with King Hiram who was able to better Solomon in solving them.

So were it not for the Biblical record, we would know virtually nothing at all about the life and times of Solomon. This is the case because in the 6th Century B.C., King Nebuchadnezzar destroyed all the historical records and libraries he could locate in order to sever the links of past times for all the peoples under his control. This destruction of history helped him to establish his power and the control of minds.

One day, as knowledge is increased, the Bible record will be vindicated and verified as an accurate record of events of history. The Biblical record may be sparse, but without it we would have no knowledge of significant sections of history. Because the Bible was written under the inspiration of Christ, it cannot be anything but a true record.

John 17:17 Sanctify them through thy truth: thy Word is truth.

For our studies, the pre-flood era is not that important to us now. Historically speaking, although very interesting, and we can learn a lot from the snippets about that time in the Bible, and we need a broad brush picture of history after the flood.

There are seven periods of Biblical history that do help to give us an overview:

One: The post flood era from Noah, including the record of the list of the nations extant at the time when Moses wrote about them in Genesis 10.

Two: The Patriarch period of Abraham, Isaac, Jacob

Three: The 215 years when Joseph and Israel were in Egypt during a period of great wealth and the glory of a very sophisticated civilisation and a population explosion until the Exodus. There was also the establishment of other nations at that time.

Four: Then the 480 year period of the dark ages after the Exodus in 1490 B.C., because the Children of Israel had lost all their expertise and any real idea of civilisation during the forty years wandering in the Sinai desert, followed by the period of the Judges and then the Kings.

Five: Then David and Solomon's time of great wealth around 1000 B.C., magnificent landscaping, buildings, artefacts all of which were stripped away after his death to leave virtually no trace.

Six: Then the 6th Century B.C., when all available records were destroyed by Nebuchadnezzar when he came to power.

Seven: Then the time of Ezra and the canonisation of the 22 books of the Old Testament in 457 B.C... when he wrote the books of I & II Chronicles (which were originally one book), Ezra, and Nehemiah and included edits and spelling changes to bring the books up to date. Ezra wrote in Hebrew and Aramaic and was skilled in both languages.

We need to go to secular historical records to gain an understanding of the period between the Canonisation by Ezra in 457 B.C., and the New Testament era beginning with John the Baptist in 4 B.C.

It is also enlightening to make study of secular history between 100 A.D., and 2000 A.D., of relevant events concerning world religions and the development of Christianity as it evolved into the Christianity extant in our era.

RELIGIONS – FORMED BEFORE THE 6th CENTURY B.C.

Hinduism – India 2000 B.C. Judaism – Moses 1500 – 1350 B.C.

RELIGIONS – FORMED AROUND THE 6th CENTURY B.C.

Zoroastrianism Near East Zoroaster 628-527 B.C. Buddhism - India Buddha 563-483 B.C. Jaianism – India Mahavira 599-527 B.C.

Taoism – China/Japan Lao Tse 580-500 B.C.

Confucianism – China/Japan Confucius 551-479 B.C.

These religions have continued to dominate the Oriental and Eastern nations which largely consist of Japhetic peoples. Japheth means enlarge, and their descendants form the majority of the population of the earth.

GREEK PHILOSOPHERS - In the 4th Century B.C., came the Greek philosophers who started a new period of philosophy. They espoused immoral concepts and foul behaviour that began to dominate the whole world's thinking.

Their ideas replaced the Sophists, who indulged in specious and false reasoning, and took the thoughts and opinions of the individual. The first was Socrates (469-399 BC) he rejected his predecessor's notions, and made the thoughts and opinions of 'the people' his starting-point. Socrates was followed by Plato, Aristotle, the Stoics, then the Epicureans, followed by the Sceptics. Many popular elements of Greek philosophy certainly became interwoven into early Christianity.

The English word Philosophy has its roots in the Greek words 'Philo' which means 'love of', and 'sophia' which means wisdom. Sophia became 'sophistry' which was defined as the art of clever deceptive argument and false reasoning, a kind of worldy 'wisdom'.

Paul speaks of the Greek influences which infected Christianity with its worldly, fleshly and perverted immoral ideas in his time. All these widely differing ways of approaching a Deity became the confused mish-mash of conflicting doctrines that still exist in 'Churchianity' today.

1 Corinthians 1:20 Where is the wise? where is the scribe? where is the disputer of this world? hath not God made foolish the wisdom of this world?

1 Corinthians 2:5 That your faith should not stand in the wisdom of men, but in the power of God. 6 Howbeit we speak wisdom among them that are perfect: yet not the wisdom of this world, nor of the princes of this world, that come to nought: 7 But we speak the wisdom of God in a mystery, even the hidden wisdom, which God ordained before the world unto our glory:

1 Corinthians 3:19 For the wisdom of this world is foolishness with God. For it is written, He taketh the wise in their own craftiness.

2 Corinthians 1:12 For our rejoicing is this, the testimony of our conscience, that in simplicity and godly sincerity, not with fleshly wisdom, but by the grace of God, we have had our conversation in the world, and more abundantly to you-ward.

Christians in the 21st century would do well to be extremely wary of the notions of 'philosophy'. The title of 'Philosopher' has an aura of professionalism and of scholarship, but a careful examination of many philosophical ideas reveals that they often present subtle reasonings that are actually opposed to the truths of the Bible.

RELIGIONS – FORMED IN THE POST CHRIST ERA

Christianity by Christ 1-33 A.D.

False Christianity mixed with pagan religions 33 A.D. - 21st Century A.D. False Christianity adopted by Rome and spread in the 1st Century A.D. False Christianity adopted by Constantine the Great in the 3rd Century A.D. Islam – Near East by Muhammed 570-632 A.D.

Sikhism – India by Guru Nanak 1469-1538 A.D. Baha'i – Near East by Baha'u'llah 1817-1892 A.D.

Important Principle and Key to understanding Bible history

Here is a very important key to the understanding of the Biblical records.

It is important to know when and where the books of the Bible were written, and realise that they would not be using the names and places that were extant at the time of the period they were writing about. Over time, geographical names change.

Those who wrote the books, wrote them with the background of the time they lived. So when Moses wrote about pre-flood times, and in describing the location of the Garden of Eden for instance, he was using terms that would be understood by his readers in the 15th Century B.C.

Genesis 2:8 And the Lord God planted a garden eastward in Eden; and there he put the man whom he had formed. 9 And out of the ground made the Lord God to grow every tree that is pleasant to the sight, and good for food; the tree of life also in the midst of the garden, and the tree of knowledge of good and evil.

Moses was in Palestine when he was writing this, and when it says 'eastward' in Eden, it is referring to an area Eastward of Palestine.

Genesis 2:10 And a river went out of Eden to water the garden; and from thence it was parted, and became into four heads. 11 The name of the first is Pison: that is it which compasseth the whole land of Havilah, where there is gold;

So there was a single river which divided into four rivers. The first one Pison is not one that can be identified with certainty in our era.

Genesis 2:12 And the gold of that land is good: there is bdellium and the onyx stone. 13 And the name of the second river is Gihon: the same is it that compasseth the whole land of Ethiopia.

When it says 'Ethiopia' (Cush), it is not talking about the 'Ethiopia' in Africa or in India. There were two areas of Cush, the other area was to the East and the North in the area of what is now called Iran.

Genesis 2:14 And the name of the third river is Hiddekel: that is it which goeth toward the east of Assyria. And the fourth river is Euphrates. Assyria was named after Ashur a decendant of Shem.

The river Hiddakel was undoubtedly the Tigris, and this is in a way confirmed by the name of the fourth river which was the Euphrates.

So the area of the Garden of Eden was in the geographical region of Mesopotamian the land between the great rivers, where Iran and Iraq are as we know it today.

When Christ through Ezra assembled the Canon in 457 B.C., he made many small edits and changes in the books so that the people of his day would be able to understand what and where he was writing about.

Sadly, ignorant people pounce on these apparent 'discrepancies' and use them to ridicule and discredit the Bible.

The account of the flood and the eight people who entered the ark, gives us the understanding of where all the people on earth today originated from.

Genesis 9:18 And the sons of Noah, that went forth of the ark, were Shem, and Ham, and Japheth: and Ham is the father of Canaan. 19 These are the three sons of Noah: and of them was the whole earth overspread.

Every one of the six or seven billion people on earth today is a descendant of these three sons of Noah.

Again let us remind ourselves that these are not the words of a man, they are the inspired Words of our Creator and Messiah, Christ Jesus.

So the list of the nations written by Moses in Genesis 10 are those nations that existed in the time of Moses.

Genesis 9:20 And Noah began to be an husbandman, and he planted a vineyard: 21 And he drank of the wine, and was drunken; and he was uncovered within his tent. 22 And Ham, the father of Canaan, saw the nakedness of his father, and told his two brethren without. 23 And Shem and Japheth took a garment, and laid it upon both their shoulders, and went backward, and covered the nakedness of their father; and their faces were backward, and they saw not their father's nakedness. 24 And Noah awoke from his wine, and knew what his younger son had done unto him.

And what had his younger son Ham done to his drunken father? He had emasculated him so that Noah would be unable to father any more children. Ham was only interested in furthering his own future, and did not want any more siblings to share his heritage, so he made sure of it.

Genesis 9:25 And he said, Cursed be Canaan; a servant of servants shall he be unto his brethren. 26 And he said, Blessed be the Lord God of Shem; and Canaan shall be his servant.

So Ham's son Canaan was cursed. Canaanites occupied the Palestine area after the flood, and inhabited the Promised Land into which the Israelites finally went after their forty years of wandering in the Sinai desert.

So Canaanites, but not all Ham's descendants, would be servants to Shem's descendants. And so many did so become, even to this day. Other descendants of Ham became peoples of great renown, authority and power. Egyptians and many other powerful nations have mainly descended from Ham.

However it was Noah's son Japheth's descendants that would expand in greater numbers.

Genesis 9:27 God shall enlarge Japheth, and he shall dwell in the tents of Shem; and Canaan shall be his servant.

Japheth means 'enlarge'. It is interesting to note that the descendants of Japheth, who are in the main the yellow people with the epicanthic fold on the eyes, comprise the greatest number of the inhabitants of this earth in China, Japan, and Mongolia. These descendants of Japheth can be mostly yellow, but some white or brown as over centuries many have intermarried.

When Japheth began their expansion, they moved Northwards into Europe into Cyprus or Chittim, Italy, and Greece, known as Javan in the Bible. Some even into North America, the American Indians and the Eskimos have similar skull shapes and facial features to the Oriental people. Later they were driven out of Europe and went East and North leaving names of places behind them.

Much like when people establish a business, then sell it to others who like to retain the original name of the founder.

The state of Massachusetts was originally populated with American Indians, the 'Massachusett' tribe of Native Americans, meaning "at or about the great hill". Over time, all of whom died out or removed to other areas to the point where today there is not one Indian still living in Massachusetts, but the name of the tribe lives on in the name of the State.

Ezekiel tells in chapter 38 where many of these people were in Ezekiel's time. Some religious denominations think that Gog and Magog, Meshech and Tubal are going to invade Israel in the latter days, but a careful study will reveal that the battle referred to will occur in the Millennial era. It is at a time when the inhabitants of Israel are dwelling safely, and this has yet to happen, and will not happen until after Christ's return.

Ezekiel 38:14 Therefore, son of man, prophesy and say unto Gog, Thus saith the Lord God; In that day when my people of Israel dwelleth safely, shalt thou not know it? 15 And thou shalt come from thy place out of the north parts, thou, and many people with thee, all of them riding upon horses, a great company, and a mighty army: 16 And thou shalt come up against my people of Israel, as a cloud to cover the land; it shall be in the latter days, and I will bring thee against my land, that the heathen may know me, when I shall be sanctified in thee, O Gog, before their eyes.

Since most historical records have been thoroughly and systematically destroyed at various times in the history of the world, it is only by believing the veracity of the Holy Scriptures and accepting the total authority of God's Word can we even begin arrive at a clear perspective and to make any sense of the history of human beings, God's Children.

The next chapter will deal with the era of the 6th Century B.C., when God moved to cause established governments to decline, and to motivate King Nebuchadnezzar of Babylon to bring in a new type of government which became the Origin of Western Civilisation.

CHAPTER 9

WORLD POWERS DECLINE - 6TH C.B.C. - A 'NEW AGE' DAWNS

In the 6th Century B.C., God intervened dramatically in world affairs and changed the course of history, and the way the world was governed from that time forward which would endure until the second coming of Christ.

To announce His intentions, and tell the world at that time what was going to happen in the future, God appointed a Prophet, a young lad about seventeen years old called Jeremiah, to bear witness to the prophecies and to record the future history of the world.

Jeremiah 1:1 The words of Jeremiah the son of Hilkiah, of the priests that were in Anathoth in the land of Benjamin:

There was a High Priest by the name of Hilkiah, and Jeremiah may have been his son, but the Bible does not say. Anathoth is a little village almost 3 miles north-east of Jerusalem.

Jeremiah 1:2 To whom the word of the Lord came in the days of Josiah (640-609 B.C.) the son of Amon king of Judah, in the thirteenth year (627 B.C.) of his reign. 3 It came also in the days of Jehoiakim (609-598 B.C.) the son of Josiah king of Judah, unto the end of the eleventh year (586 B.C.) of Zedekiah (597-586 B.C.) the son of Josiah king of Judah, unto the carrying away of Jerusalem captive (587 B.C.) in the fifth month.

Jeremiah lived at the same time as Daniel, who was somewhat younger, and their prophesies are linked by the time frame in which they were given.

Daniel 1:1 In the third year of the reign of Jehoiakim king of Judah (606 B.C.) came Nebuchadnezzar king of Babylon unto Jerusalem, and besieged it.

This was in 606 B.C., at the start of the 70 years captivity. Daniel the Prophet was among the captives in Babylon, where God was working with the mind of King Nebuchadnezzar. Jeremiah was working among captive Judah and the House of Jacob.

Jeremiah, a priest, was the 'axial' prophet in a time of momentous change. He would be working among Israel as God ushered in a 'new age' and new era during the 6th Century

B.C. Being such a young man, Jeremiah was, to say the least, daunted by the task, but he had the power and authority of YHWH with him who had known him in the womb.

Jeremiah 1:4 Then the word of the Lord came unto me, saying, 5 Before I formed thee in the belly I knew thee; and before thou camest forth out of the womb I sanctified thee, and I ordained thee a prophet unto the nations.

Jeremiah prophesied for about 40 years between 627-587 B.C. proclaiming God's prophetic warning messages to the rebellious and idolatrous Jews and Israelites.

Jeremiah 1:6 Then said I, Ah, Lord God! behold, I cannot speak: for I am a child. 7 But the Lord said unto me, Say not, I am a child: for thou shalt go to all that I shall send thee, and whatsoever I command thee thou shalt speak. 8 Be not afraid of their faces: for I am with thee to deliver thee, saith the Lord.

As time went on, Jeremiah would have good reason to be afraid of the reactions of the religious priests and lay people of Judah who heard God's frightful predictions from his lips.

Jeremiah 1:9 Then the Lord put forth his hand, and touched my mouth. And the Lord said unto me, Behold, I have put my words in thy mouth. 10 See, I have this day set thee over the nations and over the kingdoms, to root out, and to pull down, and to destroy, and to throw down, to build, and to plant.

Note that God was setting Jeremiah in a position of authority over the nations, not just Judah and Israel.

Jeremiah's commission was in six parts: Four destructive, and two constructive to build and to plant. The first four were to:

1. Root out 2. Pull down 3. Destroy 4. Throw down.

God was about to set in motion the destruction of the entire system of worldly government that had existed since the flood of Noah in 2369 B.C., until in the 6th Century B.C. The nations, the kings, all established powers would begin to go immediately into a decline, and whose influence would quickly diminish, and be heard of no more on the world scene.

God was going to announce to the world through Jeremiah, that all the power and the known systems of government that had existed in the past would be 'rooted out', 'pulled down', 'destroyed', and thrown down'. There would soon be no remnant left of the power once held by nations like Egypt, Edom, Ammon, Moab. This would also be true of Judah and Israel because of their continual idolatry and rebellion against God.

Jeremiah 9:25 Behold, the days come, saith the Lord, that I will punish all them which are circumcised with the uncircumcised; 26 Egypt, and Judah, and Edom, and the children of Ammon, and Moab, and all that are in the utmost corners, that dwell in the wilderness: for all these nations are uncircumcised, and all the house of Israel are uncircumcised in the heart.

Jeremiah would also announce God's Plan 'to Build and to Plant'.

God would take away all power held by existing nations because He planned in the 5th and 6th parts of Jeremiah's commission 'to build and to plant', a completely new type and system of Government which would soon become a world dominating power.

A new world order which would control the politics, economics, religion, and philosophies of the world, and which would endure in different forms from the 6th Century B.C., until the second coming of Christ.

God would begin to work with the mind of the most powerful ruler in the world, King Nebuchadnezzar of Babylon and use him not only to punish Judah and Israel, but to prepare the King to set the scene for global government. The nature of this government would become the framework for what is known in our era as 'Western' civilisation.

Jeremiah 1:11 Moreover the word of the Lord came unto me, saying, Jeremiah, what seest thou? And I said, I see a rod of an almond tree. 12 Then said the Lord unto me, Thou hast well seen: for I will hasten my word to perform it.

The rod of the Almond Tree, which is first to bud and blossom, was a symbol of life. The Tree of Life in the Garden of Eden was undoubtedly an Almond Tree. Aaron's rod that budded that was kept thereafter in the Ark of the Covenant which was of Almond wood. God indicated to Jeremiah that He was going to begin to perform His Will immediately.

Next God tells Jeremiah what is about the happen, in that he will shortly see turmoil like a seething pot, and that evil people will come from the North and enter the gates of Jerusalem to destroy it.

Jeremiah 1:13 And the word of the Lord came unto me the second time, saying, What seest thou? And I said, I see a seething pot; and the face thereof is toward the north. 14 Then the Lord said unto me, Out of the north an evil shall break forth upon all the inhabitants of the land. 15 For, lo, I will call all the families of the kingdoms of the north, saith the Lord; and they shall come, and they shall set every one his throne at the entering of the gates of Jerusalem, and against all the walls thereof round about, and against all the cities of Judah.

God explains to Jeremiah that the evil is coming from the North, by King Nebuchadnezzar from Babylon, to punish God's people due to their forsaking Him, and because of their persistent idolatries and adulteries with other gods.

Judah was taken captive to Babylon around 586 B.C.

Jeremiah 1:16 And I will utter my judgments against them touching all their wickedness, who have forsaken me, and have burned incense unto other gods, and worshipped the works of their own hands.

God says, and do not be afraid Jeremiah or fearful of those who hear My words through you because I am going to protect you.

Jeremiah 1:17 Thou therefore gird up thy loins, and arise, and speak unto them all that I command thee: be not dismayed at their faces, lest I confound thee before them. 18 For, behold, I have made thee this day a defenced city, and an iron pillar, and brasen walls against the whole land, against the kings of Judah, against the princes thereof, against the priests thereof, and against the people of the land. 19 And they shall fight against thee; but they shall not prevail against thee; for I am with thee, saith the Lord, to deliver thee.

Everyone in Judah was going to be against Jeremiah because he would be repeatedly proclaiming the sins of the Jews and the destruction of Jerusalem and the Temple; all those in authority, Kings, Princes, Priests and also the people; a terrifying thought, but God is with him.

The entire book of Jeremiah exemplifies the theme of the Bible that is repeated from Genesis to Revelation. Over and over again in too many places to list, God pleads with Israel to keep His laws so that He can bless them, and begs them not forsake Him, or worship other gods in idolatry, but they do not listen.

Jeremiah 25:1 The word that came to Jeremiah concerning all the people of Judah in the fourth year of Jehoiakim (606 B.C.) the son of Josiah king of Judah, that was the first year of Nebuchadrezzar king of Babylon; 2 The which Jeremiah the prophet spake unto all the people of Judah, and to all the inhabitants of Jerusalem, saying, 3 From the thirteenth year of Josiah the son of Amon king of Judah, even unto this day, that is the three and twentieth year, the word of the Lord hath come unto me, and I have spoken unto you, rising early and speaking; (for these many years) but ye have not hearkened. 4 And the Lord hath sent unto you all his servants the prophets, rising early and sending them; but ye have not hearkened, nor inclined your ear to hear. 5 They said, Turn ye again now every one from his evil way, and from the evil of your doings, and dwell in the land that the Lord hath given unto you and to your fathers for ever and ever: 6 And go not after other gods to serve them, and to worship them, and provoke me not to anger with the works of your hands; and I will do you no hurt. 7 Yet ye have not hearkened unto me, saith the Lord; that ye might provoke me to anger with the works of your hands to your own hurt.

Jeremiah spoke out to Judah over 23 years, but they just would not listen, or take any notice of God's warnings that He was giving through him. They simply hated Jeremiah for his predictions.

The extreme Patience of God is clear over more than a thousand years, but in the end, punishment from ignoring God had to come to come. God is going to use Nebuchadrezzar the king of Babylon to punish God's people, and notice that **Nebuchadrezzar** (Nebuchadnezzar), the head of gold is referred to on more than one occasion as God's servant.

Jeremiah 25:8 Therefore thus saith the Lord of hosts; Because ye have not heard my words, 9 Behold, I will send and take all the families of the north, saith the Lord, and Nebuchadrezzar the king of Babylon, *my servant*, and will bring them against this land, and against the inhabitants thereof, and against all these nations round about, and will utterly destroy them, and make them an astonishment, and an hissing, and perpetual desolations. 10 Moreover I will take from them the voice of mirth, and the voice of gladness, the voice of the bridegroom, and the voice of the bride, the sound of the millstones, and the light of the candle. 11 And this whole land shall be a desolation, and an astonishment; and these nations shall serve the king of Babylon seventy years.

Notice again, the definitive period of seventy years according to the inspired word of God. Some Scholars dispute this period.

As explained above, God was about to set in motion the destruction of the entire existing system of worldly government .The nations, the kings, all established powers that would go immediately into a decline, are listed in the 25th chapter of Jeremiah. Judah is going to be punished, and all the other nations of the earth will go into decline.

Jeremiah 25:15 For thus saith the Lord God of Israel unto me; Take the wine cup of this fury at my hand, and cause all the nations, to whom I send thee, to drink it. 16 And they shall drink, and be moved, and be mad, because of the sword that I will send among them. 17 Then took I the cup at the Lord's hand, and made all the nations to drink, unto whom the Lord had sent me: 18 To wit, Jerusalem, and the cities of Judah, and the kings thereof, and the princes thereof, to make them a desolation, an astonishment, an hissing, and a curse; as it is this day;

Then comes the list of all the nations of the earth which are going to lose their power and influence in the world.

Jeremiah 25:19 Pharaoh king of Egypt, and his servants, and his princes, and all his people; 20 And all the mingled people, and all the kings of the land of Uz, and all the kings of the land of the Philistines, and Ashkelon, and Azzah, and Ekron, and the remnant of Ashdod, 21 Edom, and Moab, and the children of Ammon, 22 And all the kings of Tyrus, and all the kings of Zidon, and the kings of the isles which are beyond the sea, 23 Dedan, and Tema, and Buz, and all that are in the utmost corners, 24 And all the kings of Arabia, and all the kings of the mingled people that dwell in the desert, 25 And all the kings of Zimri, and all the kings of Elam, and all the kings of the Medes,

The last nation to lose its power will be the King of Sheshach (or Shishak). Bible Commentaries and historians say there is no record of a 'King Sheshach', so they use this to question the accuracy of the Bible record. The reason they cannot find it is because there never was a king by that name.

The word 'Sheshach' is a cipher, a code, made up by reversing the letters of the Hebrew alphabet that make up the word 'Babylon'. Instead of BBL, taking the Hebrew letters from the end of the alphabet in reverse order it becomes SSK, or 'Sheshach'. Bible 'scholars notwithstanding, the Scriptures do not lie, nor make false statements.

Every relationship between God and man would from this day forward would be 'backwards', just like the cipher. God had 'divorced Israel for their sins.

Jeremiah 25:26 And all the kings of the north, far and near, one with another, and all the kingdoms of the world, which are upon the face of the earth: and the king of Sheshach shall drink after them.

'Sheshach' ('SSK') or 'Babylon' will drink of the Lord's wrath 'after' all the others. Although Babylon's powers will be destroyed by Cyrus in 539 B.C., the fabric of the

Babylonian system of government will not be lost, but will continue in various forms unrealised by most people right up until the second coming of Christ. The Babylonish system becomes the 'Mystery Babylon' of the book of Revelation. More will be developed on this subject.

The Prophet Daniel explains Nebuchadnezzar's dream of the awesome beast.

Daniel 1:1 In the third year of the reign of Jehoiakim king of Judah came Nebuchadnezzar king of Babylon unto Jerusalem, and besieged it. Verse 3 And the king spake unto Ashpenaz the master of his eunuchs, that he should bring certain of the children of Israel, and of the king's seed, and of the princes; 4 Children in whom was no blemish, but well favoured, and skilful in all wisdom, and cunning in knowledge, and understanding science, and such as had ability in them to stand in the king's palace, and whom they might teach the learning and the tongue of the Chaldeans... 9 Now God had brought Daniel into favour and tender love with the prince of the eunuchs 1 7 As for these four children, God gave them knowledge and skill in all learning and wisdom: and Daniel had understanding in all visions and dreams. 18 Now at the end of the days that the king had said he should bring them in, then the prince of the eunuchs brought them in before Nebuchadnezzar. 19 And the king communed with them; and among them all was found none like Daniel, Hananiah, Mishael, and Azariah: therefore stood they before the king. 20 And in all matters of wisdom and understanding, that the king enquired of them, he found them ten times better than all the magicians and astrologers that were in all his realm. 21 And Daniel continued even unto the first year of king Cyrus. (Approximately 537 B.C.)

So Daniel, who had received the finest education possible at that time, who Nebuchadnezzar had named Belteshazzar after the name of his god, was in a very strong position with

Nebuchadnezzar until Cyrus took over decades later. God had given him the wisdom and insight to interpret dreams. The king had forgotten his dream, and all the 'wise' men of his court said it was impossible for them to interpret it if he could not tell them what the dream was about. God gave Daniel the insight to do so.

The major 'key' of 'when' - When does this prophetic dream apply?

The dream Nebuchadnezzar had was relevant to his era, and also to later times as history in Babylon and to later governments who took over the world unfolded. It is also relevant to us today and in the days to come to help us understand the current hidden nature of world government until the return of Christ Jesus.

Daniel 2:28 But there is a God in heaven that revealeth secrets, and maketh known to the king Nebuchadnezzar what shall be in the **latter days**. Thy dream, and the visions of thy head upon thy bed, are these;

The dream concerned the head of gold, Nebuchadnezzar, but was also prophecies concerning the subsequent governments after his time represented by the breast of silver, the belly and thighs of brass, and the legs and feet of iron and miry clay right up to the Second Advent.

Daniel 2:31 Thou, O king, sawest, and behold a great image. This great image, whose brightness was excellent, stood before thee; and the form thereof was terrible. 32 This image's head was of fine gold, his breast and his arms of silver, his belly and his thighs of brass, 33 His legs of iron, his feet part of iron and part of clay. 34 Thou sawest **till** (note the 'when') that a stone (Christ Jesus) was cut out without hands, which smote the image upon his feet that were of iron and clay, and brake them to pieces. 35 Then was the iron, the clay, the brass, the silver, and the gold, broken to pieces together, and became like the chaff of the summer threshingfloors; and the wind carried them away, that no place was found for them: and the stone that smote the image became a great mountain (Kingdom of God), and filled the whole earth.

Christ will completely destroy for all time the Babylonish Gentile governments of this world at His Second coming, but until that time comes, Nebuchadnezzar and those who perpetuate his Babylonish system were given power over the whole world.

Daniel 2:37 Thou, O king, art a king of kings: for the God of heaven hath given thee a kingdom, power, and strength, and glory. 38 And **wheresoever the children of men** **dwell**, (Global control) the beasts of the field and the fowls of the heaven hath he given into thine hand, and hath made thee ruler over them all. Thou art this head of gold.

Nebuchadnezzar King of Babylon was the head of gold, the one who would, under God's control, construct the fabric of the new world empire. God would even cause the other nations to serve Nebuchadnezzar or suffer punishment if they did not. Indeed God sets up Kings, rulers, and governments globally even to this day.

Jeremiah 27:4 And command them to say unto their masters, Thus saith the Lord of hosts, the God of Israel; Thus shall ye say unto your masters; 5 I have made the earth, the man and the beast that are upon the ground, by my great power and by my outstretched arm, and have given it unto whom it seemed meet unto me. 6 And now have I given all these lands into the hand of **Nebuchadnezzar the king of Babylon, my servant;** and the beasts of the field have I given him also to serve him. 7 And all nations shall serve him, and his son, and his son's son, until the very time of his land come: and then many nations and great kings shall serve themselves of him. 8 And it shall come to pass, that the nation and kingdom which will not serve the same Nebuchadnezzar the king of Babylon, and that will not put their neck under the yoke of the king of Babylon, that nation will I punish, saith the Lord, with the sword, and with the famine, and with the pestilence, until I have consumed them by his hand.

God calls Nebuchadnezzar 'His servant', in that God is working with his mind in a very direct way step by step to reveal to him that YHWH is not just a local god. God is proving to him that He is the King of Kings, the Lord of Lords, and the One True Almighty God.

God is using him to build a new order at the beginning of a 'new age' which will have One God as its foundation. The 'Head' controls everything, as the new order is developed.

Many are familiar with the stories from the book of Daniel about Shadrach, Meshach, and Abednego being thrown into the fiery furnace and how Nebuchadnezzar saw four walking about in the furnace, and how they came out without even the smell of fire on them. This was one of the very dramatic ways that God got Nebuchadnezzar's attention, and demonstrated His awesome Power to him, with the result that Nebuchadnezzar began to change his attitude towards the One True God.

Daniel 3:28 Then Nebuchadnezzar spake, and said, Blessed be the God of Shadrach, Meshach, and Abednego, who hath sent his angel, and delivered his servants that trusted in him, and have changed the king's word, and yielded their bodies, that they might not serve nor worship any god, except their own God. 29 Therefore I make a decree, That every people, nation, and language, which speak any thing amiss against the God of Shadrach, Meshach, and Abednego, shall be cut in pieces, and their houses shall be made a dunghill: because there is no other God that can deliver after this sort.

He was insisting that his subjects respect the God of gods who had so miraculously delivered Daniel's friends.

Daniel 4:4 Nebuchadnezzar the king, unto all people, nations, and languages, that dwell in all the earth; Peace be multiplied unto you. 2 I thought it good to shew the signs and wonders that the high God hath wrought toward me. 3 How great are his signs! and how mighty are his wonders! his kingdom is an everlasting kingdom, and his dominion is from generation to generation.

God was gradually changing Nebuchadnezzar's mind, but not yet his heart as becomes clear.

Then Nebuchadnezzar had another dream, a warning from God for him not to get carried away with his new power. Again his astrologers and other wise men could not interpret the dream, but Daniel could. He told Nebuchadnezzar that his dream concerned a tree which had grown up strongly, but... Daniel explains the dream:

Daniel 4:24 This is the interpretation, O king, and this is the decree of the most High, which is come upon my lord the king: 25 That they shall drive thee from men, and thy dwelling shall be with the beasts of the field, and they shall make thee to eat grass as oxen, and they shall wet thee with the dew of heaven, and seven times shall pass over thee, till thou know that the most High ruleth in the kingdom of men, and giveth it to whomsoever he will. 26 And whereas they commanded to leave the stump of the tree roots; thy kingdom shall be sure unto thee, after that thou shalt have known that the heavens do rule. 27 Wherefore, O king, let my counsel be acceptable unto thee, and break off thy sins by righteousness, and thine iniquities by shewing mercy to the poor; if it may be a lengthening of thy tranquillity. 28 All this came upon the king Nebuchadnezzar.

But Nebuchadnezzar was not really listening, and his heart was still full of vanity and pride. God was still willing to wait another year for the king's mind to change.

Daniel 4:29 At the end of twelve months he (Nebuchadnezzar) walked in the palace of the kingdom of

Babylon. 30 The king spake, and said, **Is not this great Babylon, that I have built** for the house of the kingdom **by the might of my power**, and **for the honour of my majesty?**

Despite all the demonstrations of God's Power, just like the Israelites who allowed themselves to forget how God delivered them miraculously from Egypt, Nebuchadnezzar forgot where his power actually came from, and Who was working with him, and took the credit for himself.

Daniel 4:31 While the word was in the king's mouth, there fell a voice from heaven, saying, O king Nebuchadnezzar, to thee it is spoken; The kingdom is departed from thee. 32 And they shall drive thee from men, and thy dwelling shall be with the beasts of the field: they shall make thee to eat grass as oxen, and seven times shall pass over thee, until thou know that the most High ruleth in the kingdom of men, and giveth it to whomsoever he will.

His punishment was to lose his human spirit and mind, and for seven years become controlled by an 'animal' brain.

Daniel 4:33 The same hour was the thing fulfilled upon Nebuchadnezzar: and he was driven from men, and did eat grass as oxen, and his body was wet with the dew of heaven, till his hairs were grown like eagles' feathers, and his nails like birds' claws.

At the end of the seven years, Nebuchadnezzar came to himself.

Daniel 4:34 And at the end of the days, I Nebuchadnezzar lifted up mine eyes unto heaven, and mine understanding returned unto me, and I blessed the most High, and I praised and honoured him that liveth for ever, whose dominion is an everlasting dominion, and his kingdom is from generation to generation: 35 And all the inhabitants of the earth are reputed as nothing: and he doeth according to his will in the army of heaven, and among the inhabitants of the earth: and none can stay his hand, or say unto him, What doest thou? 36 At the same time my reason returned unto me; and for the glory of my kingdom, mine honour and brightness returned unto me; and my counsellors and my lords sought unto me; and I was established in my kingdom, and excellent majesty was added unto me. 37 Now I Nebuchadnezzar praise and extol and honour the King of heaven, all whose works are truth, and his ways judgment: and those that walk in pride he is able to abase.

God, with His miracles and this punishment, had changed the mind of Nebuchadnezzar, and his attitude. This was in order that he would have the intention of the 'new age' he was instrumental in initiating being dominated by Monotheism of the True God. This concept in a diffuse way and in a confused manner, **in the latter days**, (Daniel 2:28) still underpins all types of 'Western' Babylonian civilisation.

Daniel 2:42 And as the toes of the feet were part of iron, and part of clay, so the kingdom shall be partly strong, and partly broken. 43 And whereas thou sawest iron mixed with miry clay, they shall mingle themselves with the seed of men: but they shall not cleave one to another, even as iron is not mixed with clay.

At the time of the end (in our era), miscegenation would be rife, as it is today. Now Multiculturalism is widespread, but peoples of differing ethnic or racial backgrounds never really integrate any more than iron would mix well and integrate with miry clay. Some nations proudly claim that they espouse 'multi-cultralism', as if it is something to be proud of. Remember, God originally set the bounds of people's habitations. (Acts 17:6)

Verse 44 gives the 'when' this will all happen, and it is right near the end of the age, just before the return of Christ.

Daniel 2:44 And in the days of these kings shall the God of heaven set up a kingdom, which shall never be destroyed:

and the kingdom shall not be left to other people, but it shall break in pieces and consume all these kingdoms, and it shall stand for ever.

When Darius took over, Daniel was still in a very important position.

Daniel 6:1 It pleased Darius to set over the kingdom an hundred and twenty princes, which should be over the whole kingdom; 2 And over these three presidents; of whom Daniel was first: that the princes might give accounts unto them, and the king should have no damage. 3 Then this Daniel was preferred above the presidents and princes, because an excellent spirit was in him; and the king thought to set him over the whole realm. 4 Then the presidents and princes sought to find occasion against Daniel concerning the kingdom; but they could find none occasion nor fault; forasmuch as he was faithful, neither was there any error or fault found in him.

So the other political people in the court conspired against Daniel, and persuaded Darius to make a 'decree that alters not'.

Daniel 6:7 All the presidents of the kingdom, the governors, and the princes, the counsellors, and the captains, have consulted together to establish a royal statute, and to make a firm decree, that whosoever shall ask a petition of any God or man for thirty days, save of thee, O king, he shall be cast into the den of lions. 8 Now, O king, establish the decree, and sign the writing, that it be not changed, according to the law of the Medes and Persians, which altereth not. 9 Wherefore king Darius signed the writing and the decree.

Darius would live bitterly to regret this decision and so would his astrologers and wise men. As a result of his own foolishness for listening to his 'wise men', Darius the Mede reluctantly put Daniel in the lion's den, and then watched how he was miraculously preserved with God' protection. This was another of the very dramatic ways that God, YHWH got the attention of King Darius, a world ruler, and demonstrated His awesome Power to him.

Daniel 6:14 Then the king, when he heard these words, was sore displeased with himself, and set his heart on Daniel to deliver him: and he laboured till the going down of the sun to deliver him. 15 Then these men assembled unto the king, and said unto the king, Know, O king, that the law of the Medes and Persians is, That no decree nor statute which the king establisheth may be changed. 16 Then the king commanded, and they brought Daniel, and cast him into the den of lions. Now the king spake and said unto Daniel, Thy God whom thou servest continually, he will deliver thee. 21 Then said Daniel unto the king, O king, live for ever.

Rather than lose face with his court, Darius put Daniel into the lion's den, comforting himself by telling Daniel that his God would deliver him, and despite this, Daniel still showed great respect to the King.

Daniel 6: 22 My God hath sent his angel, and hath shut the lions' mouths, that they have not hurt me: forasmuch as before him innocency was found in me; and also before thee, O king, have I done no hurt. 23 Then was the king exceedingly glad for him, and commanded that they should take Daniel up out of the den. So Daniel was taken up out of the den, and no manner of hurt was found upon him, because he believed in his God. 24 And the king commanded, and they brought those men which had accused Daniel, and they cast them into the den of lions, them, their children, and their wives; and the lions had the mastery of them, and brake all their bones in pieces or ever they came at the bottom of the den.

So Darius, extremely relieved, makes another decree, because this event has put the seal on his mind that

YHWH is indeed the Almighty God, and not just merely a local god of the Jewish people.

Daniel 6:25 Then king Darius wrote unto all people, nations, and languages, that dwell in all the earth; Peace be multiplied unto you. 26 I make a decree, That in every dominion of my kingdom men tremble and fear before the God of Daniel: for he is the living God, and stedfast for ever, and his kingdom that which shall not be destroyed, and his dominion shall be even unto the end. 27 He delivereth and rescueth, and he worketh signs and wonders in heaven and in earth, who hath delivered Daniel from the power of the lions. 28 So this Daniel prospered in the reign of Darius, and in the reign of Cyrus the Persian.

Daniel 7 tells about the dream Daniel had about the four beasts that came out of the sea, and identifies Nebuchadnezzar as the 'Lion'.

Daniel 7:3 And four great beasts came up from the sea, diverse one from another. 4 The first was like a lion, and had eagle's wings: I beheld till the wings thereof were plucked, and it was lifted up from the earth, and made stand upon the feet as a man, and a man's heart was given to it. 5 And behold another beast, a second, like to a bear, and it raised up itself on one side, and it had three ribs in the mouth of it between the teeth of it: and they said thus unto it, Arise, devour much flesh. 6 After this I beheld, and lo another, like a leopard, which had upon the back of it four wings of a fowl; the beast had also four heads; and dominion was given to it. 7 After this I saw in the night visions, and behold a fourth beast, dreadful and terrible, and strong exceedingly; and it had great iron teeth: it devoured and brake in pieces, and stamped the residue with the feet of it: and it was diverse from all the beasts that were before it; and it had ten horns.

These four beasts related to world powers. The Lion was Nebuchadnezzar, the Bear was the Medo-Persian

Empire, the Leopard was the Greco-Macedonian Empire, and the terrible fourth beast is not named, but was to be the enduring but hidden Babyonian system.

Daniel 7:12 As concerning the rest of the beasts, they had their dominion taken away: yet their lives were prolonged for a season and time.

All four lost their dominion, but their lives and influence were 'prolonged' in a hidden manner until the second coming of Christ.

This future Babylonian system, the hidden order, was then to spread into North and South America, India, even China.

The area of Babylon was prophesied in Jeremiah 51 to become desolate without inhabitant, but this has never happened so it is clear that this prophecy refers to a time yet ahead of us. Notice again the principle of repetition for emphasis on all important matters in the Bible.

Jeremiah 51:29 And the land shall tremble and sorrow: for every purpose of the Lord shall be performed against Babylon, to make the land of Babylon a desolation without an inhabitant.

Jeremiah 51:37 And Babylon shall become heaps, a dwellingplace for dragons, an astonishment, and an hissing, without an inhabitant.

The 'when' this desolation will happen is at Christ's return. When Christ was accosted in the Temple by the chief priests and elders, He offended them by telling them that the Babylonish system they were serving, and the traditions of men they were actually labouring under and their notions of the Kingdom would all be swept away from them and be blown away at the coming of the Messiah.

Matthew 21:23 And when he was come into the temple, the chief priests and the elders of the people came unto him as he was teaching, and said, By what authority doest thou these things? and who gave thee this authority? ... verse 42 Jesus saith unto them, Did ye never read in the scriptures, The stone which the builders rejected, the same is become the head of the corner: this is the Lord's doing, and it is marvellous in our eyes

There is no capstone on the pyramid pictured on U.S. Currency which should show the 'all seeing' eye of God.

Matthew 21:43 Therefore say I unto you, The kingdom of God shall be taken from you, and given to a (new) nation (the real Christianity of the future) bringing forth the fruits thereof. 44 And whosoever shall fall on this stone shall be broken: but on whomsoever it shall fall, it will grind him to powder. (as they knew it was prophesied in Daniel) 45 And when the chief priests and Pharisees had heard his parables, they perceived that he spake of them. 46 But when they sought to lay hands on him, they feared the multitude, because they took him for a prophet.

Billions all over the earth have been caught up in types of false Christianity presented by false ministers preaching 'another' gospel instead of the Truth. Believing and teaching the **doctrines of Satan like the 'Immortality of the Soul'** introduced to Adam and Eve in the Garden of Eden by the serpent.

Genesis 3:3 But of the fruit of the tree which is in the midst of the garden, God hath said, Ye shall not eat of it, neither shall ye touch it, lest ye die. 4 And the serpent said unto the woman, Ye shall not surely die:

This doctrine is very popular with the majority of 'Churchianity', as well as those who embrace so-called 'new age' concepts.

The 6th Century was a momentous time in history as it was the end of the old order of things, and the beginning of a new era of a different type of world government. It is important to know that it was also the period in which most of the Oriental or Eastern religions extant today, which embrace 'Reincarnation', were formed by various notable individuals.

The next chapter will deal with the origins and goals of Western Civilisation.

CHAPTER 10
ORIGIN & GOAL OF WESTERN CIVILISATION

What was the original central goal? One World Government, and One World Religion, with one God, but when and how did this come about?

Many nations would have wanted to enslave the whole world – Egypt, Assyria and other ancient powers, all wanted to conquer and rule, but under inspiration of God in the 6th Century B.C., King Nebuchadnezzar of Babylon had a different plan. He wanted to establish a very different setup which would govern the whole world. His vision of 'Worldism' would embrace Religion, Politics, Economics, and Philosophy, in harmonious relationship.

This was to be the key to a completely new type of government that would last more than 2600 years from the 6th Century B.C., until the Second Advent.

Nations with aspirations to achieve world government have wanted to establish these principles but they have not wanted God or Christ Jesus involved.

The aims of all those who pursue world government are driven by the desire to control and actually enslave the populace. If they have used the Bible, they have misused it to support their efforts to control for their own ends. Worldwide 'Christianity', national governments, the United Nations, the W.M.F., the 'illuminati' are all based on a completely distorted and misapplied use of God's Word.

Before Babylon was established

Over many centuries, each of the nations thought that it was their specific 'gods' local to them which gave them victories and power to rule over other nations. But over time, conquer and rule ceased to be effective due to constant rebellion.

All the 'gods' which will be listed were undoubtedly rebellious spirit 'Sons of God', many of whom 'morphed' and appeared in human form, as they do to this day. Remember, we fight against principalities and powers in high places.

The Moabites had Chemosh and Milcom; The Moabite gods were many but the principle one was Chemosh. The Ammonites chief god of was Molech, also called Milcom, Malcham.

The Canaanite god was Baal who expected children to be offered as burnt sacrifices.

The Phoenicians worshipped many gods, and were great sailors who travelled and explored man areas of the world.

The Egyptians gods were many, a list of at least twenty-five is easy to find. The creator god of all things was either Re (Ra), Amun, Ptah, Khnum or Aten. Various gods were worshipped in different areas of Egypt.

Most pagan religions had their roots in the Sun and the worship of astrological bodies, in sexual and fertility rites, and the sacrifice of children. These rituals were practiced at the numerous shrines which dotted the land, as well as at the major sanctuaries.

607 B.C. KING NEBUCHADNEZZAR OF BABYLON

By 607 B.C. God had come to the end of His patience with the Jews and the Israelites, and had decided that they needed to learn a lesson by having Nebuchadnezzar invade Jerusalem, see the Temple destroyed, and for them to be taken into captivity and transported to Babylon for seventy years.

So then began a period of over forty years when God was working with the mind of the Gentile Nebuchadnezzar, King of Babylon, to cause him to come to realise, step by step, who the God of gods was.

To serve His Master Purpose, God had put into the mind of Nebuchadnezzar to want to create a different setup of 'One Worldism'.

God through Jeremiah, The 'Axial' prophet, refers to Nebuchadnezzar as 'My Servant', and it is clear in the book of Jeremiah that God had great plans for Nebuchadnezzar, but first he had some serious lessons to learn. This is another indication that God appoints world leaders to serve His purpose.

Near the end of his reign, in the 7th Century B.C., Nebuchadnezzar finally came to appreciate the absolute power of YHWH, not just as the God of the Israelites, but THE true God of all gods.

Prophecy tells of the time when Babylon would conquer and take over Jerusalem and take the Jews into captivity for seventy years.

Jeremiah 25:11 And this whole land shall be a desolation, and an astonishment; and these nations shall serve the king of Babylon seventy years.

The Book of Daniel is one of the most important books in the Bible as it contains so much information about the historically critical time in which Daniel lived, and also embodies a great deal of prophecy, that is history written in Advance that applies to our day, and until Christ returns.

It is worth emphasising that no human being can prophesy the future. Only God can see the stream of history from before the world was created until He completes His Plan. The Bible many times mentions that if a human being prophesies anything and it does not come to pass, then according to God's law that person is subject to the penalty of death.

God's Prophets of old were frequently told to warn of false teachers; and Christ Jesus warned that *many* false prophets would arise in the future, and use His name as authority for their statements and claims.

Both this Author who has compiled this book and Dr. Martin witnessed men claiming to be Apostles and Ministers of God who made many prophetic predictions, none of which came to pass. However, despite the fact that they led many astray with their false doctrines, in our era they were not immediately struck down, nor were they subjected to corporal or capital punishment.

Daniel Chapter 1 – 607 B.C.

Daniel 1:1 In the third year of the reign of Jehoiakim king of Judah came Nebuchadnezzar king of Babylon unto Jerusalem, and besieged it. 2 And the Lord gave Jehoiakim king of Judah into his hand, with part of the vessels of the house of God: which he carried into the land of Shinar to the house of his god; and he brought the vessels into the treasure house of his god.

In the third year of Jehoiakim... This chronological indication is likely to give us the beginning of the seventy years captivity that was prophesied through Jeremiah.

Nebuchadnezzar recognised the intelligence and knowledge of some of those he had captured in Jerusalem and the land of Israel.

Daniel 1:3 And the king spake unto Ashpenaz the master of his eunuchs, that he should bring certain of the children of Israel, and of the king's seed, and of the princes; 4 Children in whom was no blemish, but well favoured, and skilful in all wisdom, and cunning in knowledge, and understanding science, and such as had ability in them to stand in the king's palace, and whom they might teach the learning and the tongue of the Chaldeans.

So Nebuchadnezzar gave instructions for one of his top officials to seek out your men of royal birth, who would be given the finest education in the whole world and who would become wise, able to learn the language of the King, and suitable to stand in the King's palace as advisors.

God was with Daniel, and his three friends that were selected (all Jews), and they were well fed, and given very special treatment for three years.

Daniel 1:5 And the king appointed them a daily provision of the king's meat, and of the wine which he drank: so nourishing them three years, that at the end thereof they might stand before the king. 6 Now among these were of the children of Judah, Daniel, Hananiah, Mishael, and Azariah:

There is a lot of significance in the numbers used in the Bible, and the numbers that are often hidden in the structure of the language. For instance, the number of man is 6, the number 7 connected with God, and the number 8 is linked to Christ. The name of Jesus Christ in Greek letters adds up to 888. The numbers of the letters of the Hebrew names of Daniel and his three friends were Daniel 95, Hananiah 120, Mishael 381, and Azariah 292, add up to 888. This matter of numbers is stated simply for interest. The God of the Old Testament, Christ the Rock, was specifically working with them!

Daniel 1:7 Unto whom the prince of the eunuchs gave names: for he gave unto Daniel the name of Belteshazzar; and to Hananiah, of Shadrach; and to Mishael, of Meshach; and to Azariah, of Abednego.

Names that would be associated with the language of Babylon. And God gave these four very special skills, and they became well established and enjoyed great favour in the court of the King.

Daniel 1:17 As for these four children, God gave them knowledge and skill in all learning and wisdom: and Daniel had understanding in all visions and dreams. 18 Now at the end of the days that the king had said he should bring them in, then the prince of the eunuchs brought them in before

Nebuchadnezzar. 19 And the king communed with them; and among them all was found none like Daniel, Hananiah, Mishael, and Azariah: therefore stood they before the king. 20 And in all matters of wisdom and understanding, that the king enquired of them, he found them ten times better than all the magicians and astrologers that were in all his realm. 21 And Daniel continued even unto the first year of king Cyrus.

Wise above their years, and they certainly were ten times better than all the 'wise' men of the King. This did not endear Daniel and his friends to the local Chaldean magicians and astrologers, so they hatched a plot to get rid of them.

Daniel Chapter 2 - 603 B.C.

Daniel 2:1 And in the second year of the reign of Nebuchadnezzar Nebuchadnezzar dreamed dreams, wherewith his spirit was troubled, and his sleep brake from him. 4 Then spake the Chaldeans to the king in Syriack, O king, live for ever: tell thy servants the dream, and we will shew the interpretation. 5 The king answered and said to the Chaldeans, The thing is gone from me: if ye will not make known unto me the dream, with the interpretation thereof, ye shall be cut in pieces, and your houses shall be made a dunghill.

Nebuchadnezzar had forgotten the dream, but he still expected his 'wise men' to tell him what it meant, which of course, was humanly impossible.

Daniel 2:10 The Chaldeans answered before the king, and said, There is not a man upon the earth that can shew the king's matter: therefore there is no king, lord, nor ruler, that asked such things at any magician, or astrologer, or Chaldean. 11 And it is a rare thing that the king requireth, and there is none other that can shew it before the king, except the gods, whose dwelling is not with flesh.

Nebuchadnezzar did not like being told this,

Daniel 2:12 For this cause the king was angry and very furious, and commanded to destroy all the wise men of Babylon. 13 And the decree went forth that the wise men should be slain; and they sought Daniel and his fellows to be slain.

Daniel got to hear about the King's displeasure, and that he intended to kill all the wise men because they could not reveal the dream to the King. So Daniel went to the King and asked him for a little time, and he would be able to reveal the nature and meaning of the dream to the King.

Daniel 2:19 Then was the secret revealed unto Daniel in a night vision. Then Daniel blessed the God of heaven. 20 Daniel answered and said, Blessed be the name of God for ever and ever: for wisdom and might are his: 21 And he changeth the times and the seasons: he removeth kings, and setteth up kings: he giveth wisdom unto the wise, and knowledge to them that know understanding: 22 He revealeth the deep and secret things: he knoweth what is in the darkness, and the light dwelleth with him. 23 I thank thee, and praise thee, O thou God of my fathers, who hast given me wisdom and might, and hast made known unto me now what we desired of thee: for thou hast now made known unto us the king's matter. 24 Therefore Daniel went in unto Arioch, whom the king had ordained to destroy the wise men of Babylon: he went and said thus unto him; Destroy not the wise men of Babylon: bring me in before the king, and I will shew unto the king the interpretation.

So Daniel was brought into the presence of the King. Daniel was humble, and not about to take any credit for being able to reveal the dream. Note Chapter 2 verse 28.

Daniel 2:26 The king answered and said to Daniel, whose name was Belteshazzar, Art thou able to make known unto me the dream which I have seen, and the interpretation thereof? 27 Daniel answered in the presence of the king, and said, The secret which the king hath demanded cannot the wise men, the astrologers, the magicians, the soothsayers, shew unto the king; 28 But there is a God in heaven that revealeth secrets, and maketh known to the king Nebuchadnezzar **what shall be in the latter days**. Thy dream, and the visions of thy head upon thy bed, are these; 29 As for thee, O king, thy thoughts came into thy mind upon thy bed, what should come to pass hereafter: and he that revealeth secrets maketh known to thee what shall come to pass. 30 But as for me, this secret is not revealed to me for any wisdom that I have more than any living, but for their sakes that shall make known the interpretation to the king, and that thou mightest know the thoughts of thy heart.

Absolute humility. So now Daniel explains the dream of the image that represented the kingdoms of the earth from that time forward, right into the future time of the second coming of Christ.

Daniel 2:31 Thou, O king, sawest, and behold a great image. This great image, whose brightness was excellent, stood before thee; and the form thereof was terrible. 32 This image's head was of fine gold, his breast and his arms of silver, his belly and his thighs of brass, 33 His legs of iron, his feet part of iron and part of clay. 34 Thou sawest till that a stone was cut out without hands, which smote the image upon his feet that were of iron and clay, and brake them to pieces. 35 Then was the iron, the clay, the brass, the silver, and the gold, broken to pieces together, and became like the chaff of the summer threshingfloors; and the wind carried them away, that no place was found for them: and the stone that smote the image became a great mountain, and filled the whole earth. 36 This is the dream; and we will tell the interpretation thereof before the king.

So not only did God reveal the dream to Daniel, but He also gave him the interpretation of it to reveal to the King.

Daniel 2:37 Thou, O king, art a king of kings: for the God of heaven hath given thee a kingdom, power, and strength, and glory. 38 And **wheresoever** (global control) the children of men dwell, the beasts of the field and the fowls of the heaven hath he given into thine hand, and hath made thee ruler over them all. Thou art this head of gold.

Nebuchadnezzar was the Head of Gold. The kingdom of Babylon. The head directs and controls all the other parts of the body, in this case by setting up the characteristics of this new form of government.

Daniel 2:39 And after thee shall arise another kingdom inferior to thee, (538 B.C. the Medo-Persian Empire) and another third kingdom of brass (The Greek Empire under Alexander the Great 333 B.C.), which shall bear rule over all the earth. 40 And the fourth kingdom (Is not named, but shall be strong as iron: forasmuch as iron breaketh in pieces and subdueth all things: and as iron that breaketh all these, shall it break in pieces and bruise. 41 And whereas thou sawest the feet and toes, part of potters' clay, and part of iron, the kingdom shall be divided; but there shall be in it of the strength of the iron, forasmuch as thou sawest the iron mixed with miry clay. 42 And as the toes of the feet were part of iron, and part of clay, so the kingdom shall be partly strong, and partly broken. 43 And whereas thou sawest iron mixed with miry clay, they shall mingle themselves with the seed of men (miscegenation – rife now!): but they shall not cleave one to another, even as iron is not mixed with clay. 44 And in the days of these kings shall the God of heaven set up a kingdom, which shall never be destroyed: and the kingdom shall not be left to other people, but it shall break in pieces and consume all these kingdoms, and it shall stand for ever. 45 Forasmuch as thou sawest that the stone (Christ) was cut out of the mountain without hands (supernaturally), and that it brake in pieces the iron, the brass, the clay, the silver, and the gold; the great God hath made known to the king what shall come to pass hereafter: and the dream is certain, and the interpretation thereof sure.

The succession of Empires

Daniel 2:39 And after thee shall arise another kingdom inferior to thee...

The Medo-Persian Empire is even specifically named later on in Daniel 5:30-31, as being the kingdom that conquered Babylon. Also, the Prophet Jeremiah, about 55 years earlier in 593 B.C. had prophesied that the Medes would conquer Babylon. (See Jeremiah 51:11, 28.)

History tells us that this third kingdom of brass, the one to follow Persia, was the Grecian Empire. In a later chapter Daniel specifically prophesies that Greece will be the conqueror of Medo-Persia.--Daniel 8:21, 22. This was fulfilled in 333 B.C., 219 years after the prophecy was given!

The Greeks, symbolised by the belly, were great food gourmets, and were very preoccupied with sex, the thighs and sexual parts in the image are appropriately symbolic. The Greeks were also philosophers and had many gods, the practices of both became interwoven with Christianity then in 333 B.C., and to this day, 2300 years later!

The revealing of this dream to the King was the first step in God working with his mind and revealing His power to Nebuchadnezzar

Daniel 2:47 The king answered unto Daniel, and said, Of a truth it is, that your God is a God of gods, and a Lord of kings, and a revealer of secrets, seeing thou couldest reveal this secret.

King Nebuchadnezzar was so impressed with Daniel, that he gave him and his three friends high ruling positions in the court.

Daniel 2:48 Then the king made Daniel a great man, and gave him many great gifts, and made him ruler over the whole province of Babylon, and chief of the governors over all the wise men of Babylon. 49 Then Daniel requested of the king, and he set Shadrach, Meshach, and Abednego, over the affairs of the province of Babylon: but Daniel sat in the gate of the king.

Daniel Chapter 3 - 580 B.C.

Daniel 3:1 Nebuchadnezzar the king made an image of gold, whose height was threescore cubits, and the breadth thereof six cubits: he set it up in the plain of Dura, in the province of Babylon.

Then when the music played, everyone had to bow down to this image that Nebuchadnezzar had made or be thrown into the fiery furnace.

Daniel 3:12 There are certain Jews whom thou hast set over the affairs of the province of Babylon, Shadrach, Meshach, and Abednego; these men, O king, have not regarded thee: they serve not thy gods, nor worship the golden image which thou hast set up.13 Then Nebuchadnezzar in his rage and fury commanded to bring Shadrach, Meshach, and Abednego. Then they brought these men before the king.

They refused to worship the image and were thrown into the fiery furnace, but there appeared to be four persons in the fire, one like the Son of God. So Nebuchadnezzar watched in amazement, and commanded them to come out of the fire. They did, completely unharmed, without even the smell of smoke on them.

This was a key occasion when God was working with the mind of Nebuchadnezzar to gradually come to the realisation that He was the Almighty God.

Daniel Chapter 4 - 570 B.C.

Chapter four deals with the vision of the tree representing Nebuchadnezzar which was cut down.

Daniel 4:24 This is the interpretation, O king, and this is the decree of the most High, which is come upon my lord the king: 25 That they shall drive thee from men, and thy dwelling shall be with the beasts of the field, and they shall make thee to eat grass as oxen, and they shall wet thee with the dew of heaven, and seven times shall pass over thee, till thou know that the most High ruleth in the kingdom of men, and giveth it to whomsoever he will....

Nebuchadnezzar was not listening to Daniel, or to God.

Daniel 4:29 At the end of twelve months he walked in the palace of the kingdom of Babylon. 30 The king spake, and said, Is not this great Babylon, that I have built for the house of the kingdom by the might of **my** power, and for the honour of **my** majesty?

While the King was speaking, he became like an animal, and was driven out to pasture like one for seven years.

At the end of the seven years Nebuchadnezzar's reason returned to him, and he had learned a big lesson about God's Power, and proclaimed it to his entire kingdom.

Nebuchadnezzar then died and his kingdom was taken over by Belshazzar his grandson. Daniel Chapter 5 - 538 B.C.

Daniel 5:1 Belshazzar the king made a great feast to a thousand of his lords, and drank wine before the thousand. 2 Belshazzar, whiles he tasted the wine, commanded to bring the golden and silver vessels which his father Nebuchadnezzar had taken out of the temple which was in Jerusalem; that the king, and his princes, his wives, and his concubines, might drink therein. 3 Then they brought the golden vessels that were taken out of the temple of the house of God which was at Jerusalem; and the king, and his princes, his wives, and his concubines, drank in them.

They were drinking in vessels of god that had been stolen from God's Temple.

This was Belshazzar's way of sticking his fingers up God's nose, and as the debauchery continued, the writing appeared on the wall: MENE, MENE, TEKEL, UPHARSIN. None of the 'wise' men of the court could interpret the meaning of these words except Daniel, who told the King what it meant:

MENE: God has numbered your kingdom and finished it. TEKEL: Thou art weighed in the balances and found wanting.

PERES: The kingdom is divided and given to the Medes and Persians.

Daniel 5: 30 In that night was Belshazzar the king of the Chaldeans slain. 31 And Darius the Median took the (Babylonian) kingdom, (which, the kingdom, had been in existence) being about threescore and two years old.

Daniel Chapter 6 - 537 B.C.

Although under a new king, God was looking after the welfare of His Prophet.

Daniel 6:1 It pleased Darius to set over the kingdom an hundred and twenty princes, which should be over the whole kingdom; 2 And over these three presidents; of whom Daniel was first: that the princes might give accounts unto them, and the king should have no damage. 3 Then this Daniel was preferred above the presidents and princes, because an excellent spirit was in him; and the king thought to set him over the whole realm. 4 Then the presidents and princes sought to find occasion against Daniel concerning the kingdom; but they could find none occasion nor fault; forasmuch as he was faithful, neither was there any error or fault found in him.

So as usual, all the other high ranking men around Darius plotted and schemed how they could get rid of Daniel.

Decrees made by the Medes and the Persians could not be altered once made.

So Darius was persuaded to sign a decree that anyone who would petition any God or man other than the king would be thrown into the den of lions. Darius, like Nebuchadnezzar had a lesson to learn about the Power of God.

Then the king's high ranking men watched Daniel at prayer, and reported him to Darius, who, in order not to lose face, very regretfully threw Daniel into the lion's den. Darius spent a sleepless night, but was amazed to find Daniel alive and well the next morning. Daniel told Darius that God had shut up the mouths of the lions.

Daniel 6:23 Then was the king exceedingly glad for him, and commanded that they should take Daniel up out of the den. So Daniel was taken up out of the den, and no manner of hurt was found upon him, because he believed in his God.

So Darius threw all of Daniel's accusers into the lion's den and they killed them all in moments. Then Darius made another decree this time to all the nations of the entire world.

Daniel 6:25 Then king Darius wrote unto all people, nations, and languages, that dwell in all the earth; Peace be multiplied unto you. 26 I make a decree, That in every dominion of my kingdom men tremble and fear before the God of Daniel: for he is the living God, and stedfast for ever, and his kingdom that which shall not be destroyed, and his dominion shall be even unto the end. 27 He delivereth and rescueth, and he worketh signs and wonders in heaven and in earth, who hath delivered Daniel from the power of the lions. 28 So this Daniel prospered in the reign of Darius, and in the reign of Cyrus the Persian.

God was still working with the minds of the new rulers of His new style of government which was to last until the return of Christ.

Daniel Chapter 7 - 555 B.C.

Daniel 7 backtracks to give more information about the vision God had given to Daniel about the four great beasts that came up out of the sea, which Daniel told to Belshazzar.

Daniel 7:2 Daniel spake and said, I saw in my vision by night, and, behold, the four winds of the heaven strove upon the great sea. 3 And four great beasts came up from the sea, diverse one from another. 4 The first was like a lion, and had eagle's wings: I beheld till the wings thereof were plucked, and it was lifted up from the earth, and made stand upon the feet as a man, and a man's heart was given to it. 5 And behold another beast, a second, like to a bear, and it raised up itself on one side, and it had three ribs in the mouth of it between the teeth of it: and they said thus unto it, Arise, devour much flesh. 6 After this I beheld, and lo another, like a leopard, which had upon the back of it four wings of a fowl; the beast had also four heads; and dominion was given to it. 7 After this I saw in the night visions, and behold a fourth beast, dreadful and terrible, and strong exceedingly; and it had great iron teeth: it devoured and brake in pieces, and stamped the residue with the feet of it: and it was diverse from all the beasts that were before it; and it had ten horns. 8 I considered the horns, and, behold, there came up among them another little horn, before whom there were three of the first horns plucked up by the roots: and, behold, in this horn were eyes like the eyes of man, and a mouth speaking great things.

Verse 9 gives the 'when' of this prophecy.

Daniel 7:9 I beheld till the thrones were cast down, and the Ancient of days did sit, whose garment was white as snow, and the hair of his head like the pure wool: his throne was like the fiery flame, and his wheels as burning fire.

The detail of this prophecy gives information about the time leading up to the second coming of Christ.

Daniel 7:15 I Daniel was grieved in my spirit in the midst of my body, and the visions of my head troubled me. 16 I came near unto one of them that stood by, and asked him the truth of all this. So he told me, and made me know the interpretation of the things. 17 These great beasts, which are four, are four kings, which shall arise out of the earth. 8 But the saints of the most High shall take the kingdom, and possess the kingdom for ever, even for ever and ever. 19 Then I would know the truth of the fourth beast, which was diverse from all the others, exceeding dreadful, whose teeth were of iron, and his nails of brass; which devoured, brake in pieces, and stamped the residue with his feet; 20 And of the ten horns that were in his head, and of the other which came up, and before whom three fell; even of that horn that had eyes, and a mouth that spake very great things, whose look was more stout than his fellows. 21 I beheld, and the same horn made war with the saints, and prevailed against them; 22 Until the Ancient of days came, and judgment was given to the saints of the most High; and the time came that the saints possessed the kingdom. 23 Thus he said, The fourth beast shall be the fourth kingdom upon earth, which shall be diverse from all kingdoms, and shall devour (control) the whole earth, and shall tread it down, and break it in pieces.

Daniel 7:24 And the ten horns out of this kingdom are ten kings that shall arise: and another shall rise after them; and he shall be diverse from the first, and he shall subdue three kings.

These are ten Kings that **shall arise** *in the time ahead of us now, and they will arise in the general geographical area of Babylon. The ten kings will not arise in the area of*

Rome, or the European Union as some sects teach, they will arise in the Middle East.

Daniel 7:25 And he (the Beast) shall speak great words against the most High, and shall wear out the saints of the most High, and think to change times (the world's calendar) and (God's?) laws: and they shall be given into his hand until a time and times and the dividing of time (3½.years) 26 But the judgment shall sit, and they shall take away his dominion, to consume and to destroy it unto the end. 27 And the kingdom and dominion, and the greatness of the kingdom under the whole heaven, shall be given to the people of the saints of the most High, whose kingdom is an everlasting kingdom, and all dominions shall serve and obey him. 28 Hitherto is the end of the matter. As for me Daniel, my cogitations much troubled me, and my countenance changed in me: but I kept the matter in my heart.

Daniel Chapter 8 - 553 B.C.

Daniel 8:1 In the third year of the reign of king Belshazzar a vision appeared unto me, even unto me Daniel, after that which appeared unto me at the first.

In this chapter, Daniel has a vision of a ram with two horns, which are interpreted for Daniel as being the Kings of Media and Persia which pushed west and north and southwards, no beast could stand before him, or nothing could deliver out of his hand, he did as he pleased, and became great. Then a he-goat, which is identified as the King of Grecia and a horn which is the first king.

It also contains the prophecy of the 2300 days, and concerns the daily sacrifices, desolation and the sanctuary being trodden under foot. This prophecy in Chapter 8 concerning the end time is very complex, and needs a careful study on its own. We look to the time when knowledge will be increased.

Daniel Chapter 9 - 538 B.C.

Daniel 9 contains the '70 weeks' prophecy which is only partially understood, and again we need greater understanding which will come at the end time with the promised increase of knowledge. Daniel was still in very good standing with the King.

Daniel 9:1 In the first year of Darius the son of Ahasuerus, of the seed of the Medes, which was made king over the realm of the Chaldeans;   In the first year of his reign I Daniel understood by books the number of the years, whereof the word of the Lord came to Jeremiah the prophet, that he would accomplish seventy years in the desolations of Jerusalem.

We understand that the 70 'weeks' were 70 'weeks' of years, so 70x7= 490 years.

Daniel was praying for forgiveness for Judah and Israel in spite of their constant rejection of God.

Daniel 9:21 Yea, whiles I was speaking in prayer, even the man Gabriel, whom I had seen in the vision at the beginning, being caused to fly swiftly, touched me about the time of the evening oblation. 22 And he informed me, and talked with me, and said, O Daniel, I am now come forth to give thee skill and understanding. 23 At the beginning of thy supplications the commandment came forth, and I am come to shew thee; for thou art greatly beloved: therefore understand the matter, and consider the vision. 24 Seventy weeks are determined upon thy people and upon thy holy city, to finish the transgression, and to make an end of sins, and to make reconciliation for iniquity, and to bring in everlasting righteousness, and to seal up the vision and prophecy, and to anoint the most Holy.

Daniel 9:25 Know therefore and understand, that from the going forth of the commandment to restore and to build Jerusalem unto the Messiah the Prince shall be seven weeks, and threescore and two weeks: the street shall be built again, and the wall, even in troublous times. 26 And after threescore and two weeks shall Messiah be cut off, but not for himself: and the people of the prince that shall come shall destroy the city and the sanctuary; and the end thereof shall be with a flood, and unto the end of the war desolations are determined. 27 And he shall confirm the covenant with many for one week: and in the midst of the week he shall cause the sacrifice and the oblation to cease, and for the overspreading of abominations he shall make it desolate, even until the consummation, and that determined shall be poured upon the desolate.

Verse 25 gives us divisions of time of the 70 weeks. There will be seven 'sevens', and sixty-two 'sevens'. Seven "sevens" is 49 years, and sixty-two "sevens" is another 434 years, = 483 years, plus confirming the covenant another 'week' of seven years = 490 years.

Gabriel told Daniel that the prophecy would start when a decree was issued to rebuild Jerusalem. From the date of that decree to the time of the Messiah would be 483 years. We know from history that the command and permission to restore and rebuild Jerusalem was given by King Artaxerxes of Persia around 445 B.C.

Ezra 1:1 Now in the first year of Cyrus king of Persia, that the word of the Lord by the mouth of Jeremiah might be fulfilled, the Lord stirred up the spirit of Cyrus king of Persia, that he made a proclamation throughout all his kingdom, and put it also in writing, saying, 2 Thus saith Cyrus king of Persia, The Lord God of heaven hath given me all the kingdoms of the earth; and he hath charged me to build him an house at Jerusalem, which is in Judah.

Nehemiah 2:5 And I said unto the king, If it please the king, and if thy servant have found favour in thy sight, that thou wouldest send me unto Judah, unto the city of my fathers' sepulchres, that I may build it. 6 And the king said unto me, (the queen also sitting by him,) For how long shall thy journey be? and when wilt thou return? So it pleased the king to send me; and I set him a time.

2 Chronicles 36: 21 To fulfil the word of the Lord by the mouth of Jeremiah, until the land had enjoyed her sabbaths: for as long as she lay desolate she kept sabbath, to fulfil threescore and ten years. 22 Now in the first year of Cyrus king of Persia, that the word of the Lord spoken by the mouth of Jeremiah might be accomplished, the Lord stirred up the spirit of Cyrus king of Persia, that he made a proclamation throughout all his kingdom, and put it also in writing, saying, 23 Thus saith Cyrus king of Persia, All the kingdoms of the earth hath the Lord God of heaven given me; and he hath charged me to build him an house in Jerusalem, which is in Judah. Who is there among you of all his people? The Lord his God be with him, and let him go up.

Jeremiah 29:10 For thus saith the Lord, That after seventy years be accomplished at Babylon I will visit you, and perform my good word toward you, in causing you to return to this place.

There is still much discussion concerning the actual chronology of the dates of secular history not being consistent with the Bible record. Dr. Martin always took the Biblical revelation as the true guide from Christ, and that secular historians would need to adjust their thinking to align with the Bible, not the other way around.

A more detailed study and discussion of the seventy weeks prophecy is needed. Daniel Chapter 10 - 534 B.C.

Daniel 10:1 In the third year of Cyrus, 539-530 B.C., king of Persia a thing was revealed unto Daniel, whose name was called Belteshazzar; and the thing was true, but the time appointed was long: and he understood the thing, and had understanding of the vision.

Daniel did not understand the vision, but Gabriel gave him words of comfort.

Daniel 10:19 And said, O man greatly beloved, fear not: peace be unto thee, be strong, yea, be strong. And when he had spoken unto me, I was strengthened, and said, Let my lord speak; for thou hast strengthened me.

Daniel Chapter 11 - 534 B.C.

It is not intended to discuss this, the longest prophecy in the Bible at this time, or here in connection with the origin of Western civilisation.

Daniel Chapter 12 - 534 B.C.

Is talking about the time just before and when Christ comes, and the resurrection. There is still a great deal for us to understand, and we have the promise:

Daniel 12:8 And I heard, but I understood not: then said I, O my Lord, what shall be the end of these things? 9 And he said, Go thy way, Daniel: for the words are closed up and sealed till the time of the end. 10 Many shall be purified, and made white, and tried; but the wicked shall do wickedly: and none of the wicked shall understand; but the wise shall understand.

Cyrus claims his world control - orders rebuilding of the Temple.

Cyrus represented the silver portion of the great statue of Nebuchadnezzar.

Ezra 1:1 Now in the first year of Cyrus king of Persia, that the word of the Lord by the mouth of Jeremiah might be fulfilled, the Lord stirred up the spirit of Cyrus king of Persia, that he made a proclamation throughout all his kingdom, and put it also in writing, saying, 2 Thus saith Cyrus king of Persia, *The Lord God of heaven hath given me all the kingdoms of the earth; and he hath charged me to build him an house at Jerusalem, which is in Judah.*

Isaiah 45:28 That saith of Cyrus, He is my shepherd, and shall perform all my pleasure: even saying to Jerusalem,

Thou shalt be built; and to the temple, Thy foundation shall be laid.

From this time forward, this knowledge of the global nature government would begin to be spread around the entire world.

The notion of One God was fine, but the human governments wanted to use the knowledge to control, but they wanted to do it their way. So they misused God's name to support their ideas, which is exactly the situation now in the 21st Century.

After the silver portion of the image, the brass portion would come from the West, and Javan, or the Grecian Empire took over under the control of Alexander the Great in 333- 332 B.C.

Alexandra went to Jerusalem in 332 B.C., as he had had a vision in Macedonia telling him that the inhabitants would welcome him. According to Josephus, the renowned Jewish historian, Alexander met the High Priest, clad in his white and blue robes, wearing the symbol of YHWH, and bowed or prostrated himself before the High Priest bowing to YHWH and not the man. Alexandra did not destroy the Temple.

Alexander had begun to realise the nature of the True God as had Nebuchadnezzar, Darius and Cyrus before him. It is said that Alexander went to Egypt and was initiated into all the mysteries which usually took years to learn in just one day. The truth of the mysteries was kept from the people, and only revealed to those of top rank. Alexander wrote to his Mother telling her that the Egyptians knew that all the local gods were dead men, and that there was only One True God.

Alexander then tried to bring in one world government, with one religion, but he died in 323 B.C., after thirteen years of conquering all before him. He either died of a fever, or perhaps was murdered by four of his generals.

There is then a gap in the historical record of the development of the world government as the concept spread throughout the known world.

The Roman Empire certainly utilised some of the character of the Babylonian system of government as it spread out across the known world. Rome invaded Britain in 55 B.C., and brought with them a form of government and a rule of law which inevitably was absorbed by those they ruled.

Nero, after persecuting Christianity saw its value in controlling the populace of Rome, and wanted to move his headquarters to Jerusalem, but this never happened. After murdering Paul, Nero committed suicide in June 68 A.D.

Centuries later the Roman Empire under Constantine the Great, 272-337 A.D., embraced a form of Christianity heavily laced with pagan and heathen idolatrous traditions. At that time that form of 'Christianity' spread like wildfire around the Western world as it appealed to the people as it embraced of their traditional heathen and pagan forms of worship.

During the later centuries the Roman Catholic Church was the power in many countries of the world, upholding its beliefs and practices by whatever means were needed to control the inhabitants.

Their form of government still held the same characteristics of one religious system, one rule of law, one system of fiscal control, one political ideal of domination, and indeed perpetuated the Babylonian system of government which was taken up by civil governments all over the globe, and undergirds the whole of Western Civilisation.

In our era, the United Nations represents the desire and the wishes of the member nations to establish world government. Many people who are considered 'conspiracy theorists' believe, with apparently good reason, that there is an invisible elite who control the governments of this world behind the scenes.

True Christianity is not a form of control.

Christianity was never intended to be used to exert any form of control over others. It is this aspect of the churches of this world that completely misuse Christ's life, death and resurrection as a means of subjugating their followers.

Democracy refers to a type of political system in which, supposedly - but not in reality, the people or their representatives lawfully govern themselves, as opposed to being governed by a despot, a military dictatorship, or a monarch.

Some historians suggest that a type of democracy existed thousands of years ago. The Grecian Empire established in 333 B.C., used the idea of 'democracy', which is defined by rule of the people. Prior to that time as early as 500 B.C., The Athenian Greek philosopher's ideas were much in vogue, and dominated political life. These ideas were absorbed into the fabric of many countries and grew in importance up until the time of Christ, and then has flourished in many countries in all the centuries of the Christian era.

In the 21st century, many countries aspire to have a democratic form of government usually patterned after the system of the so-called British Mother of Parliaments.

Democracy is supposed to be the rule of the majority of the people, but this does not exist anywhere in the modern world. The ruling party rarely, almost never, represents anywhere near a majority of the electorate or of the population.

In fact, even the best run democracies are little different from a military dictatorship or rule by a ruthless despot. In a democracy, the armed forces are well in the background and only appear on the public scene if normal police procedures fail to maintain law and order. Whereas in dictatorships, and military junta, rule is very obviously by force of arms.

All governments are in the business of control, peaceful control if possible, but if not, then by naked violence.

Christ will return and put down all forms of human government and institute the Kingdom of God on earth. Initially Christ will use a great deal of force to subdue human governments in order to establish the basis for peace on earth during the thousand year millennium.

The next chapter explains what Christians have to avoid at all costs.

CHAPTER 11

WHAT MUST 21ST CENTURY CHRISTIANS AVOID LIKE THE PLAGUE?

IDOLATRY. Idolatry is one of the worst, if not the worst sin. Idolatry is mentioned in many different ways in the Bible more times than any other human transgression.

God wants us to love and appreciate Him, to respect and honour Him, to hallow His name, and to avoid at all costs Spiritual fornication.

What is Spiritual fornication? It is giving our love, time, energy, money, and attention to events, ideas, celebrations, or the observance of customs that have their roots in pagan and heathen worship of other gods. Or simply just living our lives without giving God thanks or credit for life and the wonders of His Creation.

Britain, America, Canada, Australia, and most of the countries of Europe are referred to as 'Christian' countries. But are they? Historically, were the inhabitants of these countries God-fearing peoples, or were they people who mostly practised heathen and pagan ideas of worshipping the 'gods'?

Yet these nations consider themselves as 'Christian' countries, and a high proportion of the citizens are, or think of themselves as Christians, or at least 'nominal' Christians. Nominal Christinas are those '**Christians in name only'**, who may or may not actually attend a 'church', or practice Biblical Christianity.

But do these billions of people practice true Christianity? Or is what they believe in and practice based on paganism and ancient heathen idolatrous rites? The traditional activities included in popular 'Churchianity', Christmas, Easter, and Halloween, were in existence thousands of years before Christ came into this world and created 'Christianity'.

But surely, one might say, Christmas, Easter, Halloween and other 'Christian' festivals are not bad, they are just harmless ways in which people choose to worship God. But what does God say about these activities in His Word, the Holy Bible? When all is said and done, the bottom line in the Bible from God is:

It has to be MY WAY not any way you dream up

What does the word 'Church' mean? And does it matter?

Firstly the English word 'church' is a word derived from the name of an ancient goddess called 'Circe'. Who was 'Circe' and what type of 'god' was she?

Circe, is the Greek word is Kírk. The Circe C's are hard C's, so it was pronounced Kirky, which gave rise to the Scottish and Welsh word Kirk or church. The **mythical** Circe was said to be the daughter of the Sun god Helios. Many 'church' buildings feature circular stained glass windos used originally in Sun worship.

Circe, Kirkee, was a goddess of magic, a nymph, a witch, an enchantress or sorceress. She used Pharmakeia (the origin of the English word pharmacy), which involves the administering of drugs, poisoning and magical arts to turn men into animals, all in connection with idolatry. She was thought to use the magic of metamorphosis, to change men into animals. She had the power of illusion, and practiced the dark art of necromancy, supposedly communicating with the dead, in attempts to predict the future.

In our era, there are television programs on air daily featuring 'mediums' who, like Circe, purport to be in touch with the dead and 'departed'. They invite audience participation in this public performance of necromancy which is in direct defiance of God's laws in the Bible. **The dead are dead, not in any way conscious.**

Ecclesiastes 9:10 Whatsoever thy hand findeth to do, do it with thy might; for there is no work, nor device, nor knowledge, nor wisdom, in the grave, whither thou goest.

So is the word 'church' an appropriate word to use in connection with Christ or Christianity, and the worship of the True God? No it is not!

Language, and the manner and way we use of words, is vitally important. We use specific words to convey exact meanings to each other in spoken or written language.

The use of this one word 'Church' did literally change the world. To retain his control of the Church of England King James required the translators of the original Scripture manuscripts consistently to translate the Greek word "ekklesia" as 'Church', 111 times in the King James Version, and in most other versions of the Bible.

The actual definition of the Greek word "ekklesia" is 'group' or 'assembly'. Nothing whatsoever to do with a building.

When Christ said, "Upon this rock I will build my ekklesia." (Mat 16:18) The Greek word in the original text is 'ekklesia' pronounced ek-klay-see-ah.

The dictionary definition of the word 'Church' is a 'building', a 'place of worship of any religion', or 'a body of information of beliefs'. The translators in 1611 under the direct instructions of King James, (1603-1625) of England were told not to translate any portion of the Bible in a manner which would not support the doctrines of the Church of England.

So the translators knowingly used the word 'Church' which means a 'building' to support a clergy rather than a word that would build a unified group of Christians, the body of Christ. Using the word "Church" in the Bible has implanted a completely wrong concept into the minds of everyone who reads the Bible.

The early assembly of Christian believers in the 1st Century A.D., did not have ministers in charge over the rest of the group.

As 'Churches' began to develop, they became structured with an authoritarian hierarchy that needed buildings, and a 'body' of false doctrines to control the people religiously and politically. That control is power, and power certainly tends to corrupt.

By changing the true meaning and function of the Greek word "ekklesia" to our English word "church", it gave the system of clergy power over the people. The fact that **"power corrupts and absolute power corrupts absolutely"** has been the downfall and corruption of original 'Christianity' and of the system to this day.

21st Century 'Churchianity' keeps pagan idolatry alive and well

The word 'churchianity' was coined to differentiate between 'Christianity' and its counterfeits.

Christmas was originally called 'Saturnalia' and was the worship of the Sun. Easter was the worship of the sex goddess Ishtar. Halloween reflects the fear of and worship of wicked spirits. These three festivals led to the weird customs practiced each year by religious and secular people alike in 'Christian' countries.

In Amos 5:21 God says " 21 I hate, I despise **your** feast days, and I will not smell in your solemn assemblies".

What does God say in His Word about idolatry?

Exodus 20:3 Thou shalt have no other gods before me. 4 Thou shalt not make unto thee any graven image, or any likeness of any thing that is in heaven above, or that is in the earth beneath, or that is in the water under the earth.

Almost all churches around the world contain graven images, busts or statues, stained glass windows purporting to be likenesses of Christ, Mary, angels, and 'saints'. Church buildings are adorned with demonic looking gargoyles and other stone images, and topped with steeples which were originally phallic symbols. Also 'likenesses' or pictures abound, 'relics' are preserved and adored.

What about learning and practising the ways of the pagans and heathen?

Deuteronomy 18:9 When thou art come into the land which the Lord thy God giveth thee, **thou shalt not** learn to do after the abominations of those nations. 10 There shall not be found among you any one that maketh his son or his daughter to pass through the fire, or that useth divination, or an observer of times, or an enchanter, or a witch.

Jeremiah 1:16 And I will utter my judgments against them touching all their wickedness, who have forsaken me, and have burned incense unto other gods, and worshipped the works of their own hands.

Jeremiah 10:2 Thus saith the Lord, Learn not the way of the heathen, and be not dismayed at the signs of heaven (Astrology, not astronomy); for the heathen are dismayed at them.

Every newspaper and magazine in the Western world contain astrological sections purporting to inform the reader about the aspects the affect their lives. It is all a nonsense, and should be ignored by anyone who aspires to be a true Christian.

Jeremiah 44:19 And when we burned incense to the queen of heaven (Mary?), and poured out drink offerings unto her, did we make her cakes (hot cross buns?) to worship her, and pour out drink offerings unto her, without our men?

Ezekiel 8:16 And he brought me into the inner court of the Lord's house, and, behold, at the door of the temple of the Lord, between the porch and the altar, were about five and twenty men, with their backs toward the temple of the Lord, and their faces toward the east; and they worshipped the sun (Easter Sunrise services?) toward the east.

Any form of worship and feasts that involve a connection with forms of idolatry is regarded by God as dung.

Malachi 2:3 Behold, I will corrupt your seed, and spread dung upon your faces, even the dung of your solemn feasts; and one shall take you away with it.

God does not mince words. What he feels about 'churchianity' is graphic.

Isaiah 2: 6 Therefore thou (God) hast forsaken thy people the house of Jacob, because they be replenished from the east (Easter, sun worship), and are soothsayers like the Philistines, and they please themselves (sexually) in the children of strangers. 7 Their land also is full of silver and gold, neither is there any end of their treasures; their land is also full of horses, neither is there any end of their chariots (now cars!): 8 Their land also is full of idols; they worship the work of their own hands, that which their own fingers have made:

All material things that dominate the desires and thinking of people of the world is in fact idolatry.

Mixed marriages, same-sex marriages, the proliferation of 'LGBTQI?', worshipping wealth, coveting possessions, chariots (cars!), and the 'Christian' lands and churches that are full of idols, all these are things which God hates.

Isaiah 1:14 Your new moons and **your appointed feasts my soul hateth**: they are a trouble unto me; I am weary to bear them.

God says very plainly in His Word, he **hates** these activities, so true Christians will not do, or be involved with any of these things in any manner.

What about Christmas?

Saturnalia (now 'Christmas'),celebrated for thousands of years before Christ came onto earth, was the ancient feast of Saturnalia was all about the death and rebirth of the Sun. It was celebrated around the 22nd to the 25th December, the Winter solstice when the Sun was at its lowest in the sky, and began to appear to go upwards again.

The use of an evergreen tree was to symbolise life, the wreath hung on doors represented mourning for the dying Sun. Saturnalia was practiced since time began, it was a time of debauchery, drunkenness, over eating, and the exchange of gifts. Much like Xmas now!

It has nothing whatsoever to do with the birth of Christ. Christ was either born on the Holy Day, the Day of Trumpets, 3 B.C., which occurs annually on the 'Jewish' ecclesiastical calendar on the 1st of Tishri, which is around September/October in the Gregorian Calendar now used worldwide. It would have been wintry then, and the flocks would have been brought down from the hills by that time. Or possibly the Lamb of God was born at the time of the Passover (March/April) during the lambing season in Israel then. Remember the shepherds were 'abiding in the fields' living out with their flocks, to care for the lambing ewes. When they heard of the birth of Christ, they came down to visit him in the stable, then went back to their flocks..

Public and commercial hysteria around Christmas begins around November, and consumes the attention and the finances of billions for weeks on end. Certainly nobody sees anything wrong with it. Most think it is all just harmless fun. Or is it?

What does God have to say about it?

Jeremiah 10:3 2 Thus saith the Lord, Learn not the way of the heathen, and be not dismayed at the signs of heaven; for the heathen are dismayed at them. 3 For the customs of the people are vain: for one cuts a tree out of the forest, the work of the hands of the workman, with the axe. 4

They deck it with silver and with gold; they fasten it with nails and with hammers, that it moves not.

So Christmas trees may be pretty, but they are an abomination to God, as is the practice of Sun worship, or the worship of material things.

What about Easter?

The English name Easter came from the Anglo-Saxon spring goddess Eostre. (The root of the English word for Estrogen the sex hormone.) It is also connected to Astarte, the Phoenician fertility goddess, and the Babylonian chief goddess Ishtar.

Hares and rabbits are symbols of fertility, and were used in the ancient ceremonial and symbolism of the pagan spring festivals, and by nearly everyone on earth to this day.

The hunt for Easter eggs, supposedly brought by the Easter rabbit, far from being harmless child's play, originated in a pagan fertility rite. Some still believe that the decorated Easter egg can 'magically' bring happiness, prosperity, and health.

Easter sunrise services are clearly linked to rites of ancient Sun worshippers performed at the Vernal or Spring equinox, supposedly welcoming the Sun and its great power to bring new life to all growing things.

There is no doubt that members of the early Church of false Christianity already practiced many of the ancient pagan customs, and simply overlaid them with a Christian meaning to them. This has been carried on down the generations to this day.

What about Halloween?

The Bible does not mention Halloween as such. However, both the ancient origins of Halloween and its modern customs show it to be a celebration based on false beliefs about the dead and invisible spirits, or demons.

1 Corinthians 10:19 What say I then? that the idol is any thing, or that which is offered in sacrifice to idols is any thing? 20 But I say, that the things which the Gentiles sacrifice, they sacrifice to devils, and not to God: and I would not that ye should have fellowship with devils. 21 Ye cannot drink the cup of the Lord, and the cup of devils: ye cannot be partakers of the Lord's table, and of the table of devils. 22 Do we provoke the Lord to jealousy? are we stronger than he?

Ancient Celts wore ghoulish costumes thought to appease wandering spirits, and offered sweets to the spirits to appease them. The Bible, on the other hand, does not permit merging false religious practices with the worship of God.

2 Corinthians 6:15 And what concord hath Christ with Belial? (a Hebrew word "used to characterize the wicked or worthless) or what part has he that believeth with an infidel? (one who does not believe in God) 16 And what agreement hath the temple of God with idols? for ye are the temple of the living God; as God hath said, I will dwell in them, and walk in them; and I will be their God, and they shall be my people. 17 Wherefore come out from among them, and be ye separate, saith the Lord, and touch not the unclean thing; and I will receive you. 18 And will be a Father unto you, and ye shall be my sons and daughters, saith the Lord Almighty.

The true Christian is commanded to be separate from **ALL** the pagan activities of worldly people.

Ghosts, vampires, werewolves, witches, and zombies mimicked during Halloween are associated with the evil spirit world. The Bible clearly states many times that we should resist wicked spirit forces, not celebrate with them.

Ephesians 6:11 Put on the whole armour of God, that ye may be able to stand against the wiles of the devil. 12 For we wrestle not against flesh and blood, but against principalities, against powers, against the rulers of the darkness of this world, against spiritual wickedness in high places. 3 Wherefore take unto you the whole armour of God, that ye may be able to withstand in the evil day, and having done all, to stand.

Tens of millions of Halloween pumpkins, or jack-o'-lanterns are sacrificed to evil spirits annually when they could have provided food for the hungry. Anciently, people asked for food in return for a prayer for the dead, and they would carry hollowed-out lanterns, with a candle inside representing the false notion that a soul was trapped in purgatory. None of the beliefs behind hallow e'en, the immortality of the soul, purgatory, and prayers for the dead are based on the Bible. **The dead are dead and know not anything.**

Ecclesiastes 9:5 For the living know that they shall die: but the dead know not any thing, neither have they any more a reward;

Children, dressed in ghoulish demonic costumes are encouraged by parents to go from door to door 'tricking or treating' in a demeaning and unworthy practice which could not be further removed from the actually illegal practice of true Christianity.

What about homosexuality?

Once known by all Christians, and even 'nominal Christians', to be wrong, but all the practices of "LBGTQI?" people are now becoming almost universally accepted as the norm. Now homosexual church male ministers, lesbian females, and members of Church congregations openly claim to be Christians, and protest their right to live as they choose, despite the clear laws of God

Leviticus 18:22 Thou shalt not lie with mankind, as with womankind: it is abomination.

Also, cross dressing is forbidden in God's Law. The King James language is specific.

Deuteronomy 22:5 The woman shall not wear that which pertains unto a man, neither shall a man put on a woman's garment: for all that do so are abomination unto the Lord thy God.

Romans 1:26 For this cause God gave them up unto vile affections: for even their women did change the natural use into that which is against nature: 27 And likewise also the men, leaving the natural use of the woman, burned in their lust one toward another; men with men working that which is unseemly, and receiving in themselves that recompence of their error which was meet (or 'fitting' HIV? AIDS? STD's?) 28 And even as they did not like to retain God in their knowledge, God gave them over to a reprobate mind, to do those things which are not convenient;

1 Corinthians 6:9 Know ye not that the unrighteous shall not inherit the kingdom of God? Be not deceived: neither fornicators, nor idolaters, nor adulterers, nor effeminate, nor abusers of themselves with mankind, 10 Nor thieves, nor covetous, nor drunkards, nor revilers, nor extortioners, shall inherit the kingdom of God.

Isaiah 3:9 The shew of their countenance doth witness against them; and they declare their sin as Sodom, they hide it not. Woe unto their soul! for they have rewarded evil unto themselves.

Could this be referring to those who flaunt their defiance to God when participating in homosexual 'pride' parades? Or those who openly deride or look down on heterosexual couples. Christ warned that Christians would be hated.

John 17:14 I have given them thy word; and the world hath hated them, because they are not of the world, even as I am not of the world. 15 I pray not that thou shouldest take them out of the world, but that thou shouldest keep them from the evil. 16 They are not of the world, even as I am not of the world.

Christ prayed that Christians would be kept from evil. The world is full of idolatrous temptations:

SATAN – God of this world wants your worship and adoration SELF – The Idolatry of the 'ME' generation, and basically everyone!

IDOLS - The Idolatry of stage, screen, and tv idols EVOLUTION – The Idolatry of 'wise' fools who worship the creation rather than the Creator.

WORLDLINESS - The Idolatry of human achievements STUFF - The Idolatry of 'things' and yet more material 'things'

SEX - The Idolatry of all forms of illicit sexual activity. Especially on the 'dark' side of the Internet

WEALTH - The Idolatry of the love of money

SPORT - The Idolatry of the team, the game, the person, the 'stars'.

RELIGION - The Idolatry of 'Churchianity' and false gospels POWER - The Idolatry of power and control over others WORLD – The love of all this present evil world offers

1 Corinthians 10:14 Wherefore, my dearly beloved, **flee** from **idolatry**.

Revelation 22:14 Blessed are they that do his commandments, that they may have right to the tree of life, and may enter in through the gates into the city. 15 For without are dogs, and sorcerers, and whoremongers, and murderers, and *idolaters*, and whosoever loveth and make a lie.

None of the unholy activities described in this chapter have anything to do with being a Christian; you cannot knowingly practice any of them, and be a true follower of Christ.

Matthew 4:10 Then saith Jesus unto him, Get thee hence, Satan: for it is written, Thou shalt worship the Lord thy God, and him only shalt thou serve.

True Christians who become aware of what is behind all these idolatrous activities will want to change their minds, change their ways, and seek a repentant attitude.

John 4:24 God is a Spirit: and they that worship him must worship him in spirit and in truth.

The next chapter explores the meaning and purpose of our human life and our glorious future.

CHAPTER 12
THE MEANING AND PURPOSE OF HUMAN LIFE

This chapter contains concepts that might be new to you. It also contains many scriptures with which you may be familiar. The theme of this whole book is about studying the Bible, and the vital importance of asking our Heavenly Father for Spiritual help and Guidance. So that when taking a new fresh careful look at familiar Scriptures, they may become very real, more alive, and of important relevance to the reader. There is a lot of repetition of concepts for emphasis in the Bible, and this compilation uses repetition in the same way.

Long before time began – before anything physical we know of existed – GOD WAS. God's name is the verb 'to be': 'Was-Is-Will Be'. The God Being.

The Eternal; Past, Present, and Future; the Eternal Almighty God. God is composed of Spirit. God is totally Holy; His Power Almighty.

John 4:24 God is a Spirit: and they that worship him must worship him in spirit and in truth. God is the Essence of All Power which is expressed by His Spirit which is Holy.

People call the Powers of God the Laws of Physics, or evolution which is sacrilege, stealing the credit from God. Gravity, the energy in atoms, light, time, and those listed in this volume are all Spritual Powers, so they cannot be fully understood by the carnal mind.

God's Spirit is everywhere, it is the manifestation of His Power, but it is definitely NOT a personality or a being, it is the extension of God's creative and sustaining power. A radio operates and 'speaks' when operated by the power of electricity, but nobody would suggest that the radio or the electricity is a person.

The Role of the Holy Spirit in our lives as Christians

The role of the Holy Spirit, the Spirit of God in our lives as Christians is paramount. The Holy Spirit is the agency, the very means by which They, God through Christ communicate with us to show and explain their love for us. We who in reality are Their children, and brothers and sisters of Christ. By the means of the flowing of the Holy Spirit, They reveal to us our understanding of life, and the reason for our very existence on this world.

God the Word, Christ, wrote the Bible in His own special language and style which makes it impossible for mere humans to comprehend without the help of the Holy Spirit.

Isaiah 28:10 For precept must be upon precept, precept upon precept; line upon line, line upon line; here a little, and there a little: 11 For with stammering lips and another tongue will he speak to this people.

The many story threads that are woven into the books of the Bible are made up of precepts or principles which appear as fragments, a little of the story in one place, and more detail in other places.

It is somewhat like the speech of someone who 'stammers', the whole sentence or paragraph does not come out at once. The Bible is truly written in another 'tongue' or language for which we need the Holy Spirit to comprehend it, and interpret for us as it flows through our minds and hearts in terms of thoughts, ideas, concepts and feelings.

Matthew 4:4 But he answered and said, It is written, Man shall not live by bread alone, but by every word that proceedeth out of the mouth of God.

Notice we need to live by every Word out of the mouth of God directly, not through humans or from any human organisations.

God is Love – so why is there so much suffering in the world?

1 John 4:8 He that loveth not knows not God; for God is love.

Human beings often find it baffling to reconcile a Loving God with the dreadful amount of pain, suffering and travail that human beings experience in this life. Suffering is a Gift that helps us to keep relying on God to deal with it.

James 1:2-3 ² My brethren, count it all joy when ye fall into divers temptations; ³ Knowing this, that the trying of your faith worketh patience.

1 John 3:1 Behold, what manner of love the Father hath bestowed upon us, that we should be called the sons of God: therefore the world knoweth us not, because it knew him not.

For us to understand Love we also have to have experienced the opposite. Because God is Love, we need to ponder just how much all the human sin and suffering in this life is costing God Himself in terms of pain and suffering for Him. He is going through this period willingly, as part of the process of building His Family.

We need to ask for the faith, and the belief that if there had been any other way to achieve God's Plan and Purpose, He would have done it differently. Who are we the clay, to question God the potter?

Isaiah 64:8 But now, O Lord, thou art our father; we are the clay, and thou our potter; and we all are the work of thy hand.

Our job is to believe, to know, to accept that God is pure Love, and to thank Him for our sufferings in this life, knowing that it is God's Will that we will ultimately be a part of Him.

We can see the picture in a very small way when we humans start a family and experience the pain of watching how our children suffer hurt and pain because they ignore the love, direction, and guidance we parents shower on them. But we humans are willing to bear these years of pain to have the delights of bringing little ones into this world.

So as God is watching billions of humans ignoring Him, going against all the principles of Love He has given us. He sees us fail to appreciate the magnificence of His Design in all Creation, instead the majority **embraces the folly of Evolution, a form of idolatry**.

Romans 1:19 Because that which may be known of God is manifest in them; for God hath shewed it unto them. 20 For the invisible things of him from the creation of the world are clearly seen, being understood by the things that are made, even his eternal power and Godhead; so that they are without excuse: 21 Because that, when they knew God, they glorified him not as God, neither were thankful; but became vain in their imaginations, and their foolish heart was darkened. 22 Professing themselves to be wise, they became fools, 23 And changed the glory of the uncorruptible God into an *image* made like to corruptible man, and to birds, and fourfooted beasts, and creeping things.

People scoff at the idea of Creation by a Designer. Instead, they give their hearts and minds to the ludicrous notion that many scientists now propose that everything came from nothing! That everything produced itself, and life occurred spontaneously by accident, and there is no purpose or design. They are without excuse, as the very detail that science uncovers further reveals the awesome complexity of Nature. So these often very clever and intelligent highly educated people 'professing themselves to be wise, they become fools.

Psalm 14:1 The fool hath said in his heart, There is no God. They are corrupt, they have done abominable works, there is none that doeth good.

God is also saddened by the way we humans are spoiling the beautiful Creation on this Earth that He so lovingly prepared for us. God our Father is suffering with us. He is experiencing the pain of observing uncountable trillions of sins hurting His children. But this is the price God and Christ have to pay, and are very willing to pay, to create God's future Family.

The Feminine aspect of God

The Bible tells us a lot about God, He has a face, hair. He sits, has hands and feet, although He is Spirit, His body is tangible, not like some type of fog. After Christ had been resurrected and returned to the Father He was Spirit, but when he appeared to the disciples He was in a terrestrial body, otherwise His Glory would have killed everyone who saw Him.

Every mention of God in His Word is masculine. God's Word is Truth.

When we meet God in the scriptures, we always see Him represented as Male or in the masculine gender. This is because of His Rulership, His Authority. Yet in the Kingdom of God there will be male and female. When humans are resurrected they will be male and female as they were in life.

Genesis 1:27 So God created man in his own image, **in the image of God** created he him; male and female created he them.

So God looks like a human being, and human beings look like God.

Genesis 5:2 Male and female created he them; and blessed them, and called their name Adam, in the day when they were created.

God made male and female and called their (plural) name Adam, that is God called Adam and Eve – Adam. This is another indication of unity in plurality. So Adam and Eve were 'one', as God and Christ are One. All life is male and female, even inanimate things in nature like rock are made of atoms which have polarity, a positive and a negative charge in their component parts.

These verses tell us that man and woman were created in the image of God. This reveals that there is a female or feminine aspect of God. He embodies the essence of masculine and feminine while being God the Father, distinctly masculine. We have to allow our minds to think outside the box, as our thoughts are not His thoughts, nor can they be at this time.

Isaiah 55:8 For my thoughts are not your thoughts, neither are your ways my ways, saith the Lord.

God the Father was not alone during the period **before** the Creation of all we know. He had a feminine counterpart, Sophia or Wisdom.

The book of Proverbs chapter 8 gives more information and insights about God and His relationship with Knowledge, Understanding, and Wisdom (Greek Sofia), which is a feminine word in the original Hebrew. Wisdom is personified as female, a female Essence, and we are encouraged to seek to know 'Her' better.

The first nine chapters of Proverbs were written by Joseph, and were included by Solomon in his book of Proverbs. These chapters are all about Knowledge, Understanding, and Wisdom which is always presented as female or feminine. Wisdom is 'Sophia', a skittish, witty, playful, wise female personality. She existed before the beginning of Creation, before the world was formed, She was also there when everything was created.

Proverbs 3:13 Happy is the man that findeth wisdom, and the man that getteth understanding. 14 For the merchandise of it is better than the merchandise of silver, and the gain thereof than fine gold. 15 She (wisdom) is more precious than rubies: and all the things thou canst desire are not to be compared unto her. 16 Length of days is in her right hand; and in her left hand riches and honour. 17 Her ways are ways of pleasantness, and all her paths are peace. 18 She is a tree of life to them that lay hold upon her: and happy is every one that retaineth her. 19 **The Lord by wisdom hath founded the earth; by understanding hath he established the heavens.**

God the Father and Christ by Wisdom founded the earth. She, Sofia, Wisdom, was there with Him. She is the little known and rarely mentioned feminine influence in the Life of the God Family. This creates such a wonderfully different picture of our God in our minds if we will allow it to.

Proverbs 8:1 Doth not wisdom cry? and understanding put forth her voice? 2 She standeth in the top of high places, by the way in the places of the paths. 3 She crieth at the gates, at the entry of the city, at the coming in at the doors. 4 Unto you, O men, I call; and my voice is to the sons of man. 5 O ye simple, understand wisdom: and, ye fools, be ye of an understanding heart. 6 Hear; for I will speak of excellent things; and the opening of my lips shall be right things. 7 For my mouth shall speak truth; and wickedness is an abomination to my lips. 8 All the words of my mouth are in righteousness; there is nothing froward or perverse in them. 9 They are all plain to him that understandeth, and right to them that find knowledge. 10 Receive my instruction, and not silver; and knowledge rather than choice gold. 11 For wisdom is better than rubies; and all the things that may be desired are not to be compared to it. 12 I wisdom dwell with prudence, and find out knowledge of witty inventions.

Wisdom was with God the Father before the foundation of the world. Note in this passage all the many 'when' words. They are important here, because it shows that 'Wisdom' pre-existed Creation.

Notice also that this next passage gives such detail about the earth, before the mountains, the time before fountains of water, the points of the compass, the clouds. Even that God gave His decree that the seas would be contained by the sand of the shores.

Proverbs 8:22 The Lord (The Father) possessed me (Wisdom) in the *beginning* of his way, **before** his works of old. 23 I (Wisdom) was set up (or anointed) **from everlasting, from the beginning, or ever (before) the earth was.** 24 **When** there were no depths, I (Wisdom) was brought forth; **when** there were no fountains abounding with water. 25 **Before** the mountains were settled, **before** the hills was I (Wisdom) brought forth: 26 **While** as yet he had not made the earth, nor the fields, nor the highest part of the dust of the world. 27 **When** he prepared the heavens, I was there: **when** he set a compass upon the face of the depth: 28 **When** he established the clouds above: **when** he strengthened the fountains of the deep: 29 **When** he gave to the sea his decree, that the waters should not pass his commandment: **when** he appointed the foundations of the earth:

Proverbs 8:30 indicates an intimate relationship between God the Father and Wisdom.

There is One God, and Masculine cannot be adequately expressed without Feminine. The two together make the perfectly balanced One.

Wisdom is a perfect expression of the feminine qualities.

The prosaic language of the English of 1611 does not do justice to the reality of what was being described, or the force about what was happening between God the Father, and Wisdom.

Proverbs 8:30 Then I (wisdom) was by him, as one brought up with him: and I was daily his delight, rejoicing always before him;

Proverbs 8:30 gives a fascinating insight about the connection between God and Wisdom. Wisdom was with God, personified as a Being, had a close relationship with God, as one who was brought up with him. A family type of relationship, in much the same way as someone is with another in a human family when brought up together.

It tells how Wisdom daily was delighting God the Father. Wisdom herself was rejoicing before God. The Hebrew words in this verse imply a skittish, light hearted relationship, jovial and jocular, full of fun. Note the plurality of Oneness! Wisdom personified is shown here as being daily God's delight, and rejoicing always before Him. In the Hebrew, the poetry of the language gives a very different feel from the language of the KJV!

Wisdom was "daily God's (YHWH) delight" perhaps as His "consort", and "rejoicing always" before Him. In Hebrew these expressions appear to imply play, frolicking, skittish, teasing, flirtatious, jovial, jocular, light hearted behaviour, all in a kind of serious way that is not just allegorical, but more than that. God has all the feelings that He has endowed us with, including a sense of humour, this is clear from the Scriptures.

Every human on the face of the earth can benefit from embracing Wisdom, and appreciating Her qualities and the wealth and the contentment that she (Wisdom) can bring to a person. And in the Kingdom, we will be able to appreciate Her qualities, as God clearly does.

God the Father Created His Firstborn Son

God was enjoying the functions of Wisdom, part of His co-eternal Beingness, and decided to create His Son out of his Own Spirit who would become One with the Father.

Colossians 1:15 (Christ) Who is the image of the invisible God, the firstborn of every creature:

The One, YHWH, who became Christ the Messiah was created by God, **the firstborn of every creature,** was with God before the foundation of the world.

So at this time, there was God the Father and His Son and no other living creature.

1 Corinthians 15:45 And so it is written, The first man Adam was made a living soul; the last Adam was made a quickening spirit.

The first Adam was made out of dust. The 'Last Adam' was made out of Spirit. There is One God, Christ said that He and the Father were One.

John 10:30 I and my Father are one.

John 17:11... Holy Father, keep through thine own name those whom thou hast given me, that they may be one, as we are.

In the aeons before God and His Son began the work of Creating all that there is, They were preparing a magnificent Plan. A Plan ultimately to develop and expand the God Family. Before this Plan could be executed, all the Design Work had to be done.

God and His Son not only planned the Universe, our Solar system, the Earth, and the human race en masse, but also every single human being who would be born after the Creation of the Universe was known to Them individually. Each and every person was known to the God Family long before the foundation of the world. Amazing!

Ephesians 1:4 According as he hath chosen us in him before the foundation of the world, that we should be holy and without blame before him in love:

Before the foundation of the world God and His Son foreknew every person, knew what we would be like, and they chose to create a Plan which in the process of time would elevate us from our humanity, and grant us full membership into the Family of God as His Children.

John 3:16 For God so loved the world, that he gave his only begotten Son, that whosoever believeth in him should not perish, but have everlasting life. 17 For God sent not his Son into the world to condemn the world; but that the world through him might be saved.

Christ who was God, with God, loved us so much that He was willing to plan to give up His Power and His Godhead after Creating the Universe, the world and us, to become a man, and suffer pain, humiliation, and death for us. How can one quantify such Love?

John 1:1 In the beginning was the Word, and the Word was with God, and the Word was God... Verse 14 And the Word (Christ) was made flesh, and dwelt among us, (and we beheld his glory, the glory as of the only begotten of the Father), full of grace and truth.

We learn from the His words in the Bible that the sin of each of us made the almost unbelievable suffering that Christ was willing to go through essential, because it was necessary in order to pay the price of death to absolve us from all guilt and responsibility for our rebellion against God.

Hebrews 2:9 But we see Christ, who was made a little lower than the angels for the suffering of death, crowned with glory and honour; that he by the grace of God should taste death for every man. 10 For it became him, for whom are all things, and by whom are all things, in bringing many sons unto glory, to make the captain of their salvation perfect through sufferings.

God's sufferings and Christ's sufferings are the price they pay to have all of humanity join them in Glory as their Children.

Romans 8:18 For I reckon that the sufferings of this present time are not worthy to be compared with the glory which shall be revealed in us.

Human carnal minds cannot think in the way this verse suggests. Instead we focus on all the pain and suffering, and blame God for being harsh, unfair, and cruel.

The only way we can come to think as God and Christ would have us think is to ask daily, and on a moment by moment basis, to have the Spirit of God flow in our hearts and minds. This is the only way for us to be able think differently, to appreciate what the God of Love is doing for us here on Earth, and praise Them, and thank Them for the amazing future they have planned for us.

Here is another very awesome and sobering thought. God's Son agreed to the Plan of the Father before even the first human being was made by Him. This means that for however long all the planning continued, God's Son, with all the Power and Glory of being God, knew that at a point in time, He would give it all up and become a Human Being, and suffer the horrific torture and death to pay for our sins.

Just before Christ was crucified, he could still clearly remember the Glory He had as God with His Father before He came to Earth.

John 17:5 And now, O Father, glorify thou me with thine own self with the glory which I had with thee before the world was.

1 Peter 1:19 But with the precious blood of Christ, as of a lamb without blemish and without spot: 20 Who verily was foreordained before the foundation of the world, but was manifest in these last times for you, 21 Who by him do believe in God, that raised him up from the dead, and gave him glory; that your faith and hope might be in God.

Here was Christ, just about to suffer the dreadful fate that He had planned with the Father, and He is praying to God for the human beings that God had given Him to form his Ecclesia would be resurrected to Life and witness His Glory in the Kingdom. What manner of Love is that? Understanding this puts a very much deeper meaning to the sacrifice of Christ for us.

John 17:24 Father, I **will** that they also, whom thou hast given me, be with me where I am; that they may behold my glory, which thou hast given me: for thou lovedst me before the foundation of the world.

God and His Son designed every aspect of everything we know exists, (and a great deal we do not know about yet!) long before it was brought into being by the Son. How long? Who can tell? Anyway, this is **before time as we know it began**. They also planned the eventual infinite expansion of their domain.

Isaiah 9:7 Of the increase of his government and peace there shall be no end, upon the throne of David, and upon his kingdom, to order it, and to establish it with judgment and with justice from henceforth even for ever. The zeal of the Lord of hosts will perform this.

Ponder for a moment if you will, the physical laws of gravity, magnetism, electricity, radiation, the structure and power of the atom, and all those laws of physics and mathematics that would first have to have been in place before Creation could begin.

Picture the sheer size and scope of the Universe, the intricacies of DNA, the almost mind- boggling variety of the millions of species of the fauna and flora of this world. Just think about how much Planning had to go into the perfect ecological balance of all that was going to be Created.

Interestingly there is a great deal of hostility in this world of ours today from people towards any suggestion that there is a Designer. The very idea of there being a Designer provokes great animosity in the minds of those who reject God. It cuts across the so very widely held belief in the Theory of Evolution which is a direct insult to God our Designer and Creator. It is also a form of idolatry as it replaces belief in God with belief in 'Nature' as the creator. It must grieve God to see His children rejecting Him in this way.

God the Father and His Son are the One God.

God and Christ live in Heaven

God and Christ live in Heaven, in His Palace. God is not everywhere, he lives in one place, unless He chooses to do otherwise. So how is God everywhere? God is everywhere through the Power of His Holy Spirit, which fills the universe, yet can be directed as God Wills as well. Each human being is very important to God the Father and Christ His Son.

John 14:1 Let not your heart be troubled: ye believe in God, believe also in me. 2 In my Father's house are many mansions: if it were not so, I would have told you. I go to prepare a place for you. 3 And if I go and prepare a place for you, I will come again, and receive you unto myself; that where I am, there ye may be also.

I will come back to Earth, so that you can be where I am. And after we are changed at the resurrection, we shall undoubtedly spend some part of our eternal lives in heaven.

At this time Christ is in Heaven, and we need a Divine attachment to Him, and we have that through our measure, our earnest of the Holy Spirit. Here again is the promise given to us by Christ.

John 14:15 If ye love me, keep my commandments. 16 And I will pray the Father, and he shall give you another Comforter, that he may abide with you for ever;

Without the Holy Spirit, it would be totally impossible to keep the Law of Love.

The 'Trinity' is a totally false doctrine

We indeed see 'through a glass darkly', the world is blinded. Religious leaders have made a person out of the Holy Spirit, and created the doctrine of the 'Trinity'. This false doctrine started before the 3rd Century A.D., then progressively became accepted by almost all of 'Churchianity'. Many church people do say that they cannot explain it, and this is because it is not true, and therefore cannot be explained.

Because so many do not recognise the true Nature of God, or understand the mechanism of the Holy Spirit, they go astray. This is to a large extent the fault of the false doctrine of the Trinity, that the Holy Spirit is a person, and is part of the **God/Son/Holy Spirit** Trinity. This one incorrect teaching confuses the Truth, and gives rise to many different ideas about the Holy Spirit and what the Bible teaches about it.

There is only one verse in the entire Bible which suggests the Trinity, every other mention of God refers to the One God. **This one verse is spurious**, and was added long after the Canon was completed.

1 John 5:7 *For there are three that bear record in heaven, the Father, the Word, and the Holy Ghost: and these three are one.*

You will find that the words of this verse in your Bible are in *italics* which means that they were not in the original manuscripts. It appears in one of the earliest manuscripts in the 10th century. It was clearly added sometime after the original composition, there is no evidence of this verse in any Greek manuscript until the 1500th Century A.D.

The only way we can possibly understand, and to be able to sort truth from error about the Nature of God, is to ask

God for the help of His Holy Spirit in our lives, to enlighten the Word; to trust that it is the Truth and to shine His Truth about Him into us.

God the Son, the Word, who also had the rank of YHWH, created all things

God made His Son the Executive Creator and Sustainer of all things; the Universes, the Galaxies, the Planets, our Solar system, and the Earth and all it contains.

The Word (who became Christ) was created out of Spirit by His Father; the Word used His Father's Spirit Powers to Create Spirit Beings like angels, and the Sons of God. The Word then converted the Spirit of God into matter to make the Universe, to refurbish the earth, and to make man.

In the book of Hebrews, those 'Sons of God' are referred to as His 'Fellows'.

Hebrews 1:8,9 [8] But unto the Son he saith, Thy throne, O God, is for ever and ever: a sceptre of righteousness is the sceptre of thy kingdom. [9] Thou hast loved righteousness, and hated iniquity; therefore God, even thy God, hath anointed thee with the oil of gladness above thy fellows. The Einstein Law of Relativity may be used to indicate the fact that 'energy' (God's Spirit Power) can be converted into matter. Matter can be changed into energy, but neither matter nor energy can be destroyed because they are made from God's Spirit.

By Einstein's reasoning, the amount of energy it takes to produce matter is vast. $E=MC^2$.

This formula says that E for Energy is equal to M for Matter multiplied by the speed of light squared. The speed of light squared is a huge number, 900,000,000 kilometres/second.

So it takes a huge amount of energy (God's Power) to create a small amount of matter. Just imagine how much energy it took to create the Universe!!!

We now know the incredible power that is locked up in the atom. A few pounds of matter contain enough energy to destroy our planet if that energy was irresponsibly released in a nuclear explosion. Christ knew this and warned in Matthew 24 that if He did not shorten time, no flesh would remain alive on Earth.

Mark 13:20 And except that the Lord had shortened those days, no flesh should be saved: but for the elect's sake, whom he hath chosen, he hath shortened the days.

Our Saviour is a very much more powerful individual than the images of Him portray in the places of worship of Churchianity.

Colossians 1:16 For by him (YHWH – Christ) were all things created, that are in heaven, and that are in earth, visible and invisible, whether they be thrones, or dominions, or principalities, or powers: **all things** were created by him, and for him: 17 And he is before all things, and by him all things consist.

Notice carefully that YHWH, the Father through Christ, created **all things** including the visible and the invisible, all the spirit beings, the angels and the principalities and powers. He was before all other beings, and is in control over all other beings.

God the Father through Christ creates Human Beings

God the Father appointed His Son to create the Universe, and later to reform the Earth in six days to provide a suitable home for human beings. Then Christ converted the Spirit of God into matter to make man. The Word, Christ transformed the Spirit of God into matter to make man, and breathed into his nostrils both the breath of life and the human spirit, and Adam became a living being, or soul. All life and breath come from God and are the Energy of God's Spirit in action.

The Created Adam was the most perfect specimen of a human being in every detail, but lifeless until the Word breathed into him the breath of life.. Pause for thought: Compare the modern 'scientific' thought that "everything came from nothing".

The 'Breath of Life' and its components

So God the Word then breathed into Adam's nostrils 'the breath of life'; and God has subsequently 'breathed' the 'breath of life' into every human child that has ever been born and drew its first breath. This simple statement in English has unimagined meanings in the original manuscript which are explained next.

The original narrative was written in the Hebrew language which has a number of subtle, lyrical, poetical and descriptive features that do not exist in the English language. So a look at the original Hebrew words in the Old Testament brings out meanings that are completely lost when those Hebrew words are translated into English. Strong's Concordance of Hebrew words, each numbered for easy reference, is a useful work to enable us to gain greater understanding of what God wants us to understand from His Word.

God the Son breathes 'Life' into all who have breath, but 'neshama' Intellect and other components is bestowed only to humans. God use His Power, ruwach, of His Holy Spirit breathed (5301 naphach) into Adam's nostrils the breath (5397 neshama) of life (2416 chay) and he became a living soul (5315 nephesh).

God breathed these seven components of the 'Breath of Life' into Adam

1. 'breathed' naphach is to puff, inflate, blow hard, air, oxygen, breath.

2. 'breath' neshamah is 'life' consciousness, making alive, 'chay' living, the essence of 'life' as opposed to 'death'.

3. 'breath' neshamah is an electrical stimulus to enliven the brain to control the whole body, and think sub-consciously.

4. 'breath' neshamah is divine inspiration of the 'spirit in man' that links us to God via the 'Silver Cord'. Ecclesiastes 12:6,7

5. 'breath' neshamah is the thinking 'mind' which permeates and activates every cell of the body, and can cloud intellect with emotion rather than logic.

6. 'breath' neshamah is 'Mind', 'Intellect', the God-like faculty of imagining, reasoning, decision making, understanding objectively, planning, designing, creating, especially with regard to abstract matters as in ethical and moral capacity; sensitivity to who and what we are, awareness of our potential, which enables us to grow mentally and spiritually, develop abilities and talents, and can 'change' attitudes of the emotional mind.

7. 'breath' neshamah is also the spiritual conduit of the Holy Spirit from God the Father to us. John 20:22

'Neshama' is what endows human beings with aspects of God's Mind, but of course to a very limited extent. But we can make moral judgements, feel emotions, deign, create things. No animal has 'neshama', but only an operating system providing instincts that it cannot change.

Genesis 1:26 And God (YHWH, God's Son Christ) said, Let us make man in our image, after our likeness:

Here the word God is being used in the plural. So God is 'They', a single family, consisting of the Father, and the Word saying "Let us…"

Genesis 1:26b and let them have dominion over the fish of the sea, and over the fowl of the air, and over the cattle, and over all the earth, and over every creeping thing that creeps upon the earth.

Incidentally the English word 'Human' comes from an ancient root, 'Hu' which means God. So Hu-man is God-man! When the Pharisees accused Christ of blasphemy, He reminded them of the scripture which they knew very well that states that we are gods.

Psalm 82:6 I have said, Ye are gods; and all of you are children of the most High.

So God created man, with the eventual potential of becoming 'God', and gave him dominion over the whole of the rest of the Created things on this earth. This word dominion very is important, as it only applies to man, and not to any other creature. The word 'dominion' is also an important a key which gives us insight concerning the purpose of our existence here and now and also in the future. Dominion means to have power, even absolute power.

We human beings have dominion over this earth, and frankly we are not doing a very good job of 'dressing and keeping' our domain. This is a learning experience, which is not always a very happy one, considering the way human beings are treating each other, and abusing this amazing earth and all life on it.

Especially when we understand that we humans are destined in the future to have dominion not only over the earth, but over the entire Universe and all that is in it.

Human beings have a human spirit by which God communicates with us

We are physical, God is made of Spirit, but we have God in us in the form of life which is of the Spirit. As explained earlier, there is a gift of human spirit put in humans at conception, and with the first breath as we take it, 'neshama' enlivens us, gives us consciousness, and many of the characteristics of our Father. This spirit returns to God when we die. We cannot control how long we have the spirit, or power, or when we die.

God witnesses Himself directly to each of us by His Holy Spirit working through our human spirit which we receive at birth, and which returns to God who gave it at death.

Job 32:8 But there is a spirit in man: and the inspiration of the Almighty giveth them understanding.

All animals also have a 'spirit' which makes each genus what it is, an elephant has an elephant spirit, and a dog a dog spirit, all animate life has a spirit, and they are all different. Animals are limited in intellect and behaviour by the capacity of their spirit.

What is the role of the human spirit? It gives us the capacity to be able think, to plan, to create, to design, and to love, and these are all characteristics of God. It also enables us to make a connection with God.

The human spirit is completely different from animal spirit as it is our link to God's Spirit. Our human spirit gives us the power to respond to God our Father, and by the means of God's Holy Spirit if we choose to do so. If we do, we gain understanding.

Proverbs 20:27 The spirit of man is the candle of the Lord, searching all the inward parts of the belly.

The Holy Spirit shines the Light of God's Gospel illuminating the innermost parts of our hearts and minds through our human spirit.

When we do die, the human spirit which contains a complete record of the life of that person returns to God. That spirit contains an image of all we experienced in our lifetime. Much like a tape or video that has no 'life' without a machine to play it, our spirit has no life or consciousness without a body, and is in that sense is inanimate.

Ecclesiastes 8:8 There is no man that hath power over the (human) spirit to retain the (human) spirit; neither hath he power in the day of death: and there is no discharge in that war; neither shall wickedness deliver those that are given to it.

Ecclesiastes 12:7 Then shall the dust return to the earth as it was: and the spirit shall return unto God who gave it.

This 'spirit' is filed and stored by God until it is used by Him who, at the resurrection, inserts the spirit of the person into a new body for that individual, whether to temporary human life or to eternal spiritual life depending upon circumstances at the time.

Christ tells His disciples about the 'Comforter' that He will send

In John chapters 13 through 17, Christ was talking to His disciples on the eve of His Crucifixion about the Holy Spirit, and by extension is talking to us, His ekklesia, today.

John 14:15 If ye love me, keep my commandments. 16 And I will pray the Father, and he shall give you another Comforter, that he may abide with you for ever; 17 Even the Spirit of truth; whom the world cannot receive, because it seeth him not, neither knoweth him: but ye know him; for he dwelleth with you, and shall be in you. 18 I will not leave you comfortless: I will come to you.

Christ said, "Keep *my* commandments" the Law of Love, not the ten commandments, He fulfilled them, or filled them up, and they were replaced by the infinitely more potent Law of Love. The ten commandments of Moses that were given to Israel were designed for adult children who personally had no contact with the Holy Spirit. Those laws are still in effect and always will be for carnally minded people. They do not apply in the same way to those Christians who are Spirit led.

Galatians 1:4 Now I say, That the heir, as long as he is a child, differeth nothing from a servant, though he be lord of all; 2 But is under tutors and governors until the time appointed of the father. 3 Even so we, when we were children, were in bondage under the elements of the world:

Galatians 3:24 Wherefore the law was our schoolmaster to bring us unto Christ, that we might be justified by faith. 25 But after that faith is come, we are no longer under a schoolmaster. 26 For ye are all the children of God by faith in Christ.

The Holy Spirit, the Comforter is not the intermediary or the advocate, or the mediator, but is the Power of God flowing through all His works, and through each of us. It is not a person, but is the Power of God.

1 Peter 2:5 For there is one God, and one mediator between God and men, the man Christ;

John 14:17 Even the Spirit of truth; whom the world cannot receive, because it sees him not, neither knows him: but ye know him (it); for he (it) dwells with you, and (later) shall be in you. 18 I will not leave you comfortless: I will come to you.

The Holy Spirit is the Spirit of Truth which God uses to transmit His Will to us.

1 John 2:27 But the anointing which ye have received of him abides in you, and **ye need not that any man teach you:** but as the same anointing teaches you of all things, and is truth, and is no lie, and even as it hath taught you, ye shall abide in him.

We do not need men or woman, or any organisations of this world to teach us the Truth. Christ will attend to that for us through His Spirit, causing the Holy Spirit to flow through us ,giving us the Truth, which will always be in total harmony with the Word of God, the Bible.

John 14:26 But the Comforter, which is the Holy Ghost, whom the Father will send in my name, he shall teach you all things, and bring all things to your remembrance, whatsoever I have said unto you.

Since God Created the first of His children to this day, so very few in history have had the Holy Spirit *with* them, and even fewer *in* them. Even Christ's disciples had the Holy Spirit *with* them, but not *in* them until the day of Pentecost, and even then despite the thousands who were converted, not in everyone, only those God called at that time.

John 6:44 No man can come to me, except the Father which hath sent me draw him: and I will raise him up at the last day.

All the efforts of so-called 'evangelists' notwithstanding!

The Spirit of God pervades the entire universe, it is the Power of God in action, and is on a special 'frequency' by which He communicates with us. Like the frequencies that operate a radio you cannot see or hear.. Nobody would suggest that it is the radio speaking.

The inspired Word of God, the original Scriptures of the Holy Bible contain all we need to know at this time, plus the insights God gives to each of us. The Bible in its original languages, every word was entirely inspired by Christ, through the Power of His Holy Spirit to His servants the Prophets and His disciples and servants.

We are now the Children of God, to become fully changed at the resurrection when we shall have a Spirit body. Each of us will inherit the entirety of the Universe through Christ. God and Christ are made of Spirit. Our spirit will not be like a fog, it will have form, shape and substance, but invisible to humans unless they present in a terrestrial form.

The Holy Spirit can be poured out like water, and like air and water can fill up any space, solids cannot. Air and water increase pressure with depth, but this is not so of Spirit.

When God was reforming the Earth for our habitation, His Spirit 'fluttered' over the water.

Romans 8:16 The Spirit itself beareth witness with our spirit, that we are the children of God:

In this way, the Holy Spirit works with each of us individually via the 'silver cord' to provide the 'food' of the Word that is specially applicable to us. This direct contact with God is the only way we can be sure of receiving the Truth unmixed with the ideas or errors of human beings.

It is this combination of God's Spirit and our human spirit which forms the new creature, or creation in each of us once we are humanly 'converted'.

2 Corinthians 5:17 Therefore if any man be in Christ, he is a new creature: old things are passed away; behold, all things are become new.

This is the mechanism by which God puts a part of Himself, a portion of His nature, His character, His Wisdom and His Love into His children. As we respond to these gifts, we grow in Grace and knowledge, and in Godly character.

It is truly God who does the work in us. We do not have to 'work out our own salvation' because God does it. Christ said:

John 14:10 Believest thou not that I am in the Father, and the Father in me? the words that I speak unto you I speak not of myself: but the Father that dwelleth in me, he doeth the works.

Philippians 2:13 For it is God which worketh in you both to will and to do of his good pleasure.

It is He who begins the work of training and maturing us as His children while we are still humans, with all our faults and failings.

Our glorious future as God's Children

Why are we human beings here on earth? What is the purpose of human life? What are we doing here? Why is our physical life here so short? There has to be a reason for our lives, otherwise it is pointless, but what is it? So many ask this question.

Actually, the reason and purpose for our lives is glorious beyond our imagination. It is very hard to appreciate fully, and seems totally incredible. Our destiny is to be 'Saved' from death and to live forever with God and Christ.

Salvation, or being 'Saved' is not a religious term, it is a real and practical word, humans are to be salvaged from this physical existence which is preparing us for an eternity of Spiritual life with God the Father and Christ.

When we review the responsibilities that God has, His actions, His lifestyle, His Power and Authority that they have, why would they want to share it with mere mortals? Well, They do, and the position we will have with God staggers the mind. The majesty and the glory that await us is mind-boggling.

What will we be like in the resurrection?

Human beings are promised a temporary human resurrection, when they will either be restored to mortal life, or to immortality dependent upon a number of factors. What will it be like to have a new immortal body?

Mortal bodies are made out of physical matter. We may not be able fully to understand exactly what the composition of our new body will be like, but we can have an idea.

God created His Son from Spiritual matter. Spiritual Heavenly bodies are made out of Spirit Matter. This is not a wispy fog type of body at all, but it will have a form and a shape, will be tangible, have hands, feet and a face. It will normally be invisible to humans unless the Spirit person chooses to take the form of a terrestrial body.

We know that God's invisible laws of Gravity, Centrifugal Force, Electricity, Magnetic waves and many Other Laws exist by measuring them, and by the effect they have on things we can see. We cannot see the wind, but we can see the effect it has on leaves and the waves of the sea.

Romans 1:20 For the **invisible things** of Him from the creation of the world **are clearly seen**, being understood **by the things that are made**, even his eternal power and Godhead; so that they are without excuse:

God is invisible to us, but He has a tangible body which takes up a place in space. God has a face, arms, torso, legs and feet just as we do, a body which is made up of Spiritual Matter that other Spirit beings can see perfectly well.

Philippians 3:20 For our ~~conversation~~ (citizenship) is in heaven; from whence also we look for the Saviour, the Lord Jesus Christ: 21 Who shall change our vile (physical) body, that it may be fashioned like unto His (God's) glorious (Heavenly Spiritual) body, according to the working whereby he is able even to subdue all things unto himself.

After Christ was resurrected, He could appear to His disciples who could see Him, (but did not recognise Him immediately), and handle Him, and He could also pass through walls with ease. Spirit is not intangible or ethereal, but it is invisible to us, yet is tangible and very real, being made out of Heavenly God Spirit Substance.

Notice that the dead are not in Heaven, they are buried in the earth. When the resurrection to life occurs to those 'in Christ', note that the dead in the graves will be raised **up**, and those who are alive will go *up* to meet their Lord in the air. Not to be brought down from Heaven.

1 Corinthians 6:14 And God hath both raised up the Lord, and will also raise up us by his own power.

1 Corinthians 15:35 But some man will say, How are the dead raised up? and with what body do they come? 36 Thou fool, that which thou sowest is not quickened, except it die:

Those who are changed at the time of the resurrection 'die' as their mortal body changes into Spirit. Those who are dead in their graves simply put on a new Spirit body as they come up. Human bodies are like seed which has to die in order to make a new plant, so it is with us.

1 Corinthians 15:37 And that which thou sowest, thou sowest not that body that shall be, but bare grain, it may chance of wheat, or of some other grain: 38 But God giveth it a (plant) body as it hath pleased him, and to every (different) seed his own body (or plant).

You do not sow the plant, but just the seed of a plant, then the new plant can grow. We also know that when we eat different animals, not all animal, bird or fish flesh is the same.

1 Corinthians 15:39 All flesh is not the same flesh: but there is one kind of flesh of men, another flesh of beasts, another of fishes, and another of birds. 40 There are also celestial bodies, and bodies terrestrial: but the glory of the celestial is one, and the glory of the terrestrial is another. 41 There is one glory of the sun, and another glory of the moon, and another glory of the stars: for one star differeth from another star in glory.

The Sun, the Moon the earth, the celestial bodies and the terrestrial bodies differ in composition and in their glory.

1 Corinthians 15:42 So also is the resurrection of the dead. It is sown in corruption; it is raised in incorruption: 43 It is sown in dishonour; it is raised in glory: it is sown in weakness; it is raised in power: 44 It is sown a natural body; it is raised a spiritual body. There is a natural body, and there is a spiritual body. 45 And so it is written, The first man Adam was made a living soul; the last Adam was made a quickening spirit.

What is a 'soul'? Dust + Breath of life with man's spirit = Soul

Dust -minus- Breath and spirit = dust & death of the Soul.

We do not have an Immortal Soul. The Soul that sins, it shall **die.**

Ezekiel 18:4 Behold, all souls are mine; as the soul of the father, so also the soul of the son is mine: the soul that sinneth, it shall die.

We shall be like Him as He is, and He is a quickening Spirit, One who gives life, and so will we in our future existence. At present we only pass life on by sowing seed, or having children, but when we are changed we will actually be able to impart life to things we create.

1 Corinthians 15:46 Howbeit that was not first which is spiritual, but that which is natural; and afterward that which is spiritual. 47 The first man is of the earth, earthy; the second man is the Lord from heaven. 48 As is the earthy, such are they also that are earthy: and as is the heavenly, such are they also that are heavenly. 49 And as we have borne the image of the earthy, we shall also bear the image of the heavenly. 50 Now this I say, brethren, that flesh and blood cannot inherit the kingdom of God; neither doth corruption inherit incorruption.

Human beings cannot inherit the 'full version' of the Kingdom of God, but we can be a part of the Kingdom of God in part, in type, and indeed those who are 'in Christ' are already a part of it. At the resurrection we shall also bear the image of the heavenly and be immortal. Hard to believe? Christ says we will.

The doctrine of the 'Immortality of the Soul' is a complete nonsense

If we were already immortal, what would be the point of putting on immortality? The whole notion started with the serpent telling Eve that 'you will not surely die!' The concept was popularised in Greece in the 3rd Century

B.C., absorbed into the groups of the New Testament Christians, then inducted into the Christian 'Churches' in the 3rd Century A.D. So that doctrinal lie has been popular with many religious and non-religious people ever since.

It is clear simple logic, that if mankind was immortal, then Christ did not die, or spend three days and nights in the grave. He would have died and gone straight to Heaven, so nor would there have been any need for Him to be resurrected, and therefore your sins are not forgiven.

Examine the Word of God, and be assured **for yourself** that the doctrine of the Immortality of the Soul is a lie which denies the plain words in the scriptures, the whole plan of God, and makes pointless the sacrifice of Christ our Lord, Master, and Creator.

So how will we be in the resurrection?

Colossians 1:12 Giving thanks unto the Father, which hath made us meet (fitting) to be partakers of the inheritance of the saints in light: 13 Who hath delivered us from the power of darkness, and hath translated us into the kingdom of his dear Son: 14 In whom we have redemption through his blood, even the forgiveness of sins: 15 Who is the image of the invisible God, the firstborn of every creature:

Note again that Christ, God's Son was the firstborn of *every* creature.

We have been delivered, saved, by Christ dying for us, and that was done for us mortals by the Very God who Created us, Jesus Christ our Lord. Amazing grace!

Colossians 1:16 For by him (Christ) were all things created, that are in heaven, and that are in earth, visible and invisible, whether they be thrones, or dominions, or principalities, or powers: all things were created by him, and for him: 17 And he is before all things, and by him all things consist. 18 And he is the head of the body, the ~~church~~ (His ecclesia): who is the beginning, the firstborn from the dead; that in all things he might have the preeminence. 19 For it pleased the Father that in him should all fulness dwell; 20 And, having made peace through the blood of his cross, by him to reconcile all things unto himself; by him, I say, whether they be things in earth, or things in heaven. 21 And you, that were sometime alienated and enemies in your mind by wicked works, yet now hath he reconciled 22 In the body of his flesh through death, to present you (to God the Father) holy and unblameable and unreproveable in his sight:

1 Corinthians 2:7 But we speak the wisdom of God in a **mystery**, even the hidden wisdom, which God ordained before the world unto our glory:

Ephesians 3:9 And to make all men see what is the fellowship of the **mystery**, which from the beginning of the world hath been hid in God, who created all things by Jesus Christ:

What had been held as a mystery since the world began? That **every** human being, man, woman, child, Jew, Gentile, everyone, all would all have a part in the Plan of God for age- lasting quality Spiritual life. This mystery was not revealed by Christ to Paul until 63 A.D.

Colossians 1:26 Even the **mystery** which hath been hid from ages and from generations, but now is made manifest to his saints: To whom God would make known what is the riches of the glory of this **mystery** among the Gentiles; which is Christ in you, the hope of glory:

About 30 years after He was crucified and resurrected from the dead, Christ revealed this final part of the good news, the Gospel of God to Paul personally in 63 A.D. These verses from the book of Colossians, inspired to be written down by Paul, are words directly from Christ to us in this era to inspire us concerning the reality of our future with Him.

Ponder this. How blessed are we to be able to understand the mystery which was hidden from all God's servants since time began until 63 A.D.? Salvation is not just for the Jews and Israel, but for all human beings. God's mercy is such that we can know that all humans will eventually be saved and given eternal life, even the worst humans who have ever lived.

True Christians look forward to a resurrection.

No, we do not go to heaven when we die! The Scripture says no man has ascended into Heaven except Christ. We do not have an 'Immortal Soul'.

2 Corinthians 4:13 We having the same spirit of faith, according as it is written, I believed, and therefore have I spoken; we also believe, and therefore speak; 14 Knowing that He (The Father, God almighty) which raised up the Lord shall raise up us also by (the risen) Christ, and shall present us with you.

What we do have is the prospect of being changed into Spirit and given Eternal Life at the Resurrection of the body.

2 Corinthians 5:1 For we know that if our earthly house (human body) of this tabernacle were dissolved, we have a building of God, an house (a heavenly body) not made with hands, eternal (age-lasting) in the heavens. 2 For in this we groan, earnestly desiring to be clothed upon with our house (new body) which is from heaven: 3 If so be that being clothed we shall not be found naked. 4 For we that are in this (physical temple) tabernacle do groan, being burdened: not for that we would be unclothed, but clothed upon, that mortality might be swallowed up of life. 5 Now he that hath wrought us for the selfsame thing is God, who also hath given unto us the earnest of the Spirit.

We have a house, a body, not made with hands, and to look forward to living, an age- lasting life in the heavens. We are mortal, and we will die, but that mortality will be 'swallowed up' in immortality. As Christians we are 'in Christ' and are already **in type** part of the Royal Family of God.

1 Peter 2:9 But ye are a chosen generation, a royal priesthood, an holy nation, a peculiar (special) people; that ye should shew forth the praises of him who hath called you out of darkness into his marvellous light;

1 John 3:2 Behold, what manner of love the Father hath bestowed upon us, that we should be called the sons of God: therefore the world knoweth us not, because it knew him not. 2 Beloved, **now are we** (present tense) the sons of God, and it doth not yet appear what we shall be: but we know that, when he shall appear, we shall be like him; for we shall see him as he is.

We are the Children of the Most High God, and as such we will have Life Eternal. We do not know how, or indeed when this is going to happen, it is beyond our comprehension as mortal humans, but we will be taught all about it when the time comes. There is so much for us to look forward to, not the least is the lifestyle of the God Family which puts all human ideas of the 'good life' into the shade to say the least! We will be able to enjoy both the spiritual and the physical, the celestial as well as the terrestrial. Selah! Ponder on that!

Hebrews 1:1 God, (and Christ our Creator) who at sundry times and in divers manners spake in time past unto the fathers by the prophets, 2 Hath in these last days spoken unto us by his Son, whom he hath appointed heir of **all** things, by whom also he made the worlds;

Christ the Firstborn Son of the Most High God is talking to each of us individually now, this moment, in our era, through the words He inspired Paul to write down for our inspiration and joy. Do we realise this, and appreciate what we are we are really, actually reading here? Are we believing what we are reading and 'hearing' in our minds from the Word of Christ with the help of the Holy Spirit? Utterly amazing!

Hebrews 1:3 Who (Christ) being the brightness of his glory, and the express image of his (the Father's) person, and upholding all things by the word of his power, when he (Christ) had by himself purged our sins, sat down on the right hand of the Majesty on high:

The express image – Christ looked exactly like the Father. The disciples saw and touched the resurrected Christ. This is not allegory, it is a plain description. At His resurrection, Christ went up to the Father in Heaven and was judged perfect, and is now able to present us to the Father perfect also. When we are presented we shall look just like Christ does, who looks like the Father!

God's global control of government

Proverbs 8:14 Counsel is mine, and sound wisdom: I am understanding; I have strength. 15 By me kings reign, and princes decree justice. 16 By me princes rule, and nobles, even all the judges of the earth.

God the Father is in complete control of this world, and appoints government leaders according to His will and pleasure. God has also appointed Satan to be the god of this world and is using him to further His purpose while human beings are living out their lives in order to execute His Master Plan for humankind.

2 Corinthians 4:4 In whom the god of this world hath blinded the minds of them which believe not, lest the light of the glorious gospel of Christ, who is the image of God, should shine unto them.

In our era, Satan has created 'Globalism' unlike anything previously in history. When we resist Satan, we develop Godly character.

Proverbs 8:17 I love them that love me (Wisdom); and those that seek me early shall find me. 18 Riches and honour are with me; yea, durable riches and righteousness. 19 My fruit is better than gold, yea, than fine gold; and my revenue than choice silver. 20 I lead in the way of righteousness, in the midst of the paths of judgment: 21 That I may cause those that love me to inherit substance; and I will fill their treasures.

The Resurrection of Christ

John 17:4 I have glorified thee on the earth: I have finished the work which thou gavest me to do. 5 And now, O Father, glorify thou me with thine own self with the glory which I had with thee before the world was.

Christ gave abundant evidence of His resurrection, it was not done in a corner, hundreds of people saw Christ alive after His death. Those hundreds would have told thousands more about the event. There is a historical record that tells when Tiberius Caesar heard about the resurrection, he declared to the Romans that Christ was a 'god'.

1 Corinthians 15:5 And that he (Christ) was seen of Cephas, then of the twelve: 6 After that, he was seen of above five hundred brethren at once; of whom the greater part remain unto this present, but some are fallen asleep (have died). 7 After that, he was seen of James; then of all the apostles. 8 And last of all he was seen of me (Paul) also, as of one born out of due time.

Paul was ordered to appear before the King Agrippa, who Paul confronted. Paul told Festus who accused Paul of being mad that the King clearly knew about the resurrection of Christ.

Acts 26:23 That Christ should suffer, and that he should be the first that should rise from the dead, and should shew light unto the people, and to the Gentiles. 24 And as he thus spake for himself, Festus said with a loud voice, Paul, thou art beside thyself; much learning doth make thee mad. 25 But he said, I am not mad, most noble Festus; but speak forth the words of truth and soberness. 26 For the king knoweth of these things, before whom also I speak freely: for I am persuaded that none of these things are hidden from him; for this thing was not done in a corner. 27 King Agrippa, believest thou the prophets? I know that thou believest. 28 Then Agrippa said unto Paul, Almost thou persuadest me to be a Christian.

It is the 'hope' of the resurrection that spurs us on to greater efforts in our Christian life.

1 Corinthians 15:19 If in this life only we have hope in Christ, we are of all men most miserable. 20 But now is Christ risen from the dead, and become the firstfruits of them that slept. 21 For since by man (Adam) came death, by man (Christ) came also the resurrection of the dead. 22 For as in Adam all die, even so in Christ shall all be made alive.

Note: In the resurrection we shall be raised **up** from the grave or from the surface of the earth, not down from heaven! The dead are not in heaven.

John 3:13 And no man hath ascended up to heaven, but he that came down from heaven, even the Son of man which is in heaven.

1 Corinthians 15 is called the 'resurrection chapter' in the Bible because it gives so much information about our future life as a spirit being.

1 Corinthians 15:3 For I delivered unto you first of all that which I also received, how that Christ died (was dead in the tomb three days and nights) for our sins according to the scriptures; 4 And that he was buried, and that he rose again the third day according to the scriptures:

1 Corinthians 15:23 But every man in his own order (or in the time appointed): Christ the firstfruits; afterward they that are Christ's at his coming. 24 Then cometh the end, when he shall have delivered up the kingdom to God, even

the Father; when he shall have put down all rule and all authority and power. 25 For he must reign, till he hath put all enemies under his feet. 26 The last enemy that shall be destroyed is death.

Death is an enemy, the last enemy, and when death is eventually destroyed, at the end of the 'story' as it will be when 'all is in all', there will be only Life.

1 Corinthians 15:35 But some man will say, How are the dead raised up? and with what body do they come? 36 Thou fool, that which thou sowest is not quickened, except it die: 37 And that which thou sowest, thou sowest not that body that shall be, but bare grain, it may chance of wheat, or of some other grain: 38 But God giveth it a body as it hath pleased him, and to every seed his own (Spirit) body.

Please do not think that what we are saying here is 'religious' talk. This is the Creator of the Universe, Christ, talking to us in the 21st Century, telling us what is going to happen to us, that is to you reading this, and to me writing it! It might be an idea to ask ourselves as we go along, if we are continually asking the Father, our Dad, and Christ for the help of God's Holy Spirit with our daily growth in Knowledge, Understanding and Wisdom.

If Christ is calling you now and opening your mind now to His truth, and you respond with the belief and faith He is offering to give you, and you are 'in Christ', then you will be resurrected to eternal life if you are dead when He returns. Or if you are still alive you will be changed from mortal to immortal in the twinkling of any eye. Yes you will.

However if you are not being called now and you die, then the next thing you will be conscious and aware of is the moment when you are resurrected to human life. Is this a second chance? No assuredly not. If you have not been called personally in this lifetime, then you will certainly be called when you are restored to human life, and this then will be given your first chance properly to respond to Him. Again for emphasis:

1 Corinthians 15:40 There are also celestial bodies, and bodies terrestrial: but the glory of the celestial is one, and the glory of the terrestrial is another. 41 There is one glory of the sun, and another glory of the moon, and another glory of the stars: for one star differeth from another star in glory.

Resurrected humans will instantly become Spirit beings and will differ one from another in glory, power, and appearance. We will probably be able to recognise others as they will be able to recognise us.

1 Corinthians 15:44 It is sown a natural body; it is raised a spiritual body. There is a natural body, and there is a spiritual body. 45 And so it is written, The first man Adam was made a living soul; the last Adam was made a quickening spirit.

What will we look like when we are Glorified?

Christ was and is the Express Image of the Father, so we know what the Father looks like, He looks like Christ looked when He was on earth. Christ by whom the Father made the worlds.

Hebrews 1:3 (Christ) Who being the brightness of his glory, and **the express image** of his person, and upholding all things by the word of his power, when he had by himself purged our sins, sat down on the right hand of the Majesty on high:

There was a first physical Adam and there is a second spiritual 'Adam' which is Christ.

It is absolutely incredible that the Word who was with God, and was God, completely gave up that power and position, and became a man. The Individual who previously was God with all that power, died and ceased to be alive for three days and three nights trusting the Father to restore Him to His original Glory, which of course He did.

So what will we look like when we are resurrected to Glory? This description of the Living Christ in the book of Revelation will give you an idea.

Revelation 1:13 And in the midst of the seven candlesticks one like unto the Son of man, clothed with a garment down to the foot, and girt about the paps with a golden girdle. 14 His head and his hairs were white like wool, as white as snow; and his eyes were as a flame of fire; 15 And his feet like unto fine brass, as if they burned in a furnace; and his voice as the sound of many waters. 16 And he had in his right hand seven stars: and out of his mouth went a sharp twoedged sword: and his countenance was as the sun shineth in his strength. 17 And when I saw him, I fell at his feet as dead. And he laid his right hand upon me, saying unto me, Fear not; I am the first and the last:

Like Moses when God was willing to be seen by him, YHWH had to cover Moses face in the cleft of a rock, and only see His back as he passed by or the Power YHWH gave off would have killed him.

So Christ in His Glory looks like the Sun in its strength at midday, and so shall we! He has a face with a mouth, hands, feet, hair, a torso, all resplendent with iridescent light. When we are in our new glorious body, so will we have a body like Christ has now? Yes we will. Will we be able to adopt a terrestrial body which looks just like a human being, and even pass through solid walls like Christ did? Yes we will.

Christ was dead in the grave, but He was resurrected to be a quickening Spirit. We have had the image of the earthly, but we will become the image of the heavenly and put on incorruption, never to die again. We shall have a new form and shape, and we shall also have Godly Character

Spiritually, morally, ethically, psychologically, and in every way like Christ.

1 John 3:2 Beloved, now are we the sons of God, and it doth not yet appear what we shall be: but we know that, when he shall appear, **we shall be like him**; for we shall see him as he is.

This is Christ speaking through John, the first cousin of Christ, assuring us that we will indeed be just like Christ when we are changed.

2 Peter 1:3 According as his divine power hath given unto us all things that pertain unto life and godliness, through the knowledge of him that hath called us to glory and virtue: 4 Whereby are given unto us exceeding great and precious promises: that by these ye might be partakers of the divine nature, having escaped the corruption that is in the world through lust.

Again, *please* do not read these words as 'religious' talk. These are the words of the Risen Christ giving you the substance of His exceeding great and precious promises, by which we will be partakers of the divine nature, in Glory. These are plain words of truth, and they are reality, in fact they are more real than we are. Just the night before Christ was crucified He was praying to the Father for us, repeated here:

John 17:1 These words spake Jesus, and lifted up his eyes to heaven, and said, Father, the hour is come; glorify thy Son, that thy Son also may glorify thee: 2 As thou hast given him power over all flesh, that he should give eternal life to as many as thou hast given him. 3 And this is life eternal, that they might know thee the only true God, and Jesus Christ, whom thou hast sent. 4 I have glorified thee on the earth: I have finished the work which thou gavest me to do. 5 And now, O Father, glorify thou me with thine own self with the glory which I had with thee before the world was.

Christ was asking the Father to Glorify Him, to give Him back the position He originally had with God; and that He would give eternal life, and therefore Glory, to all humans that were 'in Him'.

John 17:10 And all mine are thine, and thine are mine; and I am glorified in them. 11 And now I am no more in the world, but these are in the world, and I come to thee. Holy Father, keep through thine own name those whom thou hast given me, that they may be one, as we are. 20 Neither pray I for these alone, but for them also (us!) which shall believe on me through their word; 21 That they all may be one; as thou, Father, art in me, and I in thee, that they also may be one in us: that the world may believe that thou hast sent me. 22 And the glory which thou gavest me I have given them; that they may be one, even as we are one:

Christ is praying that **as** He is One with the Father, so shall all humans who are 'in Him' will also be One with Christ and therefore One with the Father. Amazing stuff! Believe it, have faith, and you can have this, and you will be there!! Again for emphasis:

Philippians 3:20 For our ~~conversation~~ (Gk. Citizenship) is in heaven; from whence also we look for the Saviour, the Lord Jesus Christ: 21 Who shall change our vile body, that it may be fashioned like unto his glorious body, according to the working whereby he is able even to subdue all things unto himself.

We shall have a new body which will be just like Christ's glorious body. Look in the mirror a moment, right now you are a plain old human like me, but that is going to change! We are called to become like Him.

Remember, **all** will eventually be saved, but entry into the Kingdom of God is conditional. There is a condition, we have to walk worthy, which can only be done with His help.

1 Thessalonians 2:12 That ye would walk worthy of God, who hath called you unto his kingdom and glory. 13 For this cause also thank we God without ceasing, because, when ye received the word of God which ye heard of us, ye received it not as the word of men, but as it is in truth, the word of God, which effectually worketh also in you that believe.

Many, many people cherish the notion that there is such a thing as 'Unconditional Love'. Nowhere in God's Word is this idea supported. God does not 'do' "Unconditional Love". The entire Bible from start to finish is peppered with the little but powerful word **'if'.**

God repeatedly says more times in His Word than you can count, **'If** you do this'... blessings follow. **'If** you do not do this'... punishment will come eventually.

In the book of Hebrews, which when correctly placed, is in the centre of Paul's fourteen epistles, after Peter, and before 2 Thessalonians. Christians are given a severe warning. It says that once we have been enlightened by the Holy Spirit, if we drift away, we will miss out on being in the Kingdom of God, and ruling with Christ in the Millennium.

Hebrews 6:4 For it is impossible for those who were once enlightened, and have tasted of the heavenly gift, and were made partakers of the Holy ~~Ghost~~ (Spirit), 5 And have tasted the good word of God, and the powers of the world to come, 6 If they shall fall away, to renew them again unto repentance (in this lifetime); seeing they crucify to themselves the Son of God afresh, and put him to an open shame.

So there is a price to pay for not 'walking worthy', the human notions of 'Unconditional love' notwithstanding. No true Christian will want to miss out on the opportunity to be with Christ in the Kingdom.

Is it blasphemy to suggest that we are to become God?

John 10:24 Then came the Jews round about him, and said unto him, How long dost thou make us to doubt? If thou be the Christ, tell us plainly. 25 Jesus answered them, I told you, and ye believed not: the works that I do in my Father's name, they bear witness of me. 26 But ye believe not, because ye are not of my sheep, as I said unto you. 27 My sheep hear my voice, and I know them, and they follow me: 28 And I give unto them eternal life; and they shall never perish, neither shall any man pluck them out of my hand.

Christ said plainly to the Jews, I will give my sheep eternal (quality age-lasting) life. We who are true Christians are His sheep, and we believe what Christ says. At least we do, and if we ask for His belief to live in us, we will believe.

John 10:29 My Father, which gave them me, is greater than all; and no man is able to pluck them out of my Father's hand. 30 I and my Father are one.

Again, Christ says that He and the Father are One. Plurality in unity, or unity in plurality.

John 10:31 Then the Jews took up stones again to stone him. 32 Jesus answered them, Many good works have I shewed you from my Father; for which of those works do ye stone me? 33 The Jews answered him, saying, For a good work we stone thee not; but for blasphemy; and because that thou, being a man, makest thyself God. 34 Jesus answered them, Is it not written in your law, I said, Ye are gods? (Psalm 82:6) 35 If he called them gods, unto whom the word of God came, and the scripture cannot be broken; 36 Say ye of him, whom the Father hath sanctified, and sent into the world, Thou blasphemest; because I said, I am the Son of God? 37 If I do not the works of my Father, believe me not. 38 But if I do, though ye believe not me, believe the works: that ye may know, and believe, that the

Father is in me, and I in him. 39 Therefore they sought again to take him: but he escaped out of their hand,

The Pharisees and the other religious dignitaries recoiled, and called Christ a blasphemer. They just could not take the truth. They could not deny the scriptures, so they just refused to accept that this 'scoundrel' was the Messiah they had waited for so long and would have killed Him there and then if they could.

We are gods. Blasphemous? No! Outstandingly ridiculous? Yes, but true.

Here we are making fools of ourselves on this earth for seventy years or so, and even on other places in the universe with space travel leaving millions of pieces of junk and some people behind all because we ignore the Maker's Instruction Manual written as a guide to happiness by Christ our very Creator.

Thousands of years before any form of flight, let alone space travel was possible, here is what it says in God's Word. Astonishing? God knows all things.

Deuteronomy 30:4 4 If any of thine be driven out unto the outmost parts of heaven, from thence will the LORD thy God gather thee, and from thence will he fetch thee:

What is GLORY?

We should in no way take the word 'Glory' flippantly, and better not ignorantly either. We need to have profound respect for the word which describes the power and majesty of the state we are all going to inherit.

1 Corinthians 15:42 So also is the resurrection of the dead. It is sown in corruption; it is raised in incorruption: 43 It is sown in dishonour; it is raised in glory: it is sown in weakness; it is raised in power:

So we are 'sown' in corruption, and raised in incorruption, sown in dishonour, but raised in Glory. We need to understand this word 'Glory'.

In some denominations, the congregation respond with excitement to the flow of the meeting saying "Glory, glory, glory", but clearly these religious folk do not have any idea what "Glory" means when Christ talks about it through Paul in 1 Corinthians 15.

2 Thessalonians 2:14 Whereunto he called you by our gospel, to the obtaining of the glory of our Lord Jesus Christ.

It is so sad that words like 'gospel', and 'glory' have become synonymous with the mistaken and unlearned religious way of talking of so many people, and as a result they seem to have lost their power and their relevance to human beings.

The awesome, gigantic reality and truth that these words contain is visible to so very few. If they really understood that they mean and what they imply, they would be experiencing joy unbounded in their minds. But are they? Perhaps? Hopefully!

Romans 5: 1 Therefore being justified by faith, we have peace with God through our Lord Jesus Christ: 2 By whom also we have access by faith into this grace wherein we stand, and rejoice in hope of the glory of God.

Where did Paul get this word 'glory' from? He quoted it from the scripture where Moses asked for it.

Leviticus 9:6 And Moses said, This is the thing which the LORD commanded that ye should do: and the glory of the LORD shall appear unto you.

Romans 8:14 For as many as are led by the Spirit of God, they are the sons of God.

We are the children of God, now in type, awaiting the full adoption of the resurrection to the quality of life age-lasting that we will enjoy with Christ as our King and Elder Brother, and with God as our Father.

Romans 8:15 For ye have not received the spirit of bondage again to fear; but ye have received the Spirit of adoption, whereby we cry, Abba (Dad), Father.

God talked to Moses as a friend, we who are 'in Christ' can talk to God as "Dad". How awesome is that? He is our LOVING Father, and is very approachable, and He wants us to approach His throne of Grace in the genuine contact of prayer, supplication, study and meditation.

Romans 8:16 The Spirit itself beareth witness with our spirit, that we are the children of God: 17 And if children, then heirs; heirs of God, and joint-heirs with Christ; if so be that we suffer with him, that we may be also glorified together.

Heirs inherit according to a **will**, we inherit according to the Will of God. We are joint-heirs with Christ and will be glorified together with Him. Many people might have read these scriptures, but has the reality of what they mean really sunk in? Hard to know, but it certainly does not seem to have, otherwise people would be clamouring to become Christians. The glory we will inherit absolutely cannot compare with any trials we go through in this life.

Romans 8:18 For I reckon that the sufferings of this present time are not worthy to be compared with the glory which shall be revealed in us.

Romans 8:19 For the earnest expectation of the creature waiteth for the manifestation of the sons of God. 20 For the creature (creation - us) was made subject to vanity, not willingly, but by reason of him who hath subjected the same in hope, 21 Because the creature (creation) itself also shall be delivered from the bondage of corruption into the glorious liberty of the children of God.

The phrase 'glorious liberty' is here in the KJV, but it is "the liberty of Glory" in the Greek.

More and more verses tell us that Glory is coming to true Christians

1 Peter 5:1 The elders which are among you I exhort, who am also an elder, and a witness of the sufferings of Christ, and also a partaker of the glory that shall be revealed:

1 Peter 5:4 And when the chief Shepherd shall appear, ye shall receive a crown of glory that fades not away.

1 Peter 5:10 But the God of all grace, who hath called us unto his eternal (not just eternal

an age-lasting quality of life) glory by Christ Jesus, after that ye have suffered a while (in this earthly life), make you perfect, stablish, strengthen, settle you. 11 To him be glory and dominion for ever and ever. Amen.

Our suffering is part of the training we are receiving in this mortal life which is a necessary prelude and basis to our future when we are given age-lasting spiritual life.

2 Peter 1:3 According as his divine power hath given unto us all things that pertain unto life and godliness, through the knowledge of him that hath called us to glory and virtue: 4 Whereby are given unto us exceeding great and precious promises: that by these ye might be partakers of the divine nature, having escaped the corruption that is in the world through lust.

2 Peter 1:3 is another verse to ponder on, carefully, and not just read over. We are given exceeding great and precious promises by God the Father and Jesus Christ that we will be called to Glory, and we will be partakers of the Divine Nature. We human beings, God's children, are to be deified. Selah! Thank God that Peter was not a religious person, just a plain, down to earth fisherman!

Our hope in this life is the Resurrection to Eternal Life

1 Corinthians 15:19 If in this life only we have hope in Christ, we are of all men most miserable.

But it is not only in this life we have this hope, as the real 'hope' is of Life Eternal.

Romans 8:24 For we are saved by hope: but hope that is seen is not hope: for what a man seeth, why doth he yet hope for? 25 But if we hope for that we see not, then do we with patience wait for it.

That is the patience of the saints. We groan at the state of this world and when we see what we humans are doing to wreck it. We moan about our having to deal with all the events of this present evil world. But we hope in patience for that which we have faith in although we do not see it.

Romans 8:26 Likewise the Spirit also helpeth our infirmities: for we know not what we should pray for as we ought: but the Spirit itself (not himself!) maketh intercession for us with groanings which cannot be uttered. 27 And He (Christ) that searcheth the hearts knoweth what is the mind of the Spirit (of God), because he (it) maketh intercession for the saints according to the will of God.

The Power of God, the Holy Spirit flows out from God, and helps all those within whom it dwells.

*Romans 8:28 And we **know** that all things work together for good (ultimately) to them that love God, to them who are the called according to his purpose.*

This is certainly a scripture to memorise. However much evidence we think we see to the contrary, this scripture cannot be broken, just as no Word or promises of God can.

Romans 8:29 For whom he did foreknow, he also did predestinate to be conformed to the image of his Son, that he might be the firstborn among many brethren. 30 Moreover whom he did predestinate, them he also called: and whom he called, them he also justified: and whom he justified, them he also glorified.

Predestinated when? This step by step process for each of us began before the foundation of the world, our Glory was planned for each of us before human beings were created.

Colossians 1:26 Even the **mystery** which hath been hid from ages and from generations, but now is made manifest to his saints: 27 To whom God would make known what is the riches of the glory of this mystery among the Gentiles; which is Christ in you, **the hope of glory**:

We are so unbelievably fortunate to be able to understand the 'mystery' which had been hid from all those God has worked with throughout history until 63 A.D., when He revealed it to Paul.

Please do not just read over this or any other verse that has reference to the 'mystery' or our future. Pause, consider, thank, and meditate on the incredible statement that this is: Christ in you, the hope of Glory. Selah!

Glorious can describe a lovely sight like a sunset, or a magnificent view, but when 'glory' is in reference to our future, our Salvation, and the Glory which we will have, that is a very different matter.

Hebrews 2:5 For unto the angels hath he not put in subjection the world to come, whereof we speak. 6 But one in a certain place testified, saying, What is man, that thou art mindful of him? or the son of man that thou visitest him? 7 Thou madest him a little lower (or for a little while) than the angels; thou crownedst him with glory and honour, and didst set him over the works of thy hands: 8 Thou hast put all things in subjection under his feet. For in that he put all in subjection under him, he left nothing that is not put under him. But now we see not yet all things put under him.

So mankind was put over this earth now, but when resurrected the entirety of the heavens also. All things will be under Christ's feet and under ours also. All humans will be glorified in the end, even Hitler, Putin, Stalin, Pol Pot, and the most wicked people that have ever lived, as it is God's will that **all** will come to repentance of their own accord.

Heirs together – male and female in the Kingdom

God loves privacy, and like Him, humans have a part of us that enjoys privacy too. So we shall not always be with others, we will have down time. Even through the extended time ahead, there will be evil through which good will come, but as part of the God Family we control it and live above it.

1 Peter 3:7 Likewise, ye husbands, dwell with them according to knowledge, giving honour unto the wife, as unto the weaker vessel, and as being heirs together of the grace of life; that your prayers be not hindered.

This verse in Peter's epistle is forceful in the original Greek. **Husbands and wives will be heirs together**, but more than that, joint heirs in the Kingdom, male and female. Together, but not married, as there is no marriage or sex as we know it in the Kingdom, but people will be together nevertheless. Our post resurrection life will have similar characteristics to our human life, but on a completely different plane, the God plane.

Christ was resurrected at 30-32 years old. He is the standard we look to, so we will probably be resurrected with a body of a similar age, one that is in its prime. Bearing in mind that the new body we will inherit will be free of any defects we might have had in this life.

Colossians 1:12 Giving thanks unto the Father, which hath made us meet (fit) to be partakers of the inheritance of the saints in light: 13 Who hath delivered us from the power of darkness, and hath translated us into the kingdom of his dear Son: 14 In whom we have redemption through his blood, even the forgiveness of sins: 15 Who is the image of the invisible God, the firstborn of every creature:

We will be delivered from the power of darkness, and translated into the Kingdom. We are already 'dead' to this world, when Christ died we 'died', and we are now already citizens of Heaven with Christ, sitting with Him on the right hand of the Father **in type** legally speaking, yet awaiting our actual translation at the resurrection.

Colossians 3:1 If ye then be risen with Christ, seek those things which are above, where Christ sitteth on the right hand of God. 2 Set your affection on things above, not on things on the earth. 3 For ye are dead, and your life is hid with Christ in God. 4 When Christ, who is our life, shall appear, then shall ye also appear with him in glory.

When Christ was circumcised, we were 'circumcised'; when Christ died, we 'died'; when Christ rose from the dead, we 'rose from the dead'; when Christ was judged, so were we; that is how we can be reckoned legally speaking as already being 'in Christ' sitting blameless at the right hand of the Father, and enjoying a foretaste of this future life in our minds and hearts.

Ephesians 3:1 For this cause I Paul, the prisoner of Jesus Christ for you Gentiles, 2 If ye have heard of the dispensation of the grace of God which is given me to you-ward: 3 How that by revelation (in 63 A.D.) He (Christ) made known unto me the mystery; (as I wrote afore in few words, 4 Whereby, when ye read, ye may understand my knowledge in the mystery of Christ) 5 Which in other ages was not made known unto the sons of men, as it is now revealed unto his holy apostles and prophets by the Spirit;

The Prophets of old had not been given this understanding that ALL would be saved.

Paul was taught the secret of the *mystery* personally by the living risen Christ. God had kept to Himself this part of His Plan until 63 A.D., that salvation and age-lasting life, although first to the 'Jew', would also be given to the Gentiles or the Nations. In fact He had planned that every human who had ever lived or who would ever live would become members of the God Family.

Ephesians 3:6 That the Gentiles should be fellowheirs, and of the same body, and partakers of his promise in Christ by the gospel: 7 Whereof I was made a minister, according to the gift of the grace of God given unto me by the effectual working of his power. 8 Unto me, who am less than the least of all saints, is this grace given, that I should preach among the Gentiles the unsearchable riches of Christ; 9 And to make **all** men see what is the fellowship of the mystery, which from the beginning of the world hath been hid in God, who created all things by Jesus Christ:

This is the prime example of 'progressive revelation' that God has released and revealed more and more of His Plan as centuries of human existence have passed. Prior to this revelation there was no assurance whatsoever of the Gentiles inheriting the same as Israel and the Jews.

What the 'Jews' wanted more than anything was their version of the aeonic Kingdom, the Messiah to come as a King on a white horse who would free them from the Roman occupation, not as some humble carpenter on a donkey!

Christians who have the earnest of the Holy Spirit in them, and who are walking with Christ, whether Jew, Gentile, Scythian, or whatever Nation, are 'resurrected with Him' and **are already legally, in type** 'in the Kingdom'.

John 3:36 He that believeth on the Son hath everlasting (aeonian) life: and he that believeth not the Son shall not see life; but the wrath of God abideth on him.

There are some problems with the translation of certain words in the KJV. When in 1611 King James commissioned the translation of the manuscripts by the seven sections of scholars, each was given part of the whole Bible. The King gave them specific instructions that they were not to translate anything that might appear to be against Church of England doctrines. The King did not want to offend anyone, or stir up dissension among the hierarchy of the Church. The King insisted that the Greek word 'ekklesia' should be translated as 'church' (111 times in KJV!) which is derived from the infamous goddess 'Circe', rather than 'assembly' which is its real meaning which has done untold damage.

Two other words among many others which they consistently mistranslated then, were 'olam' and 'aeonian'. These were translated 'eternal' or 'everlasting' often to refer to a future life. These English words give an incorrect meaning because 'Olam' and 'aeonian', they both simply imply an undefined period of time. However, there is no point in an 'eternal' life that has no quality, or is full of pain and suffering.

Salvation and eternal life are a gift to all, but entrance to the Kingdom is a reward

John 3:16 For God so loved the world, that he gave his only begotten Son, that whosoever believeth in him should not perish, but have everlasting life. 17 For God sent not his Son into the world to condemn the world; but that the world through him might be saved.

It is God's will that all will be saved. Since it is God's Will, then that will happen in due time. No work is required to earn salvation, it is a free gift to all human beings.

1 Timothy 2:3 For this is good and acceptable in the sight of God our Saviour; 4 Who **will** have **all** men to be saved, and to come unto the knowledge of the truth. 5 For there is one God, and one mediator between God and men, the man Christ Jesus;

However, being part of the first resurrection, and entrance into the Kingdom of God at Christ's return, will be given to those who have done the 'work'. What is the 'work' required of a Christian? Christ tells us:

John 6:28 Then said they unto him, What shall we do, that we might work the works of God? 29 Jesus answered and said unto them, This is the work of God, **that ye believe** on him whom he hath sent.

The parable that Christ gave us concerning the talents clearly lets us know that there is a reward for 'works'. Those that applied themselves to 'working' with what the master had given them, and increased their worth were praised, and assured of a reward.

Matthew 25:20 And so he that had received five talents came and brought other five talents, saying, Lord, thou deliveredst unto me five talents: behold, I have gained beside them five talents more. 21 His lord said unto him, Well done, thou good and faithful servant: thou hast been faithful over a few things, I will make thee ruler over many things: enter thou into the joy of thy lord. 22 He also that had received two talents came and said, Lord, thou deliveredst unto me two talents: behold, I have gained two other talents beside them. 23 His lord said unto him, Well done, good and faithful servant; thou hast been faithful over a few things, I will make thee ruler over many things: enter thou into the joy of thy lord.

The reward for the diligent will be to rule over many things in the Kingdom.

And the parable of the 'pounds' is another indication of reward for diligence.

Luke 19:15 And it came to pass, that when he (Christ) was returned, having received the kingdom, then he commanded these servants to be called unto him, to whom he had given the money, that he might know how much every man had gained by trading. 16 Then came the first, saying, Lord, thy pound hath gained ten pounds. 17 And he said unto him, Well, thou good servant: because thou hast been faithful in a very little, have thou authority over ten cities. 18 And the second came, saying, Lord, thy pound hath gained five pounds. 19 And he said likewise to him, Be thou also over five cities.

And when and where do we conclude that faithful stewards of God's gifts will be ruling over cities? This will be in the Kingdom of God, ruling with Christ during the millennium.

Sadly, there will be those many who will not be changed at Christ's Second Coming and will not enter the Kingdom of God at that time. There are over two billion adherents to many thousands of churches who consider themselves to be Christian, but who have their own un-Biblical version of the Gospel and view of the Scriptures. Christ warned many times of the deception which would affect many.

Matthew 24:11 And many **false prophets** shall rise, and shall **deceive many**. 12 And because iniquity (criminal activity) shall abound, the love of many shall wax cold.

Matthew 7:12 Therefore all things whatsoever ye would that men should do to you, do ye even so to them: for this is the law and the prophets. 13 Enter ye in at the strait gate: for wide is the gate, and broad is the way, that leadeth to destruction, and many there be which go in thereat:

Many will be deceived, and follow the broad, easy way that leads to destruction, and will let their love of God become lukewarm or cold. These are those who have not worked with the 'talent' or the 'pound' they were given, so it will be taken from them for the time being. They will have to wait until a future time when they can be given their first opportunity to respond to God's calling.

Matthew 25:24 Then he which had received the one talent came and said, Lord, I knew thee that thou art an hard man, reaping where thou hast not sown, and gathering where thou hast not strawed: 25 And I was afraid, and went and hid thy talent in the earth: lo, there thou hast that is thine. 26 His lord answered and said unto him, Thou wicked and slothful servant, thou knewest that I reap where I sowed not, and gather where I have not strawed:

27 Thou oughtest therefore to have put my money to the exchangers, and then at my coming I should have received mine own with usury. 28 Take therefore the talent from him, and give it unto him which hath ten talents. 29 For unto every one that hath shall be given, and he shall have abundance: but from him that hath not ('worked') shall be taken away even that which he hath.

Those who have 'worked' with God's gifts of Belief, Faith, Repentance, and grown in Grace, Knowledge and Wisdom will benefit from places of responsibility in the Kingdom, but those who have not 'worked' will have the opportunity taken away, and given their chance later.

Those who have not responded to God's calling, or worked diligently as Christians to grow in Grace and Knowledge, nor obeyed Christ's commandments to love our neighbour as ourselves in having compassion on others, in taking care of the sick, and helping those who are less well off than themselves. Or those who had been a part of churches led by men and false ministers who preach a false gospel in this life, will finally have to learn what true Christianity is really all about.

So at some time in the future, many will awake from the sleep of human death at a resurrection to human life. They will then realise that they have missed out on the first resurrection and being in the Kingdom of God.

A person can only become a Spirit led Christian at God's invitation,

John 6:44 No man can come to me, except the Father which hath sent me draw him: and I will raise him up at the last day.

Part of our 'work' as a Christian is to respond to the Gifts of Belief, Repentance, and Faith with an open mind, and a willingness to respond to His call.

Luke 12:31 But rather seek ye the kingdom of God; and all these things shall be added unto you. 32 Fear not, little flock; for it is your Father's good pleasure to give you the kingdom.

Notice, Christ speaks of a 'little flock', certainly not billions.

Matthew 7:14 Because strait is the gate, and narrow is the way, which leadeth unto life, and **few** there be that find it.

Colossians 3:24 Knowing that of the Lord ye shall receive the **reward** of the inheritance: for ye serve the Lord Christ.

Hebrews 11:6 But without faith it is impossible to please him: for he that cometh to God must believe that he is, and that he is a **rewarder** of them that **diligently** seek him.

Isaiah 40:10 Behold, the Lord God will come with strong hand, and his arm shall rule for him: behold, his **reward** is with him, and his work before him.

Matthew 16:27 For the Son of man shall come in the glory of his Father with his angels; and then he shall **reward** every man according to his works.

Christians will be rewarded in proportion to the way they have worked with the gifts they were given.

Matthew 25:34 Then shall the King say unto them on his right hand, Come, ye blessed of my Father, inherit the kingdom prepared for you from the foundation of the world:

Christians keep the Law of Love with the help of the Holy Spirit

Galatians 5:22 But the fruit of the Spirit is love, joy, peace, longsuffering, gentleness, goodness, faith, Meekness, temperance: against such there is no law.

First Corinthians 13 is called the 'Love' chapter. Although this chapter is taken directly from the King James Version, the old English word 'charity' which meant 'love' in every sense has been has been replaced by the word 'love' we now use.

1 Corinthians 13:1 Though I speak with the tongues of men and of angels, and have not Love, I am become as sounding brass (deafening din!), or a tinkling (crashing) cymbal.

2 And though I have the gift of prophecy, and understand all mysteries, and all knowledge; and though I have all faith, so that I could remove mountains, and have not Love, I am nothing. 3 And though I bestow all my goods to feed the poor, and though I give my body to be burned, and have not Love, it profiteth me nothing. 4 Love suffereth long, and is kind; Love envieth not; Love vaunteth not itself, is not puffed up, 5 Doth not behave itself unseemly, seeketh not her own, is not easily provoked, thinketh no evil; 6 Rejoiceth not in iniquity, but rejoiceth in the truth; 7 Beareth all things, believeth all things, hopeth all things, endureth all things. 8 Love never faileth: but whether there be prophecies, they shall fail; whether there be tongues, they shall cease; whether there be knowledge, it shall vanish away. 9 For we know in part, and we prophesy in part. 10 But when that which is perfect is come, then that which is in part shall be done away. 11 When I was a child, I spake as a child, I understood as a child, I thought as a child: but when I became a man, I put away childish things. 12 For now we see through a glass, darkly; but then face to face: now I know in part; but then shall I know even as also I am known. 13 And now abideth faith, hope, Love, these three; but the greatest of these is Love.

We are indeed fortunate and blessed to understand the role of the Holy Spirit in our Christian lives, that is revealed to us from God and Christ's Word of Truth.

God's Will is that Salvation is ultimately for all human beings

John 6:39 And this is the Father's will which hath sent me, that of all which he hath given me I should lose nothing (nobody), but should raise it up again at the last day. 40 And this is the **will** of him that sent me, that **every one** which sees the Son, and believeth on him, may have everlasting life: and I will raise him up at the last day. (Universal Salvation!)

John 6:47 Verily, verily (great emphasis), I say unto you, He that believeth on me hath everlasting (age- lasting) life.

What God is offering, and will be giving to human beings is an exquisite quality of an age- lasting existence, with Christ ruling us in a life of constant joy and happiness and freedom from pain and suffering. These favourite verses, are memorised by so many people, but the full truth of them is not always appreciated or understood.

John 6:54 Whoso eats my flesh, and drinks my blood (in type, not in reality!), has eternal (age-lasting) life; and I will raise him **up** at the last day.

These verses are actually saying that we 'have' (are having - present continuous tense), **already in type**, but not actually until the resurrection, a supreme quality of life forever ahead of us under the rule of our Elder Brother, Christ.

1 John 5:11 And this is the record, that God hath (already planned before the foundation of the world!) given to us eternal life, and this life is in his Son. 12 He that hath the Son hath life; and he that hath not the Son of God hath not life. 13 These things have I written unto you that believe on the name of the Son of God; that ye may know that ye have (the **PROMISE** of) eternal life, and that ye may believe on the name of the Son of God.

This is the disciple Christ loved speaking, John the one who canonised the New Testament under inspiration, through whom Christ it talking to us today.

Hebrews 10:14 For by one offering he hath perfected for ever them that are sanctified.

To be born again is to be resurrected from the dead, but in type we are already 'born again' once we have the

Holy Spirit, not just 'begotten' but 'born'. We are a 'new creature'.

1 Peter 2:2 As newborn babes, desire the sincere milk of the word, that ye may grow thereby:

A 'begotten' child in the womb does not consume milk. Once we have the Holy Spirit, we are spiritually 'born', and need to desire the milk of the word. But are still human until we are fully 'born' as Spirit into the Kingdom at Christ's Coming.

Nicodemus, a master of Israel, came to Christ at night as he did not want to be seen!

John 3:3 Jesus answered and said unto him, Verily, verily, I say unto thee, Except a man be (literally) born again, he cannot see the kingdom of God. 4 Nicodemus saith unto him, How can a man be born when he is old? can he enter the second time into his mother's womb, and be born? 5 Jesus answered, Verily, verily, I say unto thee, Except a man be born of water and of the Spirit, he cannot enter into the kingdom of God. 6 **That which is born of the flesh is flesh; <u>and that which is born of the Spirit is spirit</u>**. 7 Marvel not that I said unto thee, Ye must be born again. 8 The wind blows where it listeth, and thou hear the sound thereof, but canst not tell whence it comes, and whither it goeth: <u>**so is every one that is born of the Spirit.**</u>

As was said earlier, we cannot see the wind, we know it is there due to the effect has on things you can see, like branches and leaves. As humans we cannot see the Spirit. We are not yet composed of Spirit, but we will be, but we are already 'born' of the Spirit if we have the earnest of the Holy Spirit because we have become a new creature.

2 Corinthians 5:17 Therefore if any man be in Christ, he is a new creature (type of being): old things are passed away; behold, all things are become new.

1 Peter 1:23 Being born again, not of corruptible seed, but of incorruptible, by the word of God, which live and abide for ever.

John 3:9 Nicodemus answered and said unto him, How can these things be? 10 Jesus answered and said unto him, Art thou a master of Israel, and knowest not these things?

It is clear that many of those who call themselves "Born Again Christians" do not understand the Bible. They really do not believe or understand the true nature of their calling and of their inheritance. For if they did believe with all their heart, it would definitely change the respect they have for God and cause them to alter the way they think and live.

1 Peter 1:24 For all flesh is as grass, and all the glory of man as the flower of grass. The grass wither, and the flower thereof falls away: 25 But the word of the Lord endureth for ever. And this is the word which by the gospel is preached unto you…

1 Peter 2:1 Wherefore laying aside all malice, and all guile, and hypocrisies, and envies, and all evil speakings, 2 As newborn babes, desire the sincere milk of the word, that ye may grow thereby: 3 If so be ye have tasted that the Lord is gracious.

Peter says the "born" desire the milk of the Word. Begotten embryos in the womb do not desire milk! Babies only have a use for milk after they are physically born. We need the Spritual 'food' of the Word of God on a daily basis for our Spiritual nourishment.

The 'bad news' - The 'Day of the Lord' comes just before our Resurrection

The subject of the terrible 'Day of the Lord' merits a detailed study of its own, but the events that lead up to it are introduced very briefly here.

In Matthew 24, Christ Jesus answers the question from His disciples, who asked, what shall be the sign of your coming. Matthew 24 is worthy of much study review over and over again, as there is so much information about the years just ahead of us now. This teaching of Christ Jesus is also covered in Mark 13 and Luke 21. For a thorough study of events leading up to Christ's return, these other accounts may be compared.

Christ told His disciples about many of the traumatic events which would lead up to, and precede His Second Advent.

Worldwide religious deception is the first thing Christ mentions.

Matthew 24:4 And Jesus answered and said unto them, Take heed that no man deceive you. 5 For many shall come **in my name**, saying, I am Christ; and shall deceive **many**. 6 And ye shall hear of wars and rumours of wars: see that ye be not troubled: for all these things must come to pass, but the end is not yet. 7 For (all through history) nation shall rise against nation, and kingdom against kingdom: and there shall be famines, and pestilences, and earthquakes, in divers places. 8 All these are the beginning of sorrows.

These verses sum up the subjects which are currently daily the focus of world news in the 21st Century. Fighting and atrocities between different religious factions, many wars all over the world, hunger, disease epidemics, adverse climate changes, and a dramatic increase in earthquake activity, globally all dominate the media. It is clear that the state of the world is in considerable turmoil now, but Christ warns it will get much worse.

Matthew 24:21 For then shall be great tribulation, such as was not since the beginning of the world to this time, no, nor ever shall be. 22 And except those days should be shortened, there should no flesh be saved: but for the elect's sake those days shall be shortened.

Christians can know the truth about the great deception

The Beast, and the False Prophet will suddenly appear on the world scene, and they will convince most of the people in the world that the False Prophet is Christ the Son of God.. They will use signs and wonders, even in the heavens, and confuse the world. They will be so convincing that almost all will think that Christ has returned and set up the Kingdom, but He has not!

Matthew 24:24 For there shall arise false Christs, and false prophets, and shall shew great signs and wonders; insomuch that, if it were possible, they shall deceive the very elect. 25 Behold, I have told you before. 26 Wherefore if they (Who? The Beast and the False Prophet) shall say unto you, Behold, he (Christ) is in the desert; go not forth: behold, he (Christ) is in the secret chambers; believe it not.

Many will be convinced to think that Christ has already returned, but He has not.

How can true Christians know the truth? Simple. If they are still in a human body, Christ has not returned! We will be able to see that the setup of world domination by the Beast is nothing like the true Kingdom of God. Even if they organise the building of a new Temple, institute the sacrificial system of the Old Testament, force the observance of the Sabbath and other laws, true Christians will know it is all a sham. We shall also know because we have the protection of our knowledge of the Scriptures.

An Alien invasion or Christ returning to Earth?

Matthew 24:27 For as the lightning cometh out of the east, and shineth even unto the west; so shall also the coming of the Son of man be.

We will know all right, because as He arrives we shall be changed.

There have been many fantastic, entertaining films made about the invasion of Alien beings from outer space. These fictitious stories are very popular with some people, and almost everyone has some sort of feeling of wondering if they could possibly be true, or whether it could happen.

There is nothing in the Bible to indicate that there is life anywhere else in the Universe. This does not stop men from spending millions on SETI, the Search for Extra Terrestrial Intelligence, or trillions on space travel and exploration, while they spoil and ruin our wonderful home here on earth. This Earth is where God is nurturing His children, nowhere else as far as we can tell, and there are no indications of any such thing in the Bible.

So when Christ and His millions of angels do appear in the sky, The Beast and the False Prophet will capitalise on this notion of 'Aliens', and will have the whole world convinced that the Earth is being invaded by Aliens from outer space. As Christ streaks around the Earth on His white horse, and appears in the clouds of heaven, the Beast and the False Prophet will marshal all the armies of the world to fight Christ at His Coming.

Revelation 17:12 And the ten horns which thou sawest are ten kings, which have received no kingdom as yet; but receive power as kings one hour with the beast. 13 These have one mind, and shall give their power and strength unto the beast. 14 These shall make war with the Lamb, and the Lamb shall overcome them: for he is Lord of lords, and King of kings: and they that are with him are called, and chosen, and faithful.

The ten kings will arise in countries in the Middle East, come to power for one hour, or a very short time, and they will assemble their forces to fight Christ at His Coming.

Christ has to take severe action, and destroy all these armies, so He can come to Earth, establish peace on Earth, and set up His Kingdom.

Zechariah 14:12 And this shall be the plague wherewith the Lord will smite all the people that have fought against Jerusalem; Their flesh shall consume away while they stand upon their feet, and their eyes shall consume away in their holes, and their tongue shall consume away in their mouth.

Christ will also pour out horrendous plagues on the Earth. There will be so much destruction, that if Christ did not intervene, all life on earth would cease.

Matthew 24:22 And except those days should be shortened, there should no flesh be saved: but for the elect's sake those days shall be shortened.

There will only be a few humans left, as depicted by the many futuristic post Armageddon films. And where do the producers of such films get their ideas? From Satan, the god of this world! Christ warned that were it not for His intervention, all flesh would be destroyed.

Isaiah gives a dramatic description of the state of the earth at the return of Jesus Christ.

Isaiah 24:24 Behold, the Lord maketh the earth empty, and maketh it waste, and turneth it upside down, and scattereth abroad the inhabitants thereof. 2 And it shall be, as with the people, so with the priest; as with the servant, so with his master; as with the maid, so with her mistress; as with the buyer, so with the seller; as with the lender, so with the borrower; as with the taker of usury, so with the giver of usury (fair interest) to him. 3 The land shall be utterly emptied, and utterly spoiled: for the Lord hath spoken this word. 4 The earth mourneth and fadeth away, the world languisheth and fadeth away, the haughty people of the earth do languish. 5 The earth also is defiled under the inhabitants thereof; because they have transgressed the laws, changed the ordinance, broken the everlasting covenant. 6 *Therefore hath the curse devoured the earth, and they that dwell therein are desolate: therefore the inhabitants of the earth are burned, and few men left.*

Notice, few men left of the billions now on Earth. This destruction by Christ will be totally necessary because by the time He returns, the inhabitants of the Earth will be so depraved, so far from God, worshipping anything and everything but the True God, denying God's existence and believing in Evolution instead of Creation. This all sounds very nasty indeed, and no doubt it will be as Christ foretold, Tribulation like never before.

Matthew 24:21 For then shall be great tribulation, such as was not since the beginning of the world to this time, no, nor ever shall be. 22 And except those days should be shortened, there should no flesh be saved: but for the elect's sake those days shall be shortened.

There will also be signs and wonders in the heavens.

Matthew 24:29 Immediately after the tribulation of those days shall the sun be darkened, and the moon shall not give her light, and the stars shall fall from heaven, and the powers of the heavens shall be shaken: 30 And then shall appear the sign of the Son of man in heaven: and then shall all the tribes of the earth mourn, and they shall see the Son of man coming in the clouds of heaven with power and great glory. 31 And he shall send his angels with a great sound of a trumpet, and they shall gather together his elect from the four winds, from one end of heaven to the other.

AND - Here is the REALLY Good News – the Gospel of Christ Jesus!

So at that time, those who are true Christians, and those who are the dead in Christ will be changed in the twinkling of an eye into Spirit Beings. (Really "Born again" as Spirit!)

1 Corinthians 15:51 Behold, I shew you a mystery; We shall not all sleep (die), but we shall all be changed, 52

In a moment, in the twinkling of an eye, at the last trump: for the trumpet shall sound, and the dead shall be raised incorruptible, and we shall be changed. 53 For this corruptible must put on incorruption, and this mortal must put on immortality.

So the GOOD NEWS is, that as in the time of the flood, God will save a remnant of His human children. Christ and His Newborn resurrected Christians will be with these human beings to help them to restore and rebuild the Earth, and live the happy lives God intended for His human Children to enjoy from the beginning.

As Christ returns, and we are changed at the resurrection, new life begins

Our actual birth will be at the resurrection, but nevertheless we are new 'born' creatures now if we have tasted that the Lord is gracious with His gift of the Holy Spirit. We will have the knowledge, our mentality and the character we have now, but hugely upgraded and changed to that similar to Christ.

When we are in the Kingdom, we will then have to learn how to be a Spirit Being. We will have to grow, not in a series of seminars, but by actual experience of being a Deity. This will be a process of development, and learning what our new life and powers are all about but will not be instantaneous. It will take 'time' although we will be 'timeless'.

Isaiah 66:5 Hear the word of the Lord, ye that tremble at his word; Your brethren that hated you, that cast you out for my name's sake, said, Let the Lord be glorified: but he shall appear to your joy, and they shall be ashamed. 6 A voice of noise from the city, a voice from the temple, a voice of the Lord that rendereth recompence to his enemies. 7 Before she (Zion) travailed, she brought forth; before her pain came, she was delivered of a man child. 8 Who hath heard such a thing? who hath seen such things? Shall the earth be made to bring forth in one day? or shall a nation be born at once? for as soon as Zion travailed, she brought forth her children.

This is nothing like anyone has ever seen or heard of before, a multitude of God's Children will all be 'born' in a day to life age-lasting. It will be totally amazing.

Isaiah 66:9 Shall I bring to the birth, and not cause to bring forth? saith the Lord: shall I cause to bring forth, and shut the womb? saith thy God. 10 Rejoice ye with Jerusalem, and be glad with her, all ye that love her: rejoice for joy with her, all ye that mourn for her:

Now observe the development of those that have been 'born'. They will grow and develop as Spirit Beings like human children develop, but no doubt in a very different way.

Isaiah 66:11 That ye may suck, and be satisfied with the breasts of her consolations; that ye may milk out, and be delighted with the abundance of her glory. 12 For thus saith the Lord, Behold, I will extend peace to her like a river, and the glory of the Gentiles like a flowing stream: then shall ye suck, ye shall be borne upon her sides, and be dandled upon her knees. 13 As one whom his mother comforteth, so will I comfort you; and ye shall be comforted in Jerusalem.

We who are raised and born in a day without labour pains, will enjoy the milk of the Word direct from our Elder Brother, Christ. In type, we will relish the sensation of being satisfied at the 'breast', 'carried on the hip' as mothers carry their children, and 'dandled on the knee', during the process of being nurtured, experiencing our development, and being taught how to be a Post Resurrection Being by Christ.

What will we do when we are in Heaven or on Earth with Christ?

Christ said, "I go to prepare a place for you", in heaven. So there are places (mansions!) for us in heaven where we shall spend some part of our time after the resurrection, but the Earth is going to become God's HQ remember. But what are we going to be doing?

Hebrews 1:3 Who (Christ) being the brightness of his glory, and the express image of his (God the Father's) person, and upholding all things by the word of his power, when he had by himself purged our sins, sat down on the right hand of the Majesty on high:

What does God do? He plans, designs, creates, orders it, establishes it, sustains everything by the Word of His Power, and works on the Universe which is expanding all the time, and we shall have a part in it.

We are learning some of these skills, or have the opportunity to do so on earth in a very limited way, and we only a get a very short time to practice, mostly getting it wrong! But these abilities are part of our human training and experience which will prepare us in some mall way for spiritual rulership in the future. Again:

Isaiah 9:7 Of the increase of his government and peace there shall be no end, upon the throne of David, and upon his kingdom, to order it, and to establish it with judgment and with justice from henceforth even for ever. The zeal of the Lord of hosts will perform this.

We are definitely not going to sit on "Cloud 9" strumming a harp, or continually 'casting our crowns' before Him. We are going to be given God-plane work to do. We will be planning, designing, creating, ordering, establishing, and helping to clear up the Earth, and sustain the work of the Universe under God and Christ.

There are seven billion humans (now in 2023 nearly ten billions!) on earth at the moment, and there are a hundred billion galaxies, not stars, galaxies now. There is enough space, and enough work to go around!!

The first verb, the very first action word in the Bible is 'created'. Being 'creative' is work. Christ said,

John 5:16 And therefore did the Jews persecute Christ, and sought to slay him, because he had done these things on the sabbath day. 17 But Christ answered them, My Father works hitherto, and I work.

Notice incidentally, that Christ worked on the Sabbath day, but He did not break the Sabbath as He had already brought the change in the Law. He was Lord of the Sabbath, and we as Christians no longer have to keep the letter of the Law. Keeping the spirit is so very much harder!

So what will we be doing? We shall be working on the Earth and the Universe under the direction of the Father and Christ our Older Brother. There will be plenty to do!

We shall grow in maturity of Spirit. God's power is Infinite, but God has revealed in His Word that He has grown over time in His Creative Power, Strength and Wisdom, and is continuing to do so.

As we grow as Spirit Beings, we will have a part in cleaning up the earth which will be in a terribly desolate, ruined condition after the destructive wars, and the destruction resulting from man's attempts to fight Christ at His coming. There are indications that this cleaning up period might take 70 years before the Millennium can start in earnest. This interestingly would leave 930 years of the Millennium to run, the same as the length of Adam's life.

After Christ returns, there will be an enormous amount of work to be done to repair, restore, and prepare the devastated Earth for the peace and productivity of the Millennium, and for those who are newly Members of the God Family who will have a part in that process..

Zechariah 14:4 And his feet shall stand in that day upon the mount of Olives, which is before Jerusalem on the east, and the mount of Olives shall cleave in the midst thereof toward the east and toward the west, and there shall be a very great valley; and half of the mountain shall remove toward the north, and half of it toward the south.

Zechariah 14:8 And it shall be in that day, that living waters shall go out from Jerusalem; half of them toward the former sea, and half of them toward the hinder sea: in summer and in winter shall it be.

These waters will flow down into the Dead Sea, and 'heal' the waters so that fish will be able to live in it.

Zechariah 14:9 And the Lord shall be king over all the earth: in that day shall there be one Lord, and his name one. 10 All the land shall be turned as a plain from Geba to Rimmon south of Jerusalem: and it shall be lifted up, and inhabited in her place, from Benjamin's gate unto the place of the first gate, unto the corner gate, and from the tower of Hananeel unto the king's winepresses. 11 And men shall dwell in it, and there shall be no more utter destruction; but Jerusalem shall be safely inhabited.

The geography and topography around Jerusalem will be reformed dramatically, and a huge area will be raised up to be a high plain for all to see.

Jerusalem and the Holy Land will be rebuilt, the old ways of strife and war between brothers will be abandoned, and God's children will live together with the human beings that are left, helping them to rebuild, and to enjoy their lives in peace and safety as never before.

Every person reading this chapter would do well to pray for an attitude of gratitude and repentance; to be given the mind to believe and have faith in Christ; and to ask God for the gift of the Holy Spirit.

This amazing time is just ahead of us as the 6000 year of man's rule ends

After Christ returns, we true Christians will begin our new eternal life as fully fledged sons and daughters of God. As part of the God Family, we will enjoy life as never before, and certainly in ways we could never have imagined previously in our wildest dreams.

It can clearly be seen from this chapter, that the Holy Bible that Christ wrote for our education and inspiration, reveals in great detail the ultimate answer to all our questions about the meaning, reason, and purpose of Human existence on this Earth.

God speed the day of His Coming.. Selah.

A SHORT AUTOBIOGRAPHICAL HISTORY
BY BRIAN H. BUTLER

Looking at what is happening in my life now at very nearly eighty (now 88) years old is so extraordinary; I felt I should write (update a little) a short autobiography of my journey to introduce myself to those who might decide to read this book that I have compiled based on Dr. Ernest L. Martin's work.

From a child, I was taken to church every Sunday by my parents. Over time, they went to several different 'churches'. They wanted to be Christians, but I think they were looking for 'something' which they sought but apparently never found before they died.

Apart from a few Bible stories from Sunday School about Jonah and the 'whale', or Christ turning water into wine, or feeding the five thousand, etc., nothing I heard in churches meant anything to me. I could not understand what the 'Gospel' was, or what they were all about really.

I met my first wife in a Methodist Church in my late teens, and we were married when I was twenty-one. The church seemed to me to be more of a social club than anything else, as I never was aware of any doctrinal beliefs apart from tee-totalism. Since Christ's first miracle was to produce wine for a wedding feast, even that did not seem to make sense!

Married a couple of years, we moved a few miles away, went to the nearest church, but again I was totally unimpressed with the milksop of a minister, who said nothing I could identify with. I never went again.

By this time I had already realised that there were so many different 'churches' all claiming to be right, but how could they all be 'right' when they all taught different things? I concluded that none of them could be 'right'. According to a survey conducted in 1980, there were then over 20,000 (now 33,000!) different 'Christian' denominations around the world!

Then in 1958, at twenty-three, I got the 'flu, and noticed in the pile of Reader's Digest magazines I was reading some adverts like: "Does God Exist", and "The Proof of the Bible", so I sent off for them.

For the first time in my life, I was confronted with apparently solid facts from the Bible. I avidly read and devoured the leaflets, then took the Bible Correspondence Course that was offered. There seemed to be a thread through the literature that the writers claimed to be the only true 'church' on earth, although that was not immediately obvious.

Certainly of all the 'churches' I had previously any experience with, they were the first to actually **_appear_** to take the Bible literally, and to teach solid, clearly defined doctrines directly from it.

Without realising it, I was slowly and inexorably being brain-washed and drawn into a net, into the fatal trap of 'a mixture of truth and error', which interestingly, the author of those leaflets used to describe as being the poisonous fatal fault with all other churches.

In 1961, I had become really disillusioned with the 'world'. I left my job, sold our house and bought a small farm in Sussex, intending to live the simple, self-sufficient life with my wife and our first baby child. Actually, my new 'world' fell apart after only a few weeks, so we sold the farm, and I went back to work at my old job.

In 1962, when I was twenty-seven, I was invited to attend a church group in London. The first meeting I attended seemed to me to be a dismal and somewhat depressing affair, but the people appeared devout, and the ministers passionate about what they were teaching. I was fascinated by the *apparent* authority and respect accorded to the Bible, and began my studies in real earnest. My involvement with the church was beginning to put a strain on our marriage, but I was devoted to the 'cause' which by then I really thought, (and was told by ministers almost daily) to be "God's work".

My life as a member was all consuming, studying the Bible every day. I took some theology classes. I particularly enjoyed the riveting lectures of Dr.

Earnest L. Martin that I attended for more than two years. He seemed different from all the other ministers, he gave off a strong feeling of gentleness and warmth. His detailed knowledge and objective scholarliness of the Bible, and particularly of history, were absolutely outstanding.

Dr. Martin took groups of students to Israel annually to study, and to get the 'feel' of Bible geography and history. Dr. Martin was also a highly respected archaeologist working with some of the professors in the Hebrew University on various research projects, including the actual historical position of the Temple.

What I did not realise at all at the time, was that much of the 'theology' I was learning, consisted of what the church wanted me to study and believe. I did not know then that I was on a sort of tramline track, a narrow gauge line at that, focusing on certain things in God's Word, and ignoring others of monumental importance.

However, ultimately, 'all things work together for good to those who love Him', so I shall be eternally grateful to God for allowing me that time and experience to begin to develop a deep appreciation of the Bible really being God's Holy Word.

Even if a lot of what I was learning proved later to be a distorted gospel, and many false doctrines and incorrect applications of Scripture. I noted that Christ was most emphatic about being aware of being deceived, but never thought for a moment that I was deceived!

By Brian H. Butler - The Meaning and Purpose of Human Life

I did not realise that what I was learning was so very limited, and I was kept within the boundaries of what the church leaders wanted to indoctrinate me with. I had no idea at the time that this was the case, or that they were so wrong about so many of the doctrines they insisted were "THE truth" and taught with such fervour. The ministers were mostly sincere, (sincerity is no guarantee of truth!) and did not realize that they were teaching an almost complete distortion of the truths of the Bible.

It was not long before there were well hidden, but discernible cracks began to appear among the hierarchy of the very top ministers of the church. Some of whom were involved in seriously wrong activities like the misuse of church funds, adultery, and even incest! The splits, divisions, and disintegration of that church began in the 'seventies, and that continues to this day.

In 1975, I became disillusioned with the whole setup, and was then politely but firmly told I was no longer welcome. I was baffled, upset, and bewildered. So I went home and cried for a while. Then I also made a firm decision to take control of my own life, and to think for myself, so that nobody would ever again have the power to control my thinking or my life.

Later in 1976, I talked with a friend who said, "Dr. Martin has some really interesting information about the Bible which I think you might be interested in." At that time, I had watched the disintegration of the church which was more than very upsetting, and I was in no frame of mind to pursue other studies of the Bible, or be associated with any other groups at that time.

I had come to realise that the church that I had attended for so many years was disastrously stuck in the partial and impossible practice of attempting to obey Old Testament laws. Also that it was a group which had never really embraced the real true Gospel message of Christ in the

New Testament. I certainly did not want to be involved with any religious organisation whatsoever. I was very happy with my new occupation in Applied Kinesiology, a type of Natural Health Care which had become my passion, so I thanked him, and basically said, "No thanks". It was not my time!!

So when 'providentially' (as I now strongly believe) this new career came along right at that moment, I jumped at the chance to learn a new skill,

especially one which would enable me to follow my God given talent for teaching, and my innate desire to help and enrich the lives of other people, and incidentally be my own boss. Shortly after this time, because we had grown so far apart, sadly my wife and I parted company.

Twenty-five years later In 2000, now sixty-five, I met a lady who was born in the village where I lived in Surrey. I decided to retire, and we were married in 2002. Sadly, Dr. Martin died in 2002, but his work was being carried on to a degree by his wife and a colleague.

Over the years, I had kept in touch with a friend who used to work with me many years ago. My friend reminded me that he had told me about Dr.

Martin's research and his new understanding of what the Bible actually teaches back in 1976, but it was not my time to investigate that then.

One day in 2012, my friend and I were talking about the 'old days' when we worked together, and he mentioned that there was a website where one could access the writings of Dr. Earnest Martin.

Although after thirty-six years of **not** spending much time studying the scriptures with any real fervour and enthusiasm, I had still retained my love of the Bible as being the very Word of God, and my strong belief and faith in our Creator God.

By Brian H. Butler - The Meaning and Purpose of Human Life

In his writings and taped lectures, Dr. Martin points out an incredible truth about the billions of Bibles that have been printed since 1611. There is not one edition or version anywhere in the world that presents the Books of the Bible in the order of the original manuscripts inspired by God. I have recently learned that such a Bible has in fact now been published. A chart showing the original inspired order is in the Introduction to this book 'Why *ARE* we here?'.

In the 5th century A.D., a man called Jerome decided to shuffle all the books into an order that appealed to him, and he translated the Bible into Latin. His work, called the Vulgate, resulted in the structure of the all the versions of the Bible we have today. His order has been perpetuated in the King James version translated into English in 1611, which although it is one of the best and most reliable we have, it is in the wrong order.

The Bible with sixty-six Books in print globally (6 is the number of man!) are all jumbled up in a chaotic order compared to the majestic perfection of the number of books (49 or 7x7), and the design and structure of the original writings. This arrangement of books greatly obscures the thread of truth that otherwise would enable those guided by the Holy Spirit to see the astounding truths and the story woven into the Divine Scriptures of the Holy Bible.

Under the inspiration of Christ and the Holy Spirit, the Old Testament Books were formally Canonised by Ezra in the 5th Century B.C., and the New Testament Books were Canonised at the end of the 1st century A.D., by the Apostle John. Canonised means assembled to a strict standard in their final order.

I had continued to observe that Christianity as practised by many thousands of denominations, and billions of people worldwide, was still plagued with divisions and watered down versions of the Bible's essential teachings. In fact most were clearly 'teaching for doctrines the commandments of men' that Jesus Christ warned about. 'Christianity' I had still observed, was in chaos.

Many churches had further diluted God's laws of love, 'done away' with the Ten Commandments, and almost universally embraced many pagan and idolatrous practices that God hates. Notions like Evolution, the observation of Easter, Christmas, Hallowe'en, etc., now followed and practiced by virtually the whole 'Christian' world. God hates these feasts, 'holidays', and notions of men. The whole Bible is the history of idolatry, of human beings preferring to worship anything but their Creator, and their refusal to obey His laws.

The practice of heinous sexual activities by priests and ministers has become public knowledge in recent years. Millions have also begun even to espouse homosexuality, encourage same sex marriages and other LGBTQUI? practices which all clearly against God's Biblical principles.

Thankfully God gave me the mind not to allow any of these activities in Churchianity to diminish my faith in God's Word, the Truth of the Gospel or my appreciation of the Great God, our Father. I had studied some over the years though, and written quite a lot of articles as I learned various bits of new information about the scriptures. But I now look back with amazement at what has transpired in the last few months.

All these years later, then at seventy-eight years old, I was still in touch with my friend, (again I truly believe 'providentially') and he put me in touch with someone who was continuing the work of Dr. Martin.

In 2012, I was also in contact with another man who had known Dr. Martin for ten years before he died in 2002, who 'just happened' to have a box of tape recordings made by Dr. Martin in his garage. He was kind enough to send them to me, for which I shall be eternally grateful. So I was able to listen to, and seriously study many of the over a hundred and seventy mind expanding recordings made by Dr. Martin in the twenty-five years after he resigned from his position in 1975, and before he died in 2002.

I was once again really astonished at the simplicity, power and clarity of Dr. Martin's taped lectures, and got very excited about what I was learning. I was learning more truth in a few weeks than I had learned about the Bible in fifty years! And it was so very interesting and stimulating, especially with Dr. Martin's talent for letting the Bible tell its own story without any 'spin' from him.

Dr. Martin maintains that "The best teachers are those who tell you where to look, *but not what to see*". Not at all like the ministers of most denominations. Dr. Martin also taught me a valuable truism: "If you give a man a fish, you feed him for a day, but if you TEACH him HOW TO FISH you feed him for life." The ministers of 'Churchianity' give their flocks 'fish', but certainly do not teach them HOW to fish, simply because they do not know how to do so themselves. Dr. Martin continually stresses all the important 'keys' that unlock understanding of the Divine Truths within the scriptures.

The most important primary 'key' is that the deep meaning of the Scriptures can only be understood with the direct help of Christ and the Holy Spirit.

These 'Keys' also include the importance of context, and especially the 'to whom', the 'when', and the 'where' of each passage we are studying. Without knowing 'who' the passage is addressed to, the 'chronology', timing, and historical importance of 'when' they were written, and the 'geography' or 'where' the events occurred, it is impossible to arrive at a complete understanding of any passage. This is a unique approach to study of the Bible. I have never ever heard of anyone else explaining in such detail the importance of these 'keys', which is why I have compiled this book.

By Brian H. Butler - The Meaning and Purpose of Human Life

Now after over a year with the cassettes, I have spent most of my energy each day listening to Dr. Martin's tapes. And not just listening, but studying them intently and writing notes! So again 'providentially', I strongly feel I had been given a 'doorway' to a vast amount of true Biblical knowledge and understanding which is virtually unknown.

So this time, the truths I am learning come directly from God the Father, and the Words of Christ (who wrote the entire Bible), not through the biased filter of devious human minds. Being able to glean knowledge, understanding, and wisdom from His Word is a gift from God, the human mind CANNOT do this without that gift no matter how hard one might try.

Dr. Martin is so direct, so honest, and so enthusiastic about God and His Plan and purpose for us all, so humble in his approach to sharing knowledge;

always pointing his listeners to 'study' God's Word directly, and be taught by Christ Jesus, not by him! He is a pleasure to listen to. He makes God and the Holy Bible come more real and ALIVE!!! He explains what is there in the Book for us to discover that virtually everyone ignores or overlooks.

I have told people who have asked me about my current studies, how I feel about the Bible now. Previous to my new understanding, it was like the image I had in my mind of God, His Son Christ and the Bible They wrote was in two dimensional 'black and white' and in 'mono' sound.

Now my mental image of God and the truths of the Bible are in 'Glorious 3D Technicolour' and 'Surround Stereo Sound'! And the pictures and the sound are getting clearer each day that I spend in my studies and devotions.

What God has planned for us, His children, is truly astounding, and is unrealised or understood by so very few. I decided that I would like to share what I am learning with anyone who would like to learn how to 'fish' for the truth for themselves, so hence this book. Be warned though, this is strong stuff. Jesus Christ, the Firstborn Son of God, did not pull His punches when he confronted the world, and neither does His Word, the Holy Scriptures.

Brian H. Butler. January 2015.

P.S. Since I orginally compiled this book, I have written another five books on Theology (Theo – God, Logos – Word, in other words the Bible). They, and the reviews of them may be seen on my Amazon Books Author page at Brian H. Butler.

Now in my 89th year, I decided to update the entire book, and insert some of the things I though might enhance the story, and lead the reader to a deeper understanding.

June 2023

www.ingramcontent.com/pod-product-compliance
Lightning Source LLC
Chambersburg PA
CBHW051534010526
44107CB00064B/2718